t.

hen
party

handbook

BATH SPA
MEDIA

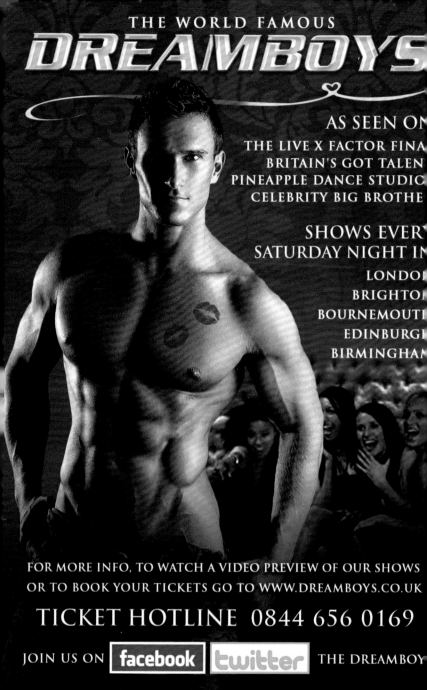

the
hen
party
handbook

The No. 1 guide to planning an
unforgettable last night of freedom

BATH SPA
MEDIA

Published by

CUTTING EDGE GUIDES

an imprint of
Bath Spa Media Ltd
The Tramshed, Beehive Yard,
Walcot Street, Bath BA1 5BB
email: guides@bathspamedia.com
www.bathspamedia.com

Also by Bath Spa Media Ltd
www.HenNightDirect.com and www.StagNightDirect.com

Creative Director Zoë Hughes Gough
Sales Director Lola Dali-Kemmery
Words by Rosie Gordon and Zoë Hughes Gough
Cover design by Clare Barber (www.cb-design.co.uk)
Book design by Lisa Hext (www.merrickspublishing.com)

Printed by Butler Tanner & Dennis
Caxton Road, Frome BA11 1NF
email: info@butlertanneranddennis.com
www.butlertanneranddennis.com

ISBN 978-0-9564368-2-5
A CIP record for this book is available from the British Library.

contents

introduction   9

part one
how to plan an unforgettable party 12
who, what, when, where…   14
how much?!   16
themes and schemes   18
the big night in   20
grand days out   24
goodnight ladies   28

part two
hen party destination guide   34
london   36
bath   66
belfast   80
birmingham   94
blackpool   108

bournemouth   122
brighton   136
bristol   150
cardiff   164
dublin   178
edinburgh   192
glasgow   206
leeds   220
manchester   234
newcastle   248
newquay   262
nottingham   276
oxford   290
york   304

picture credits   318
win a recording party for 12   320

introduction

There are few occasions in life where self-indulgence is the name of the game. But let's be clear on this. Your hen party is one. It's your party and you can do what you want to. You'll be surrounded by ladies whose sole aim in life is to launch you into married life in style. Our advice? Milk it.

This is the first guide of its kind: a UK-only, ladies-only book of inspiration and perfect plans. Find out which cities rock your world, and take your pick from top clubs, karaoke bars, restaurants, fancy dress, entertainers, DJs and many more venues and services to help you make it a party that's talked about for years to come.

The problem for brides-to-be is this. You often have to organise your hen party yourself. While obviously this means you won't end up in venues, outfits and activities that make your toes curl, on the other hand it's tough enough organising a wedding, without worrying about a hen do on top. That's probably why stag parties are often more extravagant – a best man has both the time and the inclination to organise a lavish send-off for the groom. We can't let this sexual inequality continue though, can we?

So, what to do? Nominating a head bridesmaid to do all the legwork for you is a great plan. Or get the girls over for a few glasses of wine and a brainstorm – find out how much people want to spend, the dates you can all do, the food you all like and fun stuff like themes, fancy dress and entertainment. Use the guide for inspiration – you'll be truly amazed at some of the activities available – from foreplay lessons (no, we're not joking!) through to white-water rafting, there are hundreds of weird and wonderful thrills to be had, day and night. We've included ideas for all budgets, including DIY tips for brilliant parties at home.

If you're too busy, too indecisive, or too hung over after a girls' night of 'discussion' to remember what's what, then worry not. There are many hen party organisers out there who will take one look at your budget and produce a fantastic, tailor-made event for you in the city of your choice.

So, ladies, enjoy your last maiden voyage. Whether your sailing in champagne-bucketloads of style or cobbling together your own raft, we hope you reach married shores safely and with fond (if hazy) memories of a truly legendary Hen Party.

Your hen night is an opportunity to take on a new challenge, log on to exhilaration.co.uk for ideas.

SONGMAKER

how to plan an unforgettable party

afternoon tea amazing *awesome* bars **best-ever** brilliant bubbly **bungee jump** bunny girls camp **casino** celebration **champagne** *cocktails* comedy cool cracking crazy **dancing queen** *delight* disco drinking eating enjoy entertainment excitement **extraordinary** fabulous *fancy dress* fantastic food friends fun girls **gorgeous** group *happy* hens

high spirits hilarious *ideas*
immense jollity **last night of freedom**
laughter limousine luxury marvelous
massage *music* naked **nightlife** *outrageous*
pamper party people pleasure **pole**
dancing quirky *racy* sensational
shopping sexy smiling spa stripper
stupendous ***superb*** theatre **underwear** *VIP*
wild women **x-rated** zany

who, what, when, where…

The wedding is approaching. Your dress is nearly finished, the invitations have been sent, the cake is on order, the hymns have been picked. Now for the important bit… THE HEN NIGHT!

why?

A married friend who didn't have a hen party says, 'I thought I would, but when the time came I just couldn't be bothered with the hassle of who might get on with who and picking a night out they'd all enjoy. I was so stressed out with organising the wedding that I just decided to give the hen party a miss.' And does she regret it? 'Definitely. I should have set aside the time and money to do something for myself. As it was, I hardly enjoyed any of the run up to the wedding.

Ah, what a tragic tale! So, the advice from Lady Hindsight is this: 'Make time, make yourself a priority, invite who *you* want to – not who you *should* or *shouldn't* – and remember, getting married is supposed to be enjoyable!'

Of course you could hand the whole thing over to your best mate – that's what bridesmaids are for isn't it?

when to book?

If you've just got engaged and you're already scheming for a hen do, fantastic. You can budget for something truly unforgettable, book your friends early and bag those popular venues before they get booked up. But if you're all last minute – don't panic! Pick a date (about two–four weeks before the wedding, unless you want to go to an event with a fixed date of course). Make sure the people you actually want to be there can make it. That's the crucial stuff done. Now get your budget into shape. The rest is mere detail…

if budget is no object then why not book into a sophisticated spa hotel, like Swinton Park in Yorkshire.

what's on offer?

Working out the detail is the fun part. Will you make your own cocktails or have fizz served by naked waiters? Picnic in the park or upmarket dinner? Dancing or comedy? Club dress or fancy dress? Theme, decor, dance class, DJ, boat trip, spa hotel or B&B? Or all of the above? If you want to bring in caterers or entertainers, then book them up as soon as you can. When it comes to theme, decoration and fancy dress, well they can wait until the last minute if they have to. For now, get the nuts and bolts in place, then relax and enjoy dreaming up your ideal party.

If your style is more canvas than caviar, how about a camping trip – Smugglers Haven, Newquay perhaps.

how much?!

OK, so you've constructed your ideal party in your head: the unique theme, the shiny happy people, the gorgeous male models serving you canapés, your bespoke outfit and the world-class venue...the pages in *Hello!* It's genius. Now how are you going to get this legendary event off the ground? Well, whether you're skinted or minted, it's all down to budgeting. Dull, maybe. Essential? Yes.

get it down

If you're super organised, you can factor the hen (and stag) do into your grand wedding budget and have it all on a nicely controlled simmer from word go. If you want to keep it separate, well, that makes life easy too. Your other half won't be able to interrogate you about every stripper or other *perfectly legitimate* expense you clock up. You need to set up a proper spreadsheet and factor in travel, venue hire, meals, drinks, licences for bar or music hire, entertainers, hotels...and whatever else your heart desires. Be very, very thorough at this stage and there won't be any nasty surprises down the line. If you can't afford something, use this guide to research cheaper alternatives or just cross it out and move on.

delegation, that's what you need

It's all very well talking about budgets. But what if you just don't do figures? Well, be very careful. The solution here is not *necessarily* open season on credit cards. It might work better for you to delegate the hen party to an organised and resourceful bridesmaid. Or it might make sense to hire the services of a party planner. There are many planners out there ready to take the sting out of the whole operation for you, at a price.

They will tailor-make packages for budgets big and small, ensuring you get the best rates (because they negotiate with the hotels, clubs etc) and that you don't spend wildly beyond your means.

the art of illusion

The other great thing about hiring a professional is that he or she might amaze you with theme and entertainment ideas that can be done on your budget. With their contacts, suddenly theatrical props, look-alikes, waiting staff, glamorous or bizarre venues and more will be available for your event, making a small spend look like a million dollars.

top tips

Mark Scott of Go Bananas says, 'Travel is expensive – book early to get much, much cheaper deals. Also, as soon as you know who wants to be involved, get deposits from everyone. Aim for low season and avoid special events, such as Edinburgh festival.' But his biggest tip? 'If you're partying, get a cheap hotel. As long as it's a safe place to put your bag and get a couple of hours kip, it's fine.' Go Bananas can do an Edinburgh hen weekend from just £49, so the man knows what he's talking about.

Star in your own pop video

Unforgettable pop video experiences across the UK

" Totally amazing doesn't even cover it. I can't imagine a better way of spending an afternoon with my hens, and everyone who came to my wedding got to see our video on the big screen! **"**

**Katie Rosen, 'Single Ladies'
Go-popvideo, London**

Check availability: 0845 467 6060

themes and schemes

A well-thought out theme can turn a good party into a great party, whatever budget you're juggling. It's time to get creative.

cheap and cheerful

Show me the woman who won't adopt a comedy persona when presented with a wig and assortment of 'fancy dress' from Oxfam and I'll show you my grandmother, who will just ask me what the hell I've been doing in her bedroom. My gran aside, at the very cheapest level, a box full of bad second-hand clothes in a room full of girls is the basis of a hilarious 'bad taste' party. Complete the theme with cheesy music, naff party food and games of Twister and you're on to a winner.

A colour theme for clothes (and hair!) will really make your hen party stand out.

theme your drinks

Scarlet harlots – Kir Royale
Pour a half shot of crème de cassis into a champagne flute and top up with fizz.

Latin ladies – Margarita
Shake a double shot of tequila, a shot of triple sec and shot of lime juice with ice. Wet the rim of a Margarita glass and dip into salt. Strain the cocktail into the glass.

Garishly gorgeous – Pina Colada
Blend ice with a double shot of white rum, double shot of coconut cream and three double shots of pineapple juice. When smooth and thick, pour into a chilled glass and garnish with the tackiest plastic stuff you can find.

Class acts – Cosmopolitan
Shake one and a half shots of vodka, one shot of Cointreau, one shot of cranberry juice and a dash of lime juice with cracked ice. Strain into a chilled flute or cocktail glass and garnish with a slice of lime.

the pink parade

All over the UK, every weekend, are broods of hens wearing short dresses and pink cowboy hats, carrying inflatable penises. They're usually having fun, so don't knock it…but if you want to be a bit different, tweaking basic outfits with personal touches is a simple and effective way to go. For example, if the bride's blonde, then give everyone blonde wigs. If you're at a seaside resort you all wear snorkels…and so on. Why not get your friends together over a glass of wine to mull over some ideas?

risqué business

If you're staying in, an Ann Summers party might make things a little edgier than the more predictable dinner and drinks. Or how about asking your guests to a sexy red-themed dinner party? Serve pink Kir Royales and hire a handsome butler to serve you. Butlers in the Buff and Cheeky Butlers will meet your needs.

If you're going out, there are plenty of edgy, sassy or downright dirty venues to make you feel satisfying close to crossing the nice girl/naughty girl line – just this once.

£50 off

Hen parties
Quote: The Hen
Party Handbook

The Cheerleading Company Hen Parties

Book now for your Cheerleading Company hen party. We offer dance parties including Cheerleading, Street Dance, 80's, Dirty Dancing, Grease, Fame, Moulin Rouge and more. Available in Bath, Birmingham, Bournemouth, Brighton, Bristol, Cardiff, Edinburgh, Leeds, Liverpool, London, Manchester, Newcastle, Oxford, York…and many more.

www.cheerleadingcompany.co.uk ~ admin@cheerleadingcompany.co.uk ~ 020 7274 3045

the big night in

As Dorothy so wisely noted after her house crushed the Wicked Witch of the West, 'there's no place like home'. Whether it's childcare, logistics, budget or pure love of the place, many hens have good reasons to choose home sweet home for their party.

get a man in

Inviting a performer to schmooze and amuse your guests means you're able to get on with enjoying yourself and feeling you've laid on something a little bit special. Choose from dancers, strippers, magicians, and cocktail 'mixologists' – there are performers in every region of the UK who will come to your home and wow your guests. Why not consider bronzed and toned butler to serve your nibbles. Hunkywaiters.co.uk can supply a guy with brains as well as brawn!

If the girls are unimpressed by such hi-jinks but you have kids running around, a balloon modeller or clown would be a good way of keeping them happy while you get on with the serious business of eating and drinking.

lights, canapés, action

If you're theming, decor is key. If it's a summer garden do, little tables scattered around and covered with white cloths and posies of flowers look very dainty. Plates of pretty cupcakes and elegant sandwiches or canapés laid out under strings of bunting will complete the 'garden party' scene. For a sophisticated winter bash, architectural displays of berried twigs and pussy willow can look stunning, as do twinkling white fairy lights and plenty of candles dotted around. The aroma of wine a-mulling is another winner. Colour themes work well to set a scene and make the atmosphere less 'homey' and more 'party'. Go for helium balloons and swags of brightly coloured fabric to make a splash.

larging up the lounge

If you're going for an all-out rave (and perhaps you've chosen to stay in because you have no neighbours to disturb), then disco lights, karaoke machines, glitter balls and good DJs are all available for hire, as are mobile bars and smoke or bubble machines. With all your favourite people, a clean loo, hand-picked music (why not subscribe to spotify.com for the night) and no queue for the bar, home is scoring high.

ideal home show

A low-cost night for 12 hens and chicks

5pm Kiddy entertainer arrives. Serve Pimms for the ladies.

Lay out a fabulous picnic tea – delivery of pizza for the kids, yummy deli goodies for the grown-ups, pretty cupcakes and a few bottles of fizz.

7pm Have a session with the children on the karaoke machine before their sleepover.

9pm Mixologist arrives for private cocktail lessons. Get the spotify going, hand out the canapés and get the party started.

10.30pm Now you're all cocktail experts, it's time for silly games, laughs and more karaoke...

hire a bartender

If you want to feel like celebrities for the evening, why not hire a cocktail bartender? A suave and sophisticated cocktail bartender will come to your home or rented accommodation and make cocktails for you and your hens. It's very easy and works well as pre-going out cocktails, arrival drinks, or even as a wind down on the last day over lunch. Cocktail bartenders from TheBartender are good-looking and charming with great personalities as well as fantastic drinks-making skills to boot.

It's up to you whether or not you provide drinks, glasses and accessories, or if you ask the bartender to do this for you. Most hen parties prefer a shopping list for them to purchase ingredients meaning you get to keep the drinks after your bartender has left.

If you're looking for an activity, you can experience The Cocktail Clinic; a personal, fun training session to teach you about cocktails and how to make them. All guests get three drinks each (made by yourselves!), followed by a quiz and a prize for the hen who has learnt the most. This class is available in central Bristol, Brighton or Sheffield.

To hire services for your party, contact TheBartender on **01179 028 328** or you can read more on their website **www.thebartender.co.uk**.

top 5 hen party cocktails

Mojito
Light Rum, fresh lime, mint leaves, sugar, soda
Muddled and churned to give the perfect balance of sweet and sour.

Cosmopolitan
Vodka, Cointreau, Fresh Lime, Cranberry
The 'Sex and the City' classic, served straight up in a martini glass with a flamed orange zest.

Sex on the Beach
Vodka, Peach Schnapps, Cranberry, Orange
Always gets a giggle when ordering at the bar.

Garden of Eden
Gin, Elderflower, Fresh Lime, Mint Leaves, Apple
Smells like gardens, refreshing and tasty.

Porn Star Martini
Vanilla Vodka, Passoa, Passion Fruit Juice, Fresh Lime
Shaken and served in a martini glass with a shot of champagne on the side. Shoot, lick, sip, repeat...

what hens say about us...

'The party was a huge success, with all the girls having a fabulous time and Ben being an absolute star. Unfortunately we were all too chatty and tipsy to remember to take any photos! Please pass on my thanks again to Ben for doing an excellent job and making the best cocktails and shots I have ever tasted.'
(Leanne, July 2010)

THEBAR♇ENDER

the ultimate girls night in!

get the experts in!

Experts in etiquette, charm and gorgeous men, Butlers in the Buff, the original and the best 'male order' company, offer a cheeky yet tasteful way to make hen parties unforgettable! Don't let the hen run around getting her own drinks – let a gorgeous scantily clad Butler in the Buff take the stress out of hosting for you.

The butlers can serve you and your guests champagne and nibbles, help with hen party games and look gorgeous wherever you choose to hold your hen party. What's more they do it wearing only a collar, bowtie, cuffs and a bottom-revealing apron!

top 3 reasons to hire a Butler in the Buff

1. All the butlers are absolutely gorgeous both to look at and to talk to. They will make even shyest girl giggle.

2. They are the perfect ice-breaker for groups who may not know each other. You'll soon have something to talk about.

3. Butlers in the Buff butlers are not only gorgeous, but have outstanding cocktail-making skills to boot, so why not let them mix up a Mojito, a Cosmopolitan or anything that takes your fancy?

Butlers in the Buff packages

Planning a hen weekend can be quite stressful: trying to coordinate all the guests, where to stay and what to do. But you no longer need to worry because at Butlers in the Buff they can do it all for you.

Simply decide which city you'd like to go to for your hen party and the

bookings team at Butlers in the Buff will do the rest. This includes booking the luxury apartments, a Butler in the Buff, a daytime activity on the Saturday and even where to go for your night out. So check out their packages on www.butlersinthebuff.co.uk/packages. You can choose from activities such as a spa day, wine tasting or, for the more outdoor-loving people, clay pigeon shooting or ultimate driving days. One simple call can arrange it all.

dressed for the occasion

If you have a particular theme for the hen party, the butlers can even be dressed to suit the occasion. So if you'd prefer them to wear something other than their pinny, you can tailor their outfit to match the party's theme. How about a topless butler in trousers, or even a kilt?! Or something a little more fancy – cowboy chaps or builders belt and helmet! Everyone loves a workman! Or how about Top Gun?

"I just wanted to write to say thank you so much for our Butler in the Buff, Andrew, on Saturday. From the moment he arrived he was a gentlemen and my friend, the Hen, was so surprised. He did a fabulous job at keeping us fed and full of bubbly and was thoroughly enjoyed by all the ladies. Thank you so much."

timetable for fun ✳

6.00pm Back to the house and get ready for the fun night ahead

6.45pm Butler arrives and you sneak him in so that the hen doesn't suspect!

7.00pm Give your hen the surprise of her life and let the butlering begin – starting with the all-important bubbly!

8.00pm 'Mr & Mrs' Quiz fun

8.30pm Photos of you and these gorgeous guys are essential

9.00pm Time for your butler to love and leave you

9.10pm All girls swoon over how great the butler was and how you wish your other halves would get to the gym to get a washboard stomach like theirs.

9.30pm Head to the nearest big city lights to dance the night away and reminisce about your Butler in the Buff

3.00am Dream of your lovely butler

10.30am Relive the night over breakfast with everybody's digital cameras!

Butlers in the Buff provide a premium, highly professional service that will make any hen party truly memorable.

For details on how book a butler or indeed two please call **0117 377 5693** or visit our website: **www.butlersinthebuff.co.uk**. Butlers cost from £60 per hour (with a two-hour minimum) so split that between a group of 12 hens and that's only a tenner each!

BUTLERS in the BUFF®
the male order company

grand days out

Too early for karaoke? You're right, there's a time and a place for everything. And in the daylight hours of your hen party day or weekend, there are some truly fantastic treats to be had, whatever the British weather throws at you.

the big chill

If high polish is your thing, and you have a set of girlfriends with a little cash to splash, how about a day spa or even a full-on pamper weekend? You know it will all make sense when you're wrapped in that fluffy robe with a glass of bubbly in your manicured paw. Ooh, yes. You can't beat the UK for gorgeous, ivy-clad hotels and elegant day spas with fine dining, free-flowing champagne and luxurious treatments. And if your taste is more bountiful than your bank balance, there are mobile therapists in your area to pamper you at home. A few scented candles, music and a well-stocked fridge are the only trimmings you need.

great escapes

For those of us who don't know why an emery board has two surfaces and prefer tramping through mud to slapping it on our faces, think the Great Outdoors.

There are lots of choices, and don't be afraid to exclude some hens from your daytime group – you can always catch up with them in the evening. Clay pigeon shooting, sailing and go-karting are just a few of the events you'll find here. Horse riding also makes for a fantastic short break in the countryside. Your kit is transferred between lovely B&Bs while you and Dobbin (and the rest of your group, we hope!) trot there at leisure.

let them eat cake

Why not indulge your inner Nigella with a sumptuous, home-based tea party, complete with a delivery of cupcakes and fizz? Or for something more hands-on, cookery lessons are available at many venues, specialising in anything from Moroccan spice to classic Italian, and chocolate desserts to ice-cream. They make a delicious daytime treat for a small group of friends. Go on, bring out the domestic goddess in you.

Chill out in a hot tub like this oasis of calm at Swinton Park spa, Ripon, Yorkshire. Book with Leisure Vouchers.

Clay pigeon shooting is available at outdoor activity centres around the UK with Virgin Experience Days.

No hen party is complete without a well chilled bottle of bubbly, so pop that cork and enjoy!

If white knuckle rides are your thing, there are plenty of UK theme parks to thrill you.

simple pleasures

Shopping, a long lunch and a little more shopping? Perfect. Some of the listed bars in Part Two are great for dim sum or elegant lunches in funky surroundings while you take the weight off. Tuck yourselves into a quiet booth with champagne on ice, or spread out on a sunny terrace with a cocktail, before heading back out into retail therapy. It's a hard life, isn't it?

three-ring circus

Real life can be such a bore. Yet, if you are contemplating the mechanics of a home-based do with a random selection of friends, kids and family, do not despair. Circus Whiz can nip down to your garden and erect an inflatable circus ring, and extroverts and kids can join in with various acrobatic antics. You can hire a face painter too, which the kids will love – allowing you to get on with the serious business of kicking back with a glass of Pimms. If you wake up under the trampoline painted up like Bobo the Clown, then it's been a good party. And for those of us who love a good old-fashioned fete – and who

doesn't – well Sidestalls.net can set you up with a coconut shy, hoopla, hook-a-duck and other retro delights. Go as large as you like with this theme – get your hens to dress up, hire a Victorian carousel – the sky's the limit. Candyfloss, balloons or home-made party loot bags would make the perfect finishing touches.

fairground attractions

If you're in search of thrills, there's no need to go on a pricey snowboarding break or fling yourself out of an aeroplane – what could be better than screaming your way through a rollercoaster ride? The 'official photographs' taken as you descend the deadliest loop are guaranteed to supply laughs for the night ahead. Not enough thrills for you? Perhaps you need a whole weekend at Alton Towers, complete with fairytale hotel accommodation and enough rides to guarantee you'll have screamed and giggled your vocal chords dry by the end. For smaller groups of strong-stomached friends the theme park is a winner – affordable and wicked fun.

Surfing lessons in the South West are a fun hen party activity, especially at englishsurfschool.com.

parties with splash

Fancy surfing lessons with a few friends down in Cornwall? Slides, spa and cycling at Centerparcs? How about sailing, rowing boats on a lazy river, jet-ski races or a River Thames cruise? Water babies will find lots of suggestions in this guide to whet their whistles and to suit all pockets. Cruises and row boats are great for groups where some friends are pregnant or you have a big age range. Conversation will flow, and quieter guests will love the freedom of being able to enjoy a glass of something cool as they take in the wonderful views. We're not pretending that Britain is the warmest, driest destination for watery activities, but who cares? There's something magical about partying on the water, rain or shine.

high kicks

Pole, street and belly dancing lessons have become an affordable and fun hen party staple. And now, Burlesque dance lessons are gaining huge popularity, thanks to the likes of Immodesty Blaize, who has helped bring this risqué art form back into the spotlight. Madame Peaches can offer a fun themed party learning this art form at destinations from Brighton to Edinburgh. Why not put together a routine to wow wedding guests with? For details on Burlesque and other dance styles check out madamepeaches.com. But for a room full of screaming ladies, it has to be The Devil – a strip act that will make your knees go weak. Save that for later!

go wild

If you're a bit of a petrol head, how about Castle Coombe – a beautiful, picture-postcard Wiltshire village with a deadly secret – a race track that you can take your car to (or perhaps more wisely hire a car), and drive as fast as possible. Outdoorsy types might opt for a sportier extreme thrill with white-water rafting breaks in Wales, or a good old-fashioned bit of bungee jumping at venues countrywide. And the grin you'll have all over your face after a day's 'zorbing' (doing somersaults inside a big clear plastic ball) will make it a hen party to remember. Just be careful whom you invite – your mum probably won't enjoy it!

goodnight ladies

When the sun sets on your day of pampering, wild fun or mellow treats, the hen party can really rev up a gear. No matter how loud, outrageous, elegant or memorable you want your night to be, if there's one thing that we Brits are good at, it's partying the night away.

follow that cab

Choosing how to get to your venue is crucial. Is everyone getting there under their own steam and if so, have you checked that there will be night buses, trains or cabs around to get them home again? Why not dispense with such tiresome nitty gritty by hiring yourself a chauffeur, darling? Whether it's a discreet Mercedes, a Club Class Party Bus in Manchester, the Scooby Doo mystery machine from Cardiff Limos or a flower-strewn Karma Cab in London you can arrive in style, or at least in stitches.

To get the innuendoes flowing early, hens in the London area can even travel by converted fire engine courtesy of Hot Hire. There's champagne on board and a fire bucket full of 'naughty goodies' to set the tone, as well as a fireman's helmet for each hen. Hose and helmet jokes at the ready…

The bright lights of the Big City are an intoxicating draw to any group of hens.

food – fuel up for a fun night

If you've a large group then there's a lot of sense in booking a seasoned party venue with food that everyone likes, such as gourmet pizza and pasta gem La Vittoria on The Bridge in Edinburgh. The staff won't fall over in shock at the sight of a troupe of lairy women, and your dining neighbours are more likely to join in than complain.

But don't assume a corner of TGI Fridays or another 'party restaurant' is the only option. Low budgeteers should consider a barbecue or riverside picnic for long summer nights – leaving funds free for hiring some entertainment, or perhaps for a spot of clubbing afterwards. If you book early, out of season or using all your charms, you can often get bars to hire you their private room at very reasonable rates (or even free). A thrifty tip is to opt for City or financial district bars, which tend to be both good quality and often empty at weekends, so will gladly cater for you. A private room gives you all sorts of advantages – including no competing for the waiters' attention, playing your own music and decorating the place in the theme of your choice.

As for those on user-friendly budgets, the world's your freshly-shucked oyster. Whether you want to hire an entire restaurant, have sumptuous sushi served from the very flesh of a semi-naked man, courtesy of Playtime Platters (yes, really); the purple van from Lola's on Ice to turn up with ice creams and alcoholic sorbets, or a chef to hide away in your kitchen and conjure culinary magic while you take the credit. Nothing need limit you, except your imagination.

An extravaganza of feathers and flamboyance – the Lady Boys of Bangkok on tour throughout the UK.

the art of 'boozology'

There's more than one way to get a skinful. While the end result may be similar – wobbling in front of a mirror with your best mate going 'Look, it's us', followed by getting your stiletto stuck in a drain cover, an unfortunate rendition of 'Sisters are doing it for themselves', then waking up with half a kebab stuck to your face – you could at least *start* the night with a bit of originality. Cocktail-making lessons are fantastic fun. Either book them at a good cocktail bar or hire a mixologist to bring the tools of their evil trade to your home or hired room. You

Whether you're hiring a mixologist or camping out in a cocktail bar, alcoholic concoctions are always a winner.

and the girls can craft cocktails, Tom Cruise stylie, under the watchful eye of a seasoned pro. Mine's a Cosmopolitan!

If you're starting out with drinks at home, a Spritzer (white wine and soda) or a Buck's Fizz (Champagne and orange juice) is easy to whip up and sets a less scary pace than liberally sloshing out huge glasses of Sauvignon. Fragrant mulled wine or spiced cider for winter parties raise the spirits nicely, too.

Out and about, choose from big, brash party bars, Pimms-on-the-terrace hotels, elegant wine tastings, chic cocktail bars or perfect winter pubs with open fires.... Check the listings for something that seems to ring your bell, get on the phone and book it.

belly laughs

There is no better endorsement of a hen party than everyone in fits of giggles. Booking into a comedy club (preferably a major one like Jongleurs, to guarantee class acts) makes sense on many levels. Not only will the entertainment be live and hilarious, but you and your mates will be served food and drinks at your table all night. Add to this the fabulous facts that you'll be only one of many fun-loving groups there, that there's usually a disco afterwards, and that the cocktails and beers are served in pitchers and you're laughing.

stage fright

Fancy taking in a show, you say? How very cultural. Ohh, *that* kind of show. You'll find acts such as top male strippers, The Dreamboys, at venues in London, Edinburgh, Brighton and Bournemouth, but for something a bit more exotic try The Lady Boys of Bangkok. This flamboyant extravaganza of feathers and fantasy is touring the UK and provides special hen party packages, check ladyboysofbangkok.co.uk for details. Of course there's always the legendary Madame JoJo's in the heart of Soho where Lily Savage walked the boards!

For those who really *do* like a bit of the old culture, it won't be hard to track down theatrical and musical events in your city of choice. All you need to do is sandwich the event between an early supper and a hotel with a decent bar for relaxed chats and late-night drinkies. It's a classy hen night that you can book cheaply with an agency or tailor-make yourself.

Become a pop star for a day at studios across the country, such as 'Pop Stars' in Edinburgh.

caterwauling 'I will always love you' to a crowd of people with their fingers in their ears, karaoke might be killing music but we girls just love it. The real mystery is when are those talent spotters going to make contact? Alternatively you could hire a recording studio and cut your own CD. Studios up and down the country are gearing up to welcome hen parties and make it an experience to remember. Songmaker, Go Experience and No1 Experience all have fantastic deals.

dance 'til you drop

If you fancy clubbing, you probably already know the type of clubs you like. Check the city listings to see what's on offer, and always try to book your group in. Not only will this give fair warning to the club about a descending hen party, it will also give you a chance to queue jump and get access to any special deals. Many clubs can offer a cosy little VIP lounge with waiter service and other luxuries to retreat to when you need a break from the dance floor...or somewhere to lie down!

killer tunes

Behind sound-proofed doors, all over the nation, terrible things are happening. Whether it's a small room of mates head-banging through 'Bohemian Rhapsody' with inflatable guitars, or Stacey

Brighton spice
A mid-budget night for eight cool chickens

Saturday, 2pm Check in to 3-star Kings Hotel on the seafront.

4–6pm Salsa lessons with Cubashe.

Back to the hotel to change.

8pm Early evening cocktails at smart Duke Street bar Havana.

9pm Dinner booked at El Mexicano – top-notch Latino food.

10.30pm Head back to the Lanes to the stylish Water Margin for all night DJs or live bands, cocktails and dancing...reserved to be on the safe side!

A short walk back to the hotel and sleeeep...

Sunday Brunch on the beach or a legendary Brighton pub roast.

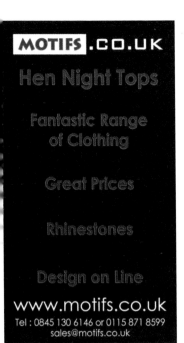

hen party destination guide

bath *belfast* **birmingham**
blackpool *bournemouth* brighton
bristol **cardiff** **dublin**

edinburgh glasgow leeds **london**
manchester newcastle **newquay**
nottingham **oxford** *york*

london

Big Ben (top), black cab (middle), London Eye (bottom).

Short of blowing your wedding fund on shipping your hens off to New York or Paris – tempting as it may be – there is no destination that can beat London for glamour, fun and sheer entertainment value. You'll find something from our listings to suit your budget and please any group, whether you're quiet, genteel ladies or eardrum-shattering banshees!

what to do

Before you land at Paddington station clutching your little case and chewing nervously on a marmalade sandwich, have a good, hard stare at this guide. London is full of surprises, and it will only take a little imagination and planning to make this a hen party to remember.

If you live in London and want to base your party at home, or you're booking a room at a London bar, you have the pick of the country's finest DJs, entertainers, therapists, cooks and mixologists to bring a touch of luxury to your party. There's even Choc Star's van (chocstar.co.uk) to deliver cocoa-based delights, for heaven's sake. If you're going out, well, you're going out in style. Gigs, shows, sport, comedy, food, cocktails, cabaret, clubbing, shopping, dancing, karaoke, markets…it's all happening here in London town.

But decisions, decisions…how – when it's hard enough to decide from a restaurant menu, lest you miss the best thing – are you going to work this one out? Hopefully our 'sounds of the city' will whittle it down for you a little. After that, practical considerations such as travelling in heels, Chantal's table manners, and your cousin's tequila-induced party stunts, will no doubt come into play. We didn't say it was easy…but we're here to help.

If you really can't decide, and it's all a bit much – you need to call on your friends. Your friends the professional party organisers, that is. They'll negotiate good deals for clubs, activities and hotels, so that you end up with something that feels like a long weekend on a Friday night budget. Or if you've managed to get your mitts on the fun-finance that most hens only dream of, they'll let their imaginations run riot and make your fantasy come true.

10 reasons…

1. **the UK's best shows**
2. **tea at Claridges**
3. **the London Eye**
4. **Thames cruises**
5. **top nightclubs**
6. **free art galleries**
7. **Carnaby Street**
8. **Selfridges shoe department**
9. **Camden Stables**
10. **chilling on the South Bank**

sounds of the city

With so much to do by day and by night in the capital we can't possibly include everything here, but hopefully these suggestions will give you some foundations to build your ideal hen party upon.

i want to break free

The frazzled bride-to-be who is, in common parlance, 'doing her nut', should take this opportunity for indulgence and serious relaxation: The Sanctuary, Covent Garden. Ahhh. There you see, it's already working. Book in on a Friday evening to use the spa pools, sleep retreat and heat and steam rooms. Choose from a range of treatments, from manicure to calming floatation. Enjoy a mouth-watering supper and a glass of champagne before drifting out at 10pm to join the rest of the girls at The Langley nearby, a cool, unpretentious little bar where you can drink and dance in stylish surrounds but keep that new found serenity intact.

Failing that, perhaps some physical exertion and fresh air will put the roses back in the bride's cheeks. A DIY school sports day with sack racing, egg and spoon etc, followed by a picnic on Hampstead Heath is inexpensive and blissfully simple. Dress up in gym kit for authenticity! Alternatively, for warm summer evenings, choose well-chilled champagne, divine deli food and live music at Kenwood House, you just can't go wrong. Check out the English Heritage website or picnicconcerts.com for 2010 listings.

Relax at The Sanctuary.

the one that i want

For posing Pink Ladies and tomboys alike, a few games of bowling can't fail. Posher poulets (that's 'chickens' in French!) head for All Star Lanes in Holborn, Brick Lane or Bayswater. Here large groups of 25 or so can book a stylish two-lane private room with a DJ and cocktail bar all to yourselves. They will even bring you canapés to nibble on while you contemplate a strike. For a slightly less upmarket but seriously authentic vibe – and the added bonus of lane-side karaoke rooms – book in at Bloomsbury Bowling. American food and hard-hitting milkshakes are on the menu, naturally. The fifties theme is readymade and you won't have to decamp to another venue for your evening entertainment – strike!

yodelay he hoooo!

When nothing will ring your bell quite as loudly as a man in leather shorts, it's time to book in to the Tiroler Hut in Notting Hill. Be warned, he'll literally ring it, as there's a cowbell show (and audience participation) whilst you tuck into steins of beer, hearty mountain fare and lashings of cheesy fun, served by Austrian wenches and goatherders. The family von Trapp would love it, and so will you. Good night, good night, good ni—ight!

Ah, hark, The Sound of Music. Yes, it's time to cut up your granny's curtains and skip over to the Prince Charles Cinema for some wimple-wobbling, lederhosen-tastic fun courtesy of Sing-a-Long-a-Sound of Music. Around four hours of dressed up, singing and heckling fun can't be bad for £15 (it all comes back to dough, right?) and there's a complementary bottle of champagne for hen groups of ten or more. Check out princecharlescinema.com for screening dates and times. Cheer for Julie, hiss for the horrid countess and of course, scoop the prize in the fancy dress competition…brilliant! And if lederhosen doesn't float your boat, but loincloths do, then why not sing-a-long-a Joseph?

Sing-a-long-a-Sound of Music at the Prince Charles cinema near Leicester Square.

don't cry for me, marg and tina

Oh, you're *singing*…sorry. Thought you were upset about something. You see it's best to keep these things well contained with a few people who understand you. And that, my lusty-lunged lovelies, is where Karaoke Box comes in. The Smithfield venue has sixteen private karaoke rooms of various sizes, with wireless mikes, flat-screen TVs, easy-touch selection screens and thousands of tracks, leather sofas, waitress service (there's a truly impressive cocktail list, plus sumptuous sushi and posh pizza) and surround sound. Youch. If you must escape, don't go too far. The bar is very cool indeed and you can dance the night away while the DJ spins your favourite tracks.

Sing your hearts out at Karaoke Box.

who let the dogs out?

Dorgs and *'orses* have been staples for London fun for many a decade and are still the ticket for a great fun day or in fact a whole night's entertainment.

Wimbledon Greyhound Stadium's Star Attraction restaurant serves up reasonably priced food and drinks to up-for-it party groups as they watch the mutts in action. There are three packages – trackside with fast food and pitchers of booze, sit down meal with pitchers of booze and a VIP option with a lovely buffet and, you guessed it, pitchers of booze. It's a piss up with live entertainment, basically, and you can't say fairer than that.

she's a lady

If you're more interested in the hats and champers end of things, a day's horseracing at Kempton Park in Sunbury is great fun. Hampton Court is just up the road – with the palace and its lovely gardens and maze, and a smattering of pubs and shops there's time for a spot of mooching in this gorgeous riverside location before you hop on a Thames cruiser and head into Putney for your night out in west London.

But Ascot, of course, is the crème de la crème for the gee gees. The racecourse to the rich and famous runs hen packages throughout the season to include grandstand admission, a race card, a £2 flutter and 2 glasses of wine, or you can opt for champagne and strawberries on the Plaza Lawn. Place your bets and remember, if Audrey Hepburn can scream it and still look knockout in that hat, so can you…'Move yer bloomin' arse!'

pour some sugar on me

With the currant (d'ohh) trend for all things cupcake, this is the tastiest little piece of zeitgeist going. After a champagne river cruise or London Eye flight, whisk your yummy mates off to an utterly fab cake shop, such as Bea of Bloomsbury, for tea, or cocktails and canapés, and sit around health-

Go Audrey Hepburn style and don a hat for Royal Ascot.

Why not try a 'stitch before you hitch' party.at Party Pants?

consciously picking the icing off the delectable, almost-too-good-to-eat cupcakes and then eating it anyway. Alternatively, book in for a baking lesson and bring out the domestic goddess lurking within.

At Cookhouse, hens will be split into two groups, one making cocktails and the other crafting canapés, under the guidance of professionals of course. The groups then swap. It's a social event and lesson rolled into one, where you'll have time to mingle and catch up with your mates as well as learning how to make delicious bite-sized delights.

Less filling but just as sweet for creative ladies are Create Boutique's workshops. You'll learn how to unleash your inner creativity, and can choose from producing your own gorgeous pashminas, making Burlesque-style nipple tassels, mixing and packaging a beauty cream, or learning how to design accessories and jewellery to echo the latest catwalk trends. Visit create-boutique.co.uk.

Creative types who are handy with a needle will also love Party Pants. This is a sewing party with a difference where you learn to 'stitch before you hitch' in a highly entertaining knicker-making workshop. The 'chief briefs' come to your venue armed with pink sewing machines and all manner of pretty adornments, as well as the all-important pants suitable for all shapes and sizes! Check out partypants.net.

i like you better when you're naked

For a little tasteful male nudity, why not try life drawing? This works well as a diet-friendly dessert option after a boozy supper or even after lunch. To serve up your model: book a private room in a restaurant or bar (or if you have rented a hen house even better), tell the ladies you've got a game where everyone has to draw something, hand out the paper and pencils, set up a decoy bowl of fruit and when everyone is suitably settled, bring in the rather more interesting subject matter! This one is certainly going to provide a talking point the next day.

born to be wild

Here's a bit of motorized fun that will both please the greens and thrill the grease monkeys – Revolution Karting is based in Mile End Park, in the city's only floodlit track. This is the site of the proposed solar dome, which will supply electricity to the local area as well as supplying buzz to your hen party. With 700 metres of straights and chicanes and London's fastest karts, you'll be hitting speeds of up to 50mph. Keep the driving theme by scooting up to Barrio North near Angel and booking into the funky caravan booth for nachos, cocktails and tequila slammers. Watch the trash without trailers partying down from your comfy perch, or join in the fun.

If you fancy an evening with a little more splash, try The Carwash at London's only club with a pool, Club Aquarium in Shoreditch. It gives you the perfect excuse to dress up and make a watery theme of the whole hen weekend.

School Disco.

Saturday night at the Portland Girl's School in the West End, grown men and women are dressed up to the Year Nines, snogging, breakdancing and misbehaving the night away. Uniform is compulsory, naturally. And don't be late, or you'll be straight to the headmasters office.

Revolution Karting.

if i could turn back time

If you seek a night as sweet, familiar and potentially unhealthy as jam roly poly, it has to be School Disco. Every

holding out for a hero

Where have all the good men gone? And where are all the gods? Ah, if only Bonnie Tyler knew what we know. Which is that strip show pros The Dream Men and Dreamboys have all got together for some regular Saturday sing 'n' strip soirees at Sound Night Club in Leicester Square. They're lovely chaps who's only mission in life is to display their mouth-watering muscles – and you don't get an offer like that everyday, except at the fishmonger's (ha ha!).

Along with topless hosts and waiters, dinner and a drink, VIP nightclub entry after the show and more goodies, it's certainly a crowd-pleasing package.

where to stay

Looking for a place to rest your weary bones in the UK's capital can be a daunting prospect. There are thousands of places all claiming to offer you the best value in town. Well we've sorted out the 'men' from the 'boys' and checked what's on offer from hospitality to hairdryers!

hotels and hostels

* shared ro⊙ without breakfas

£ under £
££ £30–£⊙
£££ over £
pppn

Best Western Mostyn Hotel £££

4 Bryanston St, Marble Arch,
London W1H 7BY
Tel. no 020 7935 2361
www.mostynhotel.co.uk
info@mostynhotel.co.uk

Situated just a 1-minute walk from Oxford Street and Marble Arch for shopping and close to Paddington station, this hotel has a prime location for hens. The comfortable, well-furnished rooms with ensuite facilities (and good power showers) feature satellite TV and all the amenities you'd expect in a three-star nationwide chain. There is a magnificent Georgian staircase and ornate ceilings in the public areas; and the Mostyn boasts two restaurants and a champagne bar.

Generator Hostel £

37 Tavistock Place, London WC1H 9SE
Tel. no 020 7388 7666
www.generatorhostels.com
london@generatorhostels.com

This great value hostel is the largest in London. Situated in Russell Square, it is well located for sightseeing and the West End. With a popular bar and nightclub there is always a party atmosphere here. Unlike many London hostels an 'all you can eat' breakfast and bed linen are included. Choose between dorms (up to 12 people in bunks) and private rooms (up to six people), mixed or female only. All rooms have a wash basin and lockers or a hanging unit. Spotless showers are available on every floor, but don't expect ensuite facilities here.

Grange Holborn Hotel £££

50–60 Southampton Row, London WC1B 4AR
Tel. no 020 7242 1800
www.grangehotels.com
holborn@grangehotels.com

If you're seeking to celebrate in style then the hen party package on offer here (or at Grange City) might be just what you're looking for. On offer is one night's accommodation in a superior room, breakfast, full use of the five-star health club, a 30-minute beauty treatment of your choice, plus a complimentary glass of champagne, sandwich platter and free nightclub pass. The rooms are en-suite with all the amenities you could wish for and if you mention it's your hen night, you might get a good luck cake too!

Grange Holborn Hotel.

Haymarket Hotel £££

1 Suffolk Place, London SW1Y 4BP
Tel. no 020 7470 4000
www.firmdale.com
haymarket@firmdale.com

In the heart of theatreland, this hotel is 'jaw droppingly beautiful' according to a recent guest. The stunning interior design is complemented by top quality amenities, including a gym, beauty treatment rooms and an inviting pool. You can have a pamper hen party in one of the rooms off the pool area, or enjoy a civilised afternoon tea in the hotel's fabulous restaurant, Brumus. If you like a bit of luxury and something a bit different, this is the hotel for you.

The funky pool at the Haymarket Hotel.

the hotel staff could not have done more to make this a memorable occasion 9

Cool rooms at the Haymarket Hotel.

Haymarket Hotel.

Hoxton Hotel £££

81 Great Eastern St, London EC2A 3HU
Tel. no 020 7550 1000
www.hoxtonhotels.com
info@hoxtonhotels.com

In the heart of The City, this uber-cool hotel is well located for Liverpool Street station and good if you are visiting City bars and clubs on your hen night. The Hoxton boasts a lively bar open 'til late and Grille, which is excellent if a little pricey. The funky rooms are small but perfectly formed with luxurious linen on the comfortable beds and excellent bathrooms complete with Aveda toiletries and decent hairdryers. Book early to get a good price.

6 **Would heartily recommend** 9

Imperial Hotel ££

Russell Square, London WC1 5BB
Tel. no 020 7837 3655
www.imperialhotels.co.uk
info@imperialhotels.co.uk

This three-star hotel is clean and fresh, although a little dated in style. It's in a great location close to Russell Square tube, 10 minutes walk to Oxford Street or Covent Garden for retail therapy. It makes a good base for theatre going or casino – 24-hour one around the corner!

A luxury room at K West Hotel.

Jurys Inn ££

60 Pentonville Road, Islington,
London N1 9LA
Tel. no 020 7282 5500
www.jurysinns.com
islington_reservations@jurysinns.com

Modern rooms with large comfortable beds
and all the amenities you could want make
this a great value-for-money choice. Just
across the road from Angel tube and one
stop away from King's Cross main line, this is
an excellent spot whether you plan to eat out
in trendy Upper Street or head into the West
End. You can book a three-bed room here,
which makes it a very economical choice. The
self-service breakfast goes on until 11am and
check out is at noon, which is very civilised for
the morning after the night before.

K West Hotel and Spa ££

Richmond Way, London W14 0AX
Tel. no 020 8008 6600
www.k-west.co.uk
info@k-west.co.uk

K West is handy for the new Westfield
Shopping Centre; it's also walking distance to
Notting Hill and Kensington High Street for
shopping or eating out. The modern large
bedrooms feature plasma screens, waffle
robes and hand-made mattresses. The
sophisticated contemporary design is
modern, but not completely minimalistic. Go
for a Spa package, or alternatively for the
'Rock'n'roll' package and get a three-hour
recording session in boutique studio around
the corner. The bar is buzzing on a Friday and
Saturday night with DJs playing until 2am.

❝ **staff were very efficient** ❞

Indulge at the K West Hotel spa.

VINOPOLIS

Organise a Hen Party to Remember

Treated like a princess

Organising a hen party and want to do something different, classy, fun and original?

Our different packages ensure that the bride-to-be celebrates her last 'single' night in style whilst learning something new!

Tasty treats!

You can choose from our **Classic Vinopolis Hen Party**, indulge in our fabulous **Champagne Hen Party** or for that extra special experience, choose our **Full Day Hen Party.** You can also upgrade any Vinopolis hen party to include a 30 minute Prosecco and tapas reception, served by your very own '**Butler in the Buff**'!

We also offer fabulously fun options with our **Inneventive Cooking Hen Party**, for a tasty afternoon of fun with food dedicated to the lady of the moment. Or for the bride that wants to be pampered, we offer a glamorous afternoon with **Candy and Bloom's** hair and make-up artists.

Unique experiences

Really girls, what more could you ask for?

Find out more at **www.vinopolis.co.uk/henparty** or call our team on 020 7940 8300

Park Inn London, Russell Square Hotel ££

92 Southampton Row,
Bloomsbury WC1B 4BH
Tel. no 020 7242 2828
www.rezidorparkinn.com
info.russellsquare@rezidorparkinn.com

With good access to King's Cross, St Pancras and Euston Stations and walking distance to Covent Garden, the West End and Oxford Street, this hotel has a prime location. Recently renovated, the rooms are comfortable and well equipped (the standard rooms even have an iron and ironing board!), the bathrooms are not huge though. The hot and cold buffet breakfast is really impressive for a hotel of this standard – that will sort the hangover out! All in all it's very good value for a four-star hotel in a central London location.

Sidney Hotel ££

68–76 Belgrave Road, Victoria,
London SW1V 2BP
Tel. no 020 7834 2738
www.sidneyhotel.com
info@sidneyhotel.com

This recently refurbished hotel is modern and stylish. The rooms are clean and well appointed, some are on the small side however, perhaps why it has a two-star rating. Very well located if you are arriving in London at either Victoria train or coach station and it's just a short walk to Sloane Square for a bit of retail therapy. The staff are friendly and helpful and our researchers gave the thumbs up to the showers and comfy beds. Check their website for offers – group bookings of five plus rooms get a discount.

St Christopher's Inn £

48–50 Camden High Street,
London NW1 0JH
Tel. no 020 7388 1012
www.st-christophers.co.uk
bookings@st-christophers.co.uk

If you're young at heart and want the slumber party experience, hostel accommodation is for you. This no-frills accommodation is clean and tidy; you can choose between mixed and female only dorms in rooms of six or eight. On the spot for clubbing at the legendary KOKOs (formerly Camden Palace), St Christopher's is close to the six Camden markets and the Lock. You're guaranteed

fresh linen and a locker in the room, but you might have to fight over the mirror. Breakfast is included in the price, so it's great value for money.

St Giles Hotel £££

Bedford Avenue, London WC1B 3GH
Tel. no 020 7300 3000
www.stgiles.com
frontoffice@stgiles.com

Location-wise the hotel is a short walk from Oxford Street, one tube-stop from Leicester Square and a good base for most of the main attractions, especially theatreland. St Giles offers an excellent room rate for a three-star central London hotel, it has decent sized rooms with ensuite shower rooms and basic but clean facilities, providing a comfortable night's stay. It has a great after-hours bar and the breakfast is plentiful and varied.

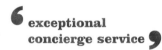

6 **exceptional concierge service** **9**

discount deals

There are plenty of bargains to be had on the many hotel booking websites. We have listed a few that hens have found useful in the past:

www.bookdirectrooms.com

www.booking.com

www.expedia.co.uk

www.hoteldirect.co.uk – this website features a 'hidden gem' deal where you get a fantastic deal, but they only tell you the star rating and the location of the hotel.

www.hotels.co.uk

www.lastminute.com

www.laterooms.com

www.travelrepublic.co.uk

Ascot

300 YEARS OF THE WORLD'S MOST FAMOUS RACECOURSE

Unique Hen and Stag Packages at Ascot

As Ascot celebrates its 300th Anniversary, 2011 has never been a better time to visit the World's Most Famous Racecourse.

Here are just some of our fantastic 2011 racedays:

Friday 6th (evening) & Saturday 7th May
Festival of Wine

Tuesday 14th to Saturday 18th June
Royal Ascot

Saturday 23rd July
King George Day and the Ascot Summer Cocktail Party

Saturday 6th August
Shergar Cup and '80s Concert

Friday 30th September & Saturday 1st October
5th Ascot CAMRA Beer Festival

Hen and Stag packages include:
Admission ticket, £2 bet, Racecard,
2 Glasses of Wine or 3 Pints of Beer.

Prices from £27pp. Stag Breakfast and Hen Champagne & Strawberry upgrades available.

**To book, call 01344 878536
or visit ascot.co.uk**

self-catering

Get the slumber party experience by renting an apartment in the capital. It may not be quite as central as some of the hotels, but is still a really good option. You can all get ready together (even friends who aren't staying) and have a few glasses of bubbly before hitting the town! There are loads of places to choose from. We suggest you try one of these online booking agents to find the ideal pad for your party.

Central London Apartments ££
Tel no. 0845 6442714
www.central-london-apartments.com
info@central-london-apartments.com

With over 180 apartments based in all areas of London, from Chelsea to the City and Bayswater to Victoria, they have something to suit everyone. There are plenty of one-night rentals available in all types of accommodation from studios to three-bed apartments in bronze, silver and gold categories starting at around £60 a night for a studio apartment for two.

Coach House London Vacation Rentals £–£££
Tel no. 020 8133 8332
www.rentals.chslondon.com
rentals@chslondon.com

This family run business has about 70 apartments on its books. Almost all of its self-catering rentals are the central London apartments and houses of residents temporarily away from the city. You have the informality, warmth and convenience of a real home in a London property, at prices to suit most pockets.

London Serviced Apartments ££
Tel no. 020 8923 0918
www.londonservicedapartments.co.uk
roy@londonservicedapartments.co.uk

Promising you the best rates on serviced apartments in London, this company has hundreds to offer. Arranged in luxury, mid-range and economy categories, you'll find something to suit every budget starting at £30 per person per night.

London School of Economics £
Tel no. 020 7955 7575
www.lsevacations.co.uk
vacations@lse.ac.uk

This award-winning, great value central London accommodation is available in University holidays only. The London School of Economics opens up its seven residencies, located around the West End all within reach of London's top attractions, to visitors with no link to the University. Ideal for groups and great for those on a budget, the rooms on offer are singles, twins and triples. B&B is also available.

Quality London Apartments ££
Tel no. 020 7476 8963
www.qualitylondonapartments.co.uk
sales@qualitylondonapartments.co.uk

This letting agent claims to have the best quality aparthotels in London. Offering apartments in three price brackets it covers all sectors of the market.

Serviced Lets Design Apartments ££
Tel no. 0871 226 1902
www.servicedlets.com

Serviced Lets specialise in modern city centre apartment homes. What makes them different to other serviced apartment agencies is that they exclusively lease all their own apartments, furnished and managed by them, guaranteeing a consistency of quality and service. Take a look at their award-winning conversion of the former Westminster Hospital – it's world class. This company also has serviced apartments for rent in Bristol and Cardiff.

Unilet Vacations £
Tel no. 020 7911 5181
www.westminster.ac.uk/vacations
summeraccommodation@westminster.ac.uk

Unilet offers accommodation in university residences located in the West End, Victoria, the South Bank, the City and Harrow-on-the-Hill with single and twin rooms available during the summer vacation. There are also a limited number of self-catering apartments on offer.

GIRLS JUST WANNA HAVE FUN!

PRISCILLA
QUEEN OF THE DESERT
the musical

Book the Ultimate PRE-SHOW PARTY for your HEN NIGHT or GIRLS' NIGHT OUT.

Cast Meet and Greet, Cocktails, Feather Boas and Show tickets in one inclusive price!

go to www.priscillatix.com

PALACE THEATRE London W1

where to eat and drink

London bars, especially the hip and trendy ones, are always choc full, so make sure you call ahead and reserve some space for your group. Some restaurants aren't keen on large groups, so you may not get your first choice of eatery. We have listed some here that happily cater for hen parties.

bars

B@1

20 Great Windmill Street, Soho,
London W1D 7LA
Tel no. 020 7479 7626
www.beatone.co.uk

With nine cocktail bars across the capital, Be At One is something of a London institution. These are genuine old-school bars and definitely a pretension-free zone! The Soho branch is the flagship, but you'll find outlets from the City to Clapham. It's free to reserve an area here for your party and the helpful bar staff will make sure your bash goes without a hitch. With a buy-one-get-one-free cocktail happy hour every day, B@1 is guaranteed to make you smile.

Barrio North

45 Essex Road, Islington,
London N1 2SF
Tel no. 020 7688 2882
www.barrionorth.com
shout@barrionorth.com

This ghetto fabulous bar, with its eccentric latino decor featuring real caravans as booths, always offers a warm welcome, however cold outside. The outstanding hand-crafted cocktails, the scintillating selection of rums and tequilas, the 'street food', together with their service with a personal touch, makes this the perfect venue if you're in the Islington area. At the weekend there's a vibrant party atmosphere as top DJs play cool tunes for the friendly up-for-it crowd.

Boundary Rooftop

2–4 Boundary Street, Shoreditch,
London E2 7DD
Tel. no 020 7729 1051
www.theboundary.co.uk/rooftop
info@theboundary.co.uk

Imagine a sun-drenched island bar then put in the East End…you have the Boundary Rooftop! Part of Terence Conran's Boundary project, it includes a large bar with seating around an open fireplace, a 48-seat grill restaurant, served by its own kitchen, and a designer garden. There are stunning 360-degree views from Canary Wharf to the City's Gherkin and Barbican to the rooftops and spires of East London. The space is replete with a large sail-like canopy, heating, festoon lighting and Welsh blankets (for when it gets chilly). If you want a hen night with a view, get the lift to the roof!

The Boundary Rooftop bar.

Buddha Bar.

Buddha Bar

8 Victoria Embankment,
London WC2R 2AB
Tel. no 020 3371 7777
www.buddhabar-london.com
enquiry@buddhabar-london.com

On the north bank of the river, just below Waterloo Bridge, this opulent bar exudes Asian exoticism. Cocktails are sophisticated and well mixed, and the pan-Asian food is exquisite, if a little on the expensive side. The lounge bar area is an elegant and impressive mezzanine overlooking the impressive ground floor dining area, all themed with Asian decor and moody lighting creating a warm and inviting ambience. The laid-back atmosphere early in the evening gets livelier as the evening progresses and the music picks up.

'been there...'

My reason for choosing London was that I live there and I'm lazy! We booked a big table at Pizza Express near Shaftesbury Avenue, then went and saw La Clique at the Hippodrome, which was the best cabaret show I've ever seen. We'd all dressed the part, so we went to this little club called Storm afterwards. It was a great night, not too mad, and we definitely picked the right show.

Cellar Door

Zero Aldwych, Covent Garden,
London W2E 7DN
Tel. no 020 7240 8848
www.cellardoor.biz
open@cellardoor.biz

If you're looking for a sexy speakeasy vibe with a very intimate atmosphere, then this could be the bar for you and your chicks. Live acts entertain from 9pm each evening (and some afternoons) serving up a range of events from seductive swing to bawdy cabaret. Indulge in their exclusive signature cocktails or try a pinch of snuff! At Cellar Door you can expect the unexpected...

Dirty Martini

11/12 Russell Street, Covent Garden,
London WC2B 5HZ
Tel. no 0207 632 2317
www.dirtymartini.uk.com
events@cgrestaurants.com

Right on the famous Covent Garden piazza beneath the cosmopolitan London restaurant Tuttons Brasserie, Dirty Martini is a great place for a hen party, whether it's for pre-dinner drinks or for late-night dancing. The intimate vaulted underground bar offers stunning cocktails, delicious bar food, laid back atmosphere & funky bar vibes making it a stylish and sexy late night venue. Book a luxurious leather seating booth for you and your hens.

Dirty Martini.

oungelover

Whitby Street, London E1 6JU
el. no 020 7012 1234
www.lestroisgarcons.com
nfo@loungelover.co.uk

This glamorous bar with its themed 'areas'
operates on a booking system so you will
eed to pick up the phone to make sure you
ave a space even if you just want to come
or a drink. Japanese-inspired food is
vailable in the form of small plates for
haring. Book an area to yourself if you've
ot a large group, choose from the luscious
Red Area with its Deco furniture or the classic
Baroque Area with a floor to ceiling tapestry
nough to set off any hen party!

Mark's Bar

Downstairs bar in Mark Hix's
Soho restaurant)
56–70 Brewer Street, Soho,
London W1F 9UP
Tel. no 020 7292 3518
www.hixsoho.co.uk

Open from noon–12.30am, this New York
style bar is cool and funky. With an
mpressive team of London's leading cocktail
shakers (and movers), the cocktail list is
egendary. But if cocktails don't float your
boat, then don't worry there is a huge wine
st and enlightened beer menu. Part of the
deal is that you order some food, but with
fabulous bar snacks, like sloe gin jelly, that's
easy! You can even book a private room for
up to 12 people.

On Anon

London Pavillion, Piccadilly Circus,
London W1V 9LA
Tel. no 020 7287 8008
www.onanon.co.uk
info@onanon.co.uk

Overlooking Piccadilly Circus, On Anon is a
great multi-room venue with a room to suit
every mood, from the relaxed Studio Bar to
the feisty Glam bar and the retro Lodge to
the lively Club! On four floors and with nine
beautifully designed individual bars there's
bound to be one that captures your
imagination. Choose from an extensive range
of cocktails, wines and premium draught
beers, perfect place anytime: for lunch, to get
the evening started or for full on clubbing.

On Anon in Piccadilly Circus.

The Moose Bar

31 Duke Street, Mayfair,
London, W1U 1LG
Tel. no 020 7644 1426

If you dream snow-capped mountains all
year round, then you'll love the Moose Bar.
With cowhide upholstery and panoramic
mountain scenes painted on the walls it is
just the right side of kitsch. Could be a good
place to go before you Sing-a-long-a-Sound
of Music! And with a very happy 'happy hour'
this is an excellent place to start your night.
There's a large basement space for some
après-drinks dancing till 3am.

The Langley

5 Langley Street, Covent Garden,
London WC2H 9JA
Tel. no 020 7836 5005
www.thelangley.co.uk
info@thelangley.co.uk

Covent Garden media and fashion types
know a good thing when they see one. That's
why The Langley remains a design classic –
complete with menus to match. Go kitsch at
its retro Geneva bar or retire cosily
underground in The Vault. Whatever your
bag, you're bound to enjoy The Langley's
fantastic wines and cocktails, go for a platter
to share or choose 3 dishes for £10. There's
a great choice of private rooms and booths
that can be reserved for your hen party. And
when it's time to get on down, there's
absolutely no shortage of funky beats.

restaurants

Barrica ££–£££

62 Goodge St, Fitzrovia, W1T 4NE
Tel. no 020 7436 9448
www.barrica.co.uk
info@barrica.co.uk

Typically Iberian in style, this classic Spanish tapas bar has a really fantastic selection of great wines, such as the trendy white, Albariño from Galicia. The Spanish waiting staff are all very helpful and will help you choose a good combination of dishes, from the jamón ibérico de bellota to the Padrón peppers – deep-fried and salted they're delish, but be warned that one in ten retains a fierce spiciness that brings tears to the eyes. For pudding, indulge in the tarta santiago, a dense almond cake that is unsurpassable. A great party restaurant.

Café des Amis ££

11–14 Hanover Place,
London WC2E 9JP
Tel. no 020 7379 3444A
www.cafedesamis.co.uk

Situated in the heart of theatreland, this is the ideal venue for pre- or post-show food. The fantastic French cuisine served in elegant surroundings has all the chic of Paris without the Eurostar fiasco! Start your decadent night with cocktails in the Wine & Champagne bar and continue your celebration in the Long Acre private dining room. For a special ladies lunch or a 'Sex in the City' evening say 'au revoir' to singledom at Café des Amis…

Los Locos ££

24–26 Russell Street, Covent Garden,
London WC2B 5HF
Tel. no 020 7379 0220
www.los-locos.co.uk
info@los-locos.co.uk

This Tex-Mex party restaurant in Covent Garden has seen more than a few hen parties and they know how to make it a memorable night. There are three different party menus for groups of eight or more, each with plenty of choice from latino favourites, plus the hen gets a free sharing cocktail and souvenir t-shirt and everyone else gets shooters! 'Special entertainment' is even allowed if arranged in advance. Los Locos is restaurant, bar and club all under one roof, why go anywhere else?

Smollensky's Bar and Grill ££

105 The Strand,
London WC2R 0AA
Tel. no 020 7497 2101
www.smollenskys.com

Smollensky's on The Strand is a bright and spacious restaurant with a large and buzzing bar area. The restaurant at Smollensky's on The Strand is a cosmopolitan dining area with a distinct 'New York' feel, offering stunning modern American cuisine with some interesting twists. Choose the party menu for your hen night; there's something for everyone on there at a set price. Book the VIP stage area and let your hen night begin in this party central restaurant.

Tiroler Hut £–££

Westbourne Grove, Bayswater,
London W2
Tel. no 020 7727 3981
www.tirolerhut.co.uk
reservations@tirolerhut.co.uk

After 40 plus years of providing food and entertainment, Joseph your host knows a thing or two about throwing a party. This crazy Austrian restaurant, with staff dressed in traditional Alpine regalia and playing everything from accordion to cow bells offers you a night to remember. Vast platters of sausages, smoked meats, fried potatoes, sauerkraut and other Tirolean delights will be served up. Grab yourself a stein of beer and yodel the night away.

TGI Friday's ££

25–29 Coventry Street, London W1D 7A
Tel. no 0844 372 7914
www.tgifridays.co.uk
leicestersquare@tgifridays.co.uk

This nationwide bar and grill needs no introduction, there's one in every city and large town in the UK, but sometimes the familiar is comforting and the food is always good. So if you love all things American, the TGI's staff will dazzle you with their smiles and service making this a night to remember. All your favourites make an appearance on the menu: potato skins, nachos, burgers, salmon and tuna steaks, so order a Long Island Ice Tea and let Friday's do the rest.

RƎVOLUTION
MASTERCLASS

GET BEHIND THE BAR AND BECOME A COCKTAIL MASTER IN THIS 90 MINUTE INTERACTIVE SESSION!

- ✪ **COCKTAILS**
- ✪ **TASTING**
- ✪ **TOOLS**
- ✪ **SKILLS**
- ✪ **GAMES**

HEN GOES FREE!
MINIMUM 8 PEOPLE

QUOTE PROMO CODE 'MARTINI' FOR FREE HEN OFFER
PACKAGES FROM ONLY £24.95 PER PERSON PLUS
NEW PARTY FOOD OPTIONS NOW AVAILABLE

TO BOOK...
ONLINE: REVOLUTION-BARS.CO.UK
PHONE: 0800 6300 860
ASK: A MEMBER OF STAFF

ANY OCCASION, ANY SIZE... REVOLUTION IS THE PERFECT PLACE TO EAT, DRINK & PARTY!

Available in Soho, The City, Clapham, Clapham Junction, Richmond and Sutton
All rights reserved - offer can be withdrawn at any time - deposit required - please drink responsibly

where to party

The capital of choice, London has such a variety of places to party that one night may not be enough. Whether you want shows or cabaret, karaoke or clubbing, you'll find something here for everyone. So get the bling on and apply that lip gloss, it's time to party!

Club Aquarium

256–264 Old Street, London EC1V 9DD
Tel no. 020 7251 6136
www.clubaquarium.co.uk
info@clubaquarium.co.uk

The only club in London with its own swimming pool, Club Aquarium in Shoreditch encourages you to party in swimwear 'Tropicana style'. If you're prepared to get wet, then you can recline in the Jacuzzi sipping cocktails. When you've dried off, head to the dancefloor: on Saturdays the music ranges from 70s and 80s Carwash to the super-camp, hen party favourite Adonis Cabaret.

Fabric

77a Charterhouse Street, London
EC1M 3HN
Tel no. 020 7336 8898
www.fabriclondon.com

This superclub serves up a line-up of superstar DJs pumping out heavy drum'n'bass and hip hop beats with the bass cranked up to the max. If you're a serious clubber, you're going love Fabric and especially lounging on its comfy beds. Make sure you're suitably attired, Saturday night is a seriously glamorous affair.

Jewel

29–30 Maiden Lane, London WC2E 7JS
Tel no. 020 7845 9980
www.jewelbar.com
info@jewelcoventgarden.co.uk

If you delve into the back streets of Covent Garden, just behind the Piazza, you'll find the hidden gem. Jewel Covent Garden and its

sister bar in Piccadilly have a little more sparkle than some of their jaded competitors. With plenty of drinks offers early on, it's a great place to start the evening off. The menu here is truly international so there's bound to be something to whet your appetite. Then after you've eaten immerse yourself in a world of distinctive global house music and high class style on Saturdays until 1am.

Jewel bar in Covent Garden.

Singstar at Karaoke Box Smithfield.

Karaoke Box Smithfield
12 Smithfield Street, London EC1A 9LA
Tel no. 020 7329 9991
www.karaokebox.co.uk
smithfield@karaokebox.co.uk

This is the perfect partnership between karaoke and bar-club and it's all about having fun. Whether you just come for a drink and a dance or if you book one of the 16 luxurious private rooms for your own exclusive karaoke session, this is going to be a night to remember. You can order stone-baked pizza, platters of sushi, champagne or cocktails all at the push of a button and they will be delivered direct to your room for your enjoyment.

KOKO
1a Camden High Street,
London NW1 7JE
Tel no. 0870 432 5527
www.koko.uk.com

One time theatre and infamously The Camden Palace until 2004, this venue is known throughout the world. It was where Madonna played her first UK gig and was 'home' to many New Romantic bands and local boys, Madness. Now after a multi million pound refurb KOKO has risen from the ashes once again providing quality live entertainment and club nights to North London.

Madame JoJo's
8–10 Brewer Street, London W1F 0SE
Tel no. 020 7734 3040
www.madamejojos.com
paris@madamejojos.com

Saturday nights at Madame JoJo's means the world famous Kitsch Cabaret: an evening of feathers, glitz and dazzling live music. It's sparkling with a million sequins and it's just waiting for you and your hen night. A blend of old-school music hall and Las Vegas floorshow, classic revue with a modern twist; you will enjoy a unique theatrical experience: drinks, supper and dancing, top notch cabaret with live singing, magic, comedy, high-kicking glamour and belting showstoppers. Check the website for other cabaret nights.

Medieval Banquet
St Katherine Dock, London E1W 1BP
Tel no. 020 7480 5353
www.medievalbanquet.com
info@medievalbanquet.com

Eat, drink and be merry. What more is there to a hen party? Well at Medieval Banquet there are fighting knights, strolling players and dancing wenches providing a magical medieval pageant for your delight, while you quaff mead (wine or beer actually), cry wassail and feast on medieval fare. After the show, there is music and dancing until late. All for one very reasonable rate.

Pacha

Terminus Place, Victoria,
London SW1
Tel no. 020 7833 3139
www.pachalondon.com
info@pachalondon.com

A little slice of the Ibiza club scene in
London, Pacha is for you if you love uplifting
house but can't afford a trip to the Balearic
Islands. An all new state-of-the-art sound and
light system along with refreshed decor and
a luxe private VIP room for 20 people. In
2010 the club promises a new roof terrace
offering an al fresco clubbing experience like
no other venue in London. Check the website
for more details.

Storm

28a Leicester Square,
London WC2H 7LE
Tel no. 020 7839 2633
www.stormlondon.co.uk
info@stormlondon.co.uk

This ever-popular intimate little club is right in
the centre of the West End. At the weekend
you'll find a range of music including RnB,
funky house, old school garage and hip hop.
If you're up for all night dancing, Storm takes
you right through to 5am.

Supperclub

12 Acklam Road, London W10 5QZ
Tel no. 020 8964 6600
www.supperclub.com

Brand new on the London scene this avant
garde club incorporates many of the
provocative elements of its big sister in
Amsterdam. Situated at the funky end of
Portobello Road, this edgy club offers an
exciting and memorable night out. Start off
Bar Rouge with drinks and live performance
move on to Salle Neige for an fine dining
experience with a difference – a reclining
one! Yes, you eat on beds. Later the room
transforms into a nightclub for dancing. A
totally unique night out.

The Ministry of Sound

103 Gaunt Street, London SE1 6DP
Tel no. 020 7378 6528/0870 060 0010
www.ministryofsound.com

Needing no introductions, this is the club th
shot to fame in the 90s and has now becom
a household name. The concept was simple
excellent house music blasting out through
an unsurpassable sound system
complemented by a great light show and
uber cool design. Still drawing huge crowds
to sample their special brand of clubbing Th
Ministry is a serious clubber's choice.

The Salle de Neige at Supperclub.

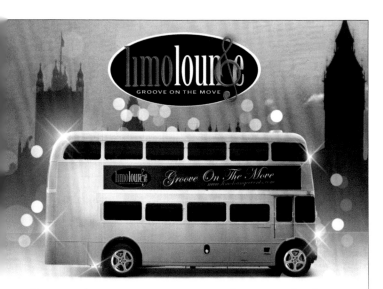

Stand out on your hen night
...travel in style

The Limo Lounge is a 1962 London Route Master with a modern twist. It offers an exclusive private hire service allowing you to experience a unique alternative whilst you groove on the move. As soon as you are aboard, you will immediately be surrounded by a setting that can only be described as ultimate luxury and comfort.

Leather Seating
Fully Stocked Bar
Large LCD Screen
DVD / Ipod Docking
Indoor & Outdoor Sound
Dj Facilities

Tel: 020 8295 1888 **Mob:** 07814 755 416
Web: www.limoloungeevents.com

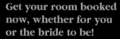

bath

Bath Abbey (top), Pulteney Bridge (middle), The Royal Crescent (bottom).

Pitchforks at the ready, we're hitting Somerset – glorious home of cider, festivals, proper cheese and The Wurzels. However, if you want 'ahh' rather than 'arr', stunning Bath fits the bill – after all, it's had glamour and luxurious living sewn up since the Romans installed the baths here. And great nightlife's the icing on the Bath Bun.

what to do

Bath is small but perfectly formed and makes a great city for a hen do. For starters, there's the sheer 'mmm' factor – amber-stoned Georgian buildings, a wide, lazy river and lots of gorgeous boutiques. Daytime activities include spa, boating, retail therapy, long lunches and picnics; at night there's top-notch comedy and several very funky little clubs.

Naturally, Bath's fancy-dress inspiration is plentiful, you'll see folks wandering around wearing anything from Jane Austen flouncery to togas. Not to mention the Barber and yellow tartan trouser combo favoured by many local men. The clubs are relaxed about dress code – anything goes and you won't feel self-conscious. If you do, simply drink a lot of cider. It cures all such ills.

You're too refined for cider? Well, pardon moi. Flounce down to one of the fab little wine bars dotted around the city or choose from any number of superb little restaurants. Bath's not exactly cosmopolitan but it has something for everyone.

To sum it up, Bath's about the body. Eat, drink, spa. Ahhh!

10 good reasons

1. it's soooo pretty
2. crazy golf in Victoria Park
3. the capital of spa
4. Komedia
5. picnics on Solsbury Hill
6. good restaurant scene
7. historic and charming
8. rowing on the River Avon
9. Petanque in Queen's Square
10. cool little clubs

Find out what a roman pamper day was all about at the historic Roman Baths.

sounds of the city

Old Style Love As a bride embarks on this important stage in her life, she often asks, 'What's missing? What should I be bringing to this marriage?' Tragically, the answer is all too often 'the ability to make my own nipple tassles and garter'. It's true that hubby aint gonna be too impressed with some mass-produced nonsense tied round your leg on the Big Night, so you'll be relieved to hear that The Makery offers lessons in these important life skills. Take your ladies along and learn to sew your way to wedded bliss. There are also classes in drawing the male nude (valuable research); making bath bombs to get your wedding night off to an explosive, yet hygienic, start; and jewellery, fascinator or lingerie making. All in all, a really good giggle.

Makin' whoopee Whoopie cakes, cupcakes, wedding cakes...if you feel the need to gorge on gorgeous iced delights, go to Green Park Station market on a Saturday morning and look for the Bath Cake Company. Cupcake decoration classes of two and a half hours can be run from your rented accommodation for up to ten hens. The theme is generally anything pretty – but you can name something a little bit different if you like. Those with a sweet tooth, go to bathcakecompany.co.uk.

Get down on it For daytime laughs, join the pole dancing craze with the lovely Alice at Pole Dancing Bath. For once, don't slather yourself in lotion after your morning shower, otherwise you won't be able to get up the pole, let alone slither gracefully down it. Pick a song and style of music you like, then turn up in heels and shorts and Alice will teach you a sexy routine. Pole dancing is not only the key to extracting favours from your loved one in the bedroom, it's also a great firming and toning workout, and quite addictive into the bargain. The great thing about this hen activity is that you might be able to persuade the fiancé to pay for it...leave the web browser open at poledancingbath.com.

Perfect day Spa is a well-practiced art in Bath and a traditional way to while away a few hours in this splendiferous Georgian city. Our recommended sunny day in Bath is this: head straight

Get creative at The Makery in Walcot Street, Bath.

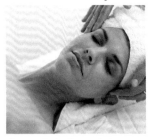

to the baths for a few hours of rooftop swimming, steaming and chilling. Have a genteel coffee and cake in the nearby Pump Rooms before trotting over to the Bathwick boating station. Here, you can hire a variety of vessels including punts and large gondola type affairs. Now break out the champagne and strawberries. You'll eventually land at The Bathampton Mill, a lovely spot for an al fresco or sofa-bound boozy lunch. Suitably refreshed, the row back to Bath centre is mercifully downstream. Follow with top class stand-up or dressed-up cabaret nights at Komedia (komedia.co.uk) for the perfect day.

Picture this Imagine the scene. You and your best friends relaxing with a glass of bubbly in your chi chi Bath accommodation. A night on the town ahead, but first – a ring on the doorbell announces the arrival of your very own pamper party. Frances and her therapist friends will provide massage, facials, pedicure, manicure, reflexology, make-up lessons and more – take a look at the website skinperfect.biz to tailor a fabulous few hours of being completely and utterly spoiled. Frances can arrange your party anytime, anywhere and for any number. Bliss, and from only £20 per head.

Red, red wine The chaps at the Tasting House in Larkhall, Bath are lovely and very knowledgeable in all things wine. Book your party in for a relaxed and civilised evening tasting and appreciating fine wines on the sofas in their cosy little shop. With a glass of good champagne on arrival and a selection of delicious nibbles, it makes a gorgeous hen party for those who prefer a little refinement while they get hammered. Hic.

'been there...'

We wanted to do a spa day, so we chose Bath. The new spa is modern but not really posh, it was so nice looking over the rooftops as we swam around in the sun. We went for lunch at Jamie's Italian, which is lush, then I had a treatment at Neal's Yard while the girls went shopping. We went to Opa and Po Na Nas later on. Bath is a really chilled out, beautiful city.

Take in the fantastic views from the rooftop pool at Bath's Thermae Spa.

where to stay

For classy little boutique hotels, you just can't beat Bath. If you like a more unique feel, then you've chosen well. Bath does cater for those on a budget too, though.

hotels & hostels

Belushi's £

9 Green Street, Bath BA1 2JY
Tel. no 01225 481444
www.belushis.com/bath
party@belushis.com

This low cost hostel style accommodation in the centre of the city features dorm rooms with bunks. There is a lively Belushi bar restaurant on site and breakfast is included in the rate. Clean linen is provided, but you need to suppy your own towel.

Harington's Hotel £££

8–10 Queen Street, Bath BA1 1HE
Tel. no 01225 461728
www.haringtonshotel.co.uk
post@haringtonshotel.co.uk

This bijou boutique hotel is right in the centre of Bath and just a couple of minutes walk from the Thermae Spa. Despite its central location it's in a quiet secluded street offering convenience and tranquility. The Harington also has apartments ideal for groups.

Macdonald Bath Spa H£££

Sydney Road, Bath, BA2 6JF
Tel. no 0844 879 9106
www.macdonaldhotels.co.uk/bathspa
enquiries@macdonald-hotels.co.uk

This 5-star hotel is luxury at its best offering first-class accommodation and spa facilities. The hotel accommodates hen parties with tailormade spa treatments and pyjama parties this hotel ticks all the boxes!

The Halcyon £££

2–3 South Parade Bath BA2 4AA
Tel. no 01225 331200
www.thehalcyon.com
info@thehalcyon.com

Bath's brand new boutique hotel offers pure luxury right in the heart of Bath. The standard rooms, all designed by an award-winning interiors expert, feature quality beds with sumptuous linen, 32" plasma TVs, walk-in showers and White Company products.

Travelodge Central£

1 York Buildings, George Street, Bath BA1 2EB
Tel. no 0871 984 6219
www.travelodge.co.uk

For location and convenience you can't beat Bath's Travelodge Central. It's literally stumbling distance from a number of great bars, restaurants and clubs. However, this does mean it can be a little noisy, but hey, you're going to be out partying anyway!

✳ **shared room without breakfast**

£ under £30
££ £30–£60
£££ over £60
pppn

Belushi's, Bath.

self-catering

1 Circus Place
1 Circus Place, Bath BA1 2PG
Tel. no 01225 446 888
www.visitbath.co.uk/site/accommodation
tourism@bathtourism.co.uk
Set just a stone's throw away from the Circus
and the Royal Crescent, Circus Place is the
perfect place for a luxury break in the West
Country.

Bath Holiday Rentals ££
Regency House, 2 Wood Street,
Queen Square, Bath BA1 2JQ
Tel. no 01225 482 225
www.bathholidayrentals.com
alexa@bathholidayrentals.com

You'll get a warm and friendly service from
this Bath-based company offering
luxurious, short-term lets. The
majority of properties are close
to the heart of the city at some
of the most prestigious
addresses.

Burlington Street Apartment
13 Burlington Street, Bath
BA1 2SA
Tel. no 01225 830 830
www.bathandcountryholidays.co.uk
info@bathandcountryholidays.co.uk
Located in a fabulous Georgian Townhouse,
this apartment offers 4-star luxury. The
perfect place to relax and unwind after
exploring what Bath's city centre has to offer
and indulging in a little retail therapy.

Laura's Townhouse Apartments ££
14 Beauford Square, Bath BA1 1HJ
Tel. no 01225 464 238
www.laurastownhouseapartments.co.uk
laura@laurastownhouseapartments.co.uk

Laura's offers stunning townhouse and
apartment self-catering accommodation in
listed buildings in the heart of Bath. All
tastefully furnished and with modern comforts
of home, such as widescreen TV, DVD, Wi-Fi
and Ipod dock. Properties sleep up to 12.

Take a limo into town from Riverside Apartment.

Riverside Apartment £
Batheaston, Bath
Tel. no 01225 852 226
www.riversapart.co.uk
sheilapex@questmusic.co.uk

At Riverside Apartment you get the
best of both worlds, a beautiful
rural setting on the River Avon
only 10 minutes from the
centre of Bath (by limo of
course). Your friendly host will
arrange pamper days, a
recording studio party, catering
and other services to order for
a truly tailormade hen party.

shared room without breakfast
£ under £30
££ £30–£60
£££ over £60
pppn

The Residence £
Ormonde Lodge, Weston Road,
Bath BA1 2XZ
Tel. no 01225 750 180
www.theresidencebath.com
info@theresidencebath.com

Two splendid Georgian properties sleeping
up to 15 people are available from this
company. One is a 10 minute walk from the
centre of Bath, the other just outside the city.

Waterfront House
230 Lower Bristol Rd, Bath BA2 3DQ
Tel. no 01225 310 033
www.waterfronthousebath.co.uk
info@amberleyhouse.net

Situated on the River Avon, up to six guests
can enjoy the comforts of the apartment in a
picturesque setting.

where to eat and drink

You're spoilt for choice when it comes to eating and drinking in Bath. There's a wealth of lively bars and a choice of fine dining or budget eateries.

bars & pubs

Ha Ha Bar and Grill
The Tramshed, Beehive Yard,
Bath BA1 5BD
Tel. no 01225 421 200
www.hahaonline.co.uk
haha.bath@bayrestaurantgroup.com

Situated just off Walcot Street, Bath's Boho area, Ha Ha is a spacious bar and restaurant with a large heated outdoor area, usable all year round. You can reserve an exclusive area for your party and select from the wine list or sample something from the Grill.

Hall and Woodhouse
1 Old King Street, Bath BA1 2JW
Tel. no 01225 469 259
www.hall-woodhousebath.co.uk
bath@hall-woodhousebath.co.uk

Newly opened in 2010, this super-sized bar bar and restaurant offers customers a tantalising selection of food and offers an extensive wine. A former auction house, the interior is stunning – the main feature being a central staircase leading up to the restaurant on the first floor. You can also dine on the rooftop terrace with views over the city.

Revolution
York Buildings, George Street,
Bath BA1 2EB
Tel. no 01225 336 168
www.revolution-bars.co.uk/bath

This stunning venue, a former post office, is a great place to spread out for a leisurely lunch or party hard into the evening. With cocktail lessons and chocolate fondues on offer, the helpful management will put together a night to remember. And you can dance on until late with Bath's finest DJs.

Sub 13
4 Edgar Buildings, George Street,
Bath BA1 2EE
Tel. no 01225 466 667
www.sub13.net
drinks@sub13.net

This super chic underground bar is located at the top of town close to Revolution. Sub 13 is an intimate bar with vaulted ceilings and cosy booths, it also has a large outdoor area for sipping cocktails on those balmy summer evenings. The experienced bartenders will mix you a quality cocktail from the extensive list at Sub 13. There's always a party atmosphere here and a very personal vibe.

Try one of the splendid cocktails at Sub 13 in Bath.

cafés & restaurants

Clarkes ££
7 Argyle Street, Bath BA1
Tel. no 01225 444 440
www.clarkesbath.co.uk
clarkesbath@btconnect.com

Set in one of Bath's most famous Georgian streets, just a short walk from Pulteney Bridge, Clarkes is a great choice for a hen night meal. The emphasis is on tasty, inventive cuisine with a French influence. You can choose to dine in the stylish but informal ground floor dining room or the more intimate, luxurious dining room on the lower level, which is also available for private hire. On the first floor, you can start your night with cocktail or glass of wine in the colourful Chazz Bar.

Jamie's Italian £££
10 Milsom Place, Bath
BA1 1BZ
Tel. no 01225 510 051
www.jamieoliver.com/italian/bath

Housed in an ecletic Georgian property right in the heart of Bath, this all day eatery is just what you'd expect from the phenomenon that is 'Jamie'. With hams, salamis and other mouth-watering ingredients hanging over the bar as you enter, you know from the start that this is going to be a true foodie experience.

Firehouse Rotisserie ££
2 John Street, Bath BA1 2JL
Tel. no 01225 482 070
www.firehouserotisserie.co.uk

Voted one of the top five American restaurants in the UK by Channel 4, Firehouse offers superb Californian cuisine in a relaxed but buzzy atmosphere. Choose between one of their gourmet brick-fired pizzas and a great selection of fish and meat dishes.

Opa £££
14 North Parade, Bath BA2 4AJ
Tel. no 01225 317 900
www.opabath.com

This Greek meze restaurant serves a wide range of authentic dishes and always has good fresh fish. The underground vaulted cellars next to the river transform into a lively club around 11pm and you can dance to a mix of cheesy disco and dance tunes until late in the evening.

The Arch ££–£££
2–3 Queen Street, Bath BA1 1HE
Tel. no 01225 444403
www.thearchbath.co.uk

Enjoy a modern British menu featuring rustic and classic dishes at this flamboyant restaurant in the heart of Bath. Choose from casual, fine dining or set menu.

The Jazz Cafe £
1 Kingsmead Street,
Bath BA1 2AA
Tel. no 01225 329 002
www.bathjazzcafe.co.uk
ch@bathjazzcafe.co.uk

Overlooking Kingsmead Square, this friendly individual licensed café serves fantastic all-day breakfasts, a great choice of lunches and afternoon tea. The atmosphere is always chilled out with a wide variety of jazz music being played and occasional live jazz sets. The Jazz Cafe is also available for private hire for your own exclusive hen do.

**2 courses
+ half a bottle
of wine**

**£ under £20
££ £20–£35
£££ over £35**

Hire a private dining room at The Arch in Bath.

where to party

It may be way out west, but Bath has a lively nightime scene. If you scratch the surface of the usual cheesy clubs, you'll find unique events and venues.

Club XL

Blue Rooms

George Street, Bath BA1 2EB
Tel. no 01225 470 040
www.bluerooms.net
info@bluerooms.net

This stylish bar and club serves an extraordinary range of spirits, claiming 'if you can't find it here it probably hasn't been invented'. Dance under the starlight ceiling until the wee small hours or book a VIP area for an exclusive experience.

Celsius

1–3 South Parade, Bath
Tel. no 01225 312 800
www.celsiusicebar.co.uk
info@celsiusbar.co.uk
Bath wasn't the first place we would have looked for an underground ice cave and yet,

bucking the local inclination for all things thermal, Celsius Ice Bar welcomes you to its freezing lair. Huge padded jackets and gloves are supplied, and drinks are served in ice glasses. Warm up with cool tunes at normal room temperature in the club afterwards. Cool, yet hot. Not for those with sensitive teeth.

Club XL

90B Walcot Street, Bath BA1 5BG
Tel. no 0845 555 1111
www.clubxl.co.uk
info@clubxl.co.uk

Located in Bath's bohemian Walcot Street, Club XL caters for all tastes and will welcome your hen night with open arms. If you're looking for a VIP experience to add a bit of style and glamour to your hen night, why not take the membership option.

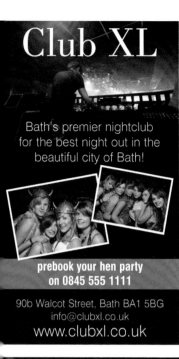

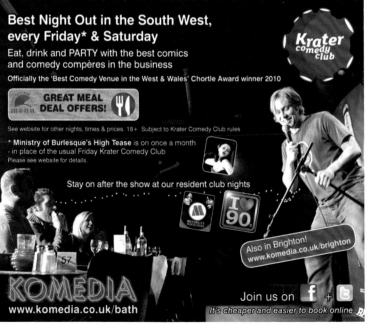

The fabulous Komedia in the exquisitely renovated Beau Nash Theatre.

Komedia
22–23 Westgate Street, Bath BA1 1EP
Tel. no 0845 293 8480
www.komedia.co.uk/bath
info@komedia.co.uk

Based in the centre of Bath, Komedia is famed for its award-winning formula of great shows, fab food, excellent drinks' choice and welcoming atmosphere. With everything from hilarious stand-up comedy and the sassiest of sultry cabaret, to screenings of your favourite films – sing-a-long style – and followed up with dancing to 90s tunes on a Friday and Motown tracks on a Saturday night, it's the perfect venue for any hen party!

Po Na Na
8–9 North Parade, Bath BA2 4AL
Tel. no 01225 424 952
www.bathponana.com
bathpnn@ponana.com

This Moroccan styled club in four underground caverns has lots of intimate seating booths for your party. Friday nights are full of guilty pleasures with Bath's biggest cheese party featuring your fave floor fillers and a karaoke singalong room. Saturday nights see superstar DJ Ross Deviant playing an eclectic mix of quality anthems from a variety of genres.

Second bridge
10 Manvers Street, Bath BA1 1JQ
Tel. no 01225 464 449
www.secondbridge.co.uk
mail@secondbridge.co.uk

Bustling with party animals from all walks of life, The Second Bridge caters for a wide range of musical tastes playing the latest in Funky house anthems to R&B classics. You'll be left spoilt for choice!

The Lounge
43 St. James's Parade, Bath BA1 1UQ
Tel. no 01225 424 321
www.loungecocktailbar.com
salvo@loungecocktailbar.com

This Italian cocktail bar never fails to impress with a wide choice of drinks from mojitos to champagne.

The Weir Lounge
Spring Gardens Road, Bath BA2 6PW
Tel. no 01225 447 187
www.weirlounge.co.uk
info@weirlounge.co.uk

Set alongside the River Avon, The Weir Lounge offers an outdoor terrace where guests can enjoy a few alfresco drinks before partying at this exclusive venue in style.

RƎVOLUTION
MASTERCLASS

GET BEHIND THE BAR AND BECOME A COCKTAIL MASTER IN THIS 90 MINUTE INTERACTIVE SESSION!

- ★ **COCKTAILS**
- ★ **TASTING**
- ★ **TOOLS**
- ★ **SKILLS**
- ★ **GAMES**

HEN GOES FREE!
MINIMUM 8 PEOPLE

QUOTE PROMO CODE 'MARTINI' FOR FREE HEN OFFER
PACKAGES FROM ONLY £24.95 PER PERSON PLUS
NEW PARTY FOOD OPTIONS NOW AVAILABLE

TO BOOK...
ONLINE: REVOLUTION-BARS.CO.UK
PHONE: 0800 6300 860
ASK: A MEMBER OF STAFF

ANY OCCASION, ANY SIZE... REVOLUTION IS THE PERFECT PLACE TO EAT, DRINK & PARTY!

Revolution Vodka Bar, York Buildings, George Street, Bath
All rights reserved - offer can be withdrawn at any time - deposit required - please drink responsibly

belfast

City Hall (top), Ferris Wheel (middle), River Lagan at night (bottom).

Ireland's buzzing capital is increasingly being recognised as one of the world's greatest city break destinations. With its long and varied musical heritage, Belfast has always been a place to enjoy the 'craic' – that's Irish for 'good time'. Rich in historic charm and modern wow-factor, it's a hen party destination with real class.

what to do

Our research has led to several key discoveries about Belfast. With limited space in which to publish these findings, a catch-all statement must suffice: it's brilliant!

Think of Northern Ireland's capital and the chances are that those old 80s news images of war-scarred streets will come to mind. But those days are past, and modern Belfast is an absolutely superb venue for a city break. The people are famously friendly, and the place is loved for being unpretentious and vibrant.

If you want to name two things the Irish are famous for, it's boozing and music. Therefore, you shouldn't be surprised to find that the capital is humming with a great party vibe.

For the more adventurous and outdoorsy among you, the landscape around Belfast is largely unspoilt and utterly stunning. The view from volcanic crag Scrabo is a 19-mile panorama including the Isle of Man, the Mourne Mountains and Scotland's coast. If you're into walking, riding or more extreme outdoor pursuits, it's pretty much paradise.

Strangford Lough is the place for craziness such as rock hopping. Dotted around the countryside are various hostelries where you can enjoy some good, old-fashioned Irish hospitality.

Taking a well-earned break from shopping!

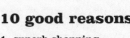

10 good reasons

1. **superb shopping**
2. **attractive city centre**
3. **extreme water sports**
4. **great live music scene**
5. **excellent clubs**
6. **chic, not pretentious**
7. **hospitable and lively**
8. **the botanic gardens**
9. **stunning scenery**
10. **horse riding nearby**

Botanical Gardens.

sounds of the city

Gotta get away Northern Ireland is.breathtakingly beautiful. If you've never been before, try to get out of the city and have a look around. Contact the Northern Walking Partnership (northernwalking.com) or Ulster Rambles (ulsterrambles.com) to get onto organised walks, or get in touch with one of Belfast's riding clubs, such as Lagan Valley Equestrian Centre (www.ridingclubs.org), to arrange a fabulous, scenic hack.

Let me entertain you Ireland has an incredibly rich heritage of music and song. From Boyzone to the Boomtown Rats, the average karaoke menu will feature hits aplenty from the land of the leprechauns. Rude not to hammer out a few local faves after a couple of pints of strawberry daiquiri, surely? The best spots for karaoke are The Globe in Queen's Quarter, the stylish but fun Union Street in the Cathedral Quarter and The Galleon in Antrim.

Ice, ice baby For a rather more thrilling spectator sport than watching your mates swaying to Wind Beneath My Wings at the 'kroaky', check out the Odyssey Arena's ice hockey team, LBM Belfast Giants. Rough play, clashing sticks and a bloodthirsty crowd make this a really great night out with a difference. The Arena also hosts shows from the likes of Russell Brand, The Backstreet Boys and the Arctic Monkeys, so check the website www.odysseyarena.com to find out what's on when you hit town.

King of the swingers From the Havana Nights Social Club, with Latin tunes and dance lessons, to The Empire Laughs Back comedy club featuring stars such as Ardal O'Hanlon and Michael McIntyre, The Belfast Empire always has something really good going on. Tribute and covers bands are often playing, and themed club nights are classy and inspired.

Dancing in the city If your hens like to strut their stuff try some dance classes. Tony and Carolina at Latin Salsa will provide an unforgettable party offering beginners Salsa, Merengue, Cha Cha Cha and more. Or let your inhibitions go and burn some calories with Polercise – the latest dance craze.

Sample a Spanish themed night with Latin Salsa.

Bring me sunshine If there's a lingering disappointment that you're not all flying off to Ibiza for a week, don't fret. The Bambu Beach Club has all the beach-ready bar staff, games and promotions you could possibly need to pretend you're on the white isle, not the emerald one. This is the option for the ultimate, dress up and party night.

The real thing So you're after the authentic Belfast vibe? A properly organised crawl around the city's oldest pubs is one of the best ways to explore the city and get to know the locals. Belfast is stuffed with gorgeous old drinkeries. Expect live folk bands, a good mix of people and a non-poseur vibe along the way. We suggest that you include the likes of Crown Liquor Saloon, McHugh's, The Front Page, and Bittle's Bar.

Didn't we almost have it all? Bar Twelve is a classy bar on Botanic Avenue where you'll be able to grab a sofa and down a few champagne cocktails while you listen to the DJ. On site is the Metro Brasserie for good food, and maybe you'll treat yourself to a night of boutique hotel heaven at the Crescent Townhouse. Always nice to find one venue that has everything so that you don't have to walk far in those fabulous four-inch heels.

'been there...'

We'd heard loads of good things about Belfast and there were some cheap flights going, so we all headed over there for a joint hen and stag weekend. The boys stayed in a different hotel but we all met up in the daytime before splitting up in the evenings. Loved the Crown Bar, saw a great band at the Empire, loved the zoo! Shops were pretty good too.

If you're looking to settle into one venue for quite a few hours, then AM:PM is perfect. The Botanic Avenue bar has an events suite if you want want private space and your own bar. At the Arthur Street AM:PM things are a little funkier – cosy into this bijou venue for a champagne lunch followed by several atmospheric hours in the company of some of Belfast's finest DJs.

Learn some sassy pole-dance moves with a Polercise party.

where to stay

This cosmopolitan city is now a popular destination for weekend breaks and, as a result, has a large number of hotels and serviced apartments at excellent rates.

hotels

Benedicts Hotel ££
7–21 Bradbury Place/
Shaftesbury Square, Belfast BT7 1RQ
Tel. no 028 9059 1999
www.benedictshotel.co.uk
info@benedictshotel.co.uk

On the spot for great pubs and restaurants, this friendly hotel is modern with a traditional twist. The ensuite rooms offer excellent amenities with a luxurious feel, representing fabulous value for money. There's a well-renowned restaurant on the first floor and a lively bar downstairs, so you don't even have to step outside to start the celebrations.

Crescent Townhouse ££
13 Lower Crescent, Belfast BT7 1NR
Tel. no 028 9032 3349
www.crescenttownhouse.com
info@crescenttownhouse.com

In the heart of Queen's Quarter, this is Belfast's original boutique hotel. Elegant and intimate the Crescent presents superb accommodation behind a stunning 19th-century facade. Beautifully appointed en-suite rooms offer fantastic value and with the Metro Brasserie and Bar Twelve on site this is a gem. Rooms are limited so don't wait.

Lagan Backpackers Hostel £
121 Fitzroy Avenue, Belfast BT7 1HU
Tel. no 028 9033 9965
www.laganhostel.com
stay@laganhostel.com

Located close to Botanic Avenue and the buzzing nightlife in Belfast, the idea at Lagan is a simple one. You get a comfortable bed

**shared room
without
breakfast**

£ under £30
££ £30–£60
£££ over £60
pppn

and good cooked breakfast and friendly service for an excellent price. Like most hostels, there's a choice of dorms with three–six bunk beds or private rooms, clean linen is included, but there are no en-suite facilities and you need to bring a towel. However, with prices from £13 per night what have you got to complain about?

Park Inn ££
4 Clarence Street West,
Belfast BT2 7GP
Tel. no 028 9067 7700
www.belfast.parkinn.com
info.belfast@rezidorparkinn.com

This large three-star hotel is located near the ferris wheel and city hall just two minutes from the bus and train station, so it's right in the heart of the city. It's clean, modern, with a very bold colour scheme, and provides all the amenities you'd expect in a chain hotel. Friendly and professional staff will make your stay a pleasant one. Park Inn offers on site parking at a reasonable rate and the grill breakfast is excellent.

Relax in the warm environment at Park Inn, Belfast.

Tara Lodge ££

36 Cromwell Rd, Belfast BT7 1JW
Tel. no 028 9059 0900
www.taralodge.com
info@taralodge.com

Located once again in Queen's Quarter, on Botanic Avenue, this luxury B&B is the perfect spot for partygoers. It's just a few minutes walk from bars and restaurants to suit all tastes and budgets. With a four-star AA rating Tara lodge exudes style; it has all the facilites you could want in the rooms. Book early.

self-catering

Brookhill Luxury Serviced Apartments ££

41 Eglantine Avenue, Belfast, BT9 6EW
Tel. no 07751 240 654
www.brookhillapartments.co.uk
brookhillapartments@hotmail.com

These luxury four-star apartments are bright and spacious with modern decor and excellent facilities. Situated in a quiet tree-lined avenue close to Lisburn Road, Queen's, for nightlife, these apartments are well located. Fully furnished, the two-bedroom apartments tend to feature two double beds.

Cordia Serviced Apartments ££

355–367 Lisburn Road Belfast, BT9 7EP
Tel. no 028 9087 8782
www.servicedapartmentsbelfast.net
mail@cordiaapartments.com

These stylish apartments are only 2 minutes from Great Victoria Street bus and railway station and the city centre. Belfast's fashionable boutiques, restaurants, cafés, and bars are within walking distance and there's a supermarket next door to stock up on beers. A generous welcome pack provides all the essentials and free parking is available in an underground car park.

Corporate Apartments ££

Ormeau Avenue, Belfast BT2 8HB
Tel. no 075 2566 4068
www.corporate-apartments.co.uk
info@corporate-apartments.co.uk

The Lucas Building is an uber cool base for any hen party. The two-bedroom apartments are spacious and well equipped with sophiscated decor. There is free parking and a welcome pack of groceries on arrival. Also available are Great Victoria Street Apartments

Malone Grove Apartments ££

60 Eglantine Avenue, Malone Road, Belfast BT9 6DY
Tel. no 028 9038 8060
www.malonelodgehotelbelfast.com
info@malonelodgehotel.com

These five-star apartments feature one, two and three bedrooms and cater for up to six guests. Adjacent to one of Belfast's boutique hotels, as a guest here you'll benefit from all the hotel facilities, including free parking and fitness suite. A breakfast pack is provided.

Pearl Court Apartments £

11 Malone Road, Belfast BT9 6RT
Tel. no 028 9066 6145
www.pearlcourt.com
info@pearlcourt.com

Located in the Queen's Quarter, luxurious and spacious self-contained apartments. The four-bedroom duplex apartmen is especialy good value for groups of up to seven people.

shared room without breakfast

£ under £30
££ £30–£60
£££ over £60
pppn

Titanic Apartments £

66 Lisburn Rd, Belfast BT1
Tel. no 028 9033 3367

These brand new luxury two-bedroom apartments, sleeping up to five people (with one fold-up bed) are in downtown Queen's Quarter. On-street parking, linen and towels included. Great value.

> We wanted something a bit more flexible than a bog standard B&B or hotel and serviced apartments were a great alternative. We all got dressed and had a glass of bubbly before hitting the town.

where to eat and drink

Head to Belfast's buzzing Golden Mile to sample the trendy bars, restaurants and clubs. There's a vibrant night time scene happening here, perfect for your hen party!

pubs and bars

Bar Twelve
13 Lower Crescent, Belfast BT7 1NR
Tel. no 028 9032 3349
www.crescenttownhouse.com
info@crescenttownhouse.com

The cosy sofas and warm ambience of this bar, located in the Crescent Townhouse Hotel, make it the perfect place to kick back and have a good chat.

Bittles Bar
Victoria Square, Belfast BT1 4QA
Tel. no 02890 311088

Beautiful old bar in a narrow building off Victoria Square. As the night wears on trendy types pile in as a DJ plays disco until dawn. Try a sweet-hot whisky with lemon and cloves.

McHugh's
29–31 Queen's Square, Belfast BT1 3FG
Tel. no 028 9050 9999
www.mchughsbar.com
info@mchughsbar.com
Open: all day every day

This atmospheric bar/gastropub is in Belfast's oldest building. There's live music and DJs in the basement bar and a large restaurant serving traditional food with a twist.

The Crown Liquor Saloon
46 Great Victoria Street, Belfast BT2 7BA
Tel. no 028 9024 3187
www.crownbar.com
info@crownbar.com

Dubbed Belfast's most beautiful bar, there's a lot more to The Crown than stunning wood panelling. There's a wide selection of wines and beers and an extensive menu.

McHugh's bar in Queen's Square.

The Globe
36 University Road, Belfast BT9 1NH
Tel. no 028 9050 9840
www.theglobebar.com
info@theglobebar.com

This popular bar in the University Quarter has a buzzing atmosphere with karaoke and DJs on every night. The friendly staff will make sure you have a good time, and with drinks offers and meal deals we know you will.

The Front Page
106–110 Donegall Street, Belfast BT1 2GX
Tel. no 01232 324 924
www.thefrontpagebar.com
info@thefrontpagebar.com

This family owned pub is renowned for live music and showcases the best of the local Irish talent. It still retains much of its fantastic Victorian panelling and stained glass.

The Galleon
18 High Street, Antrim, BT41 4AN
Tel. no 028 94467748

Join the locals for a few bevvies and a spot of karaoke at this lively pub situated in Antrim.

restaurants

AM:PM ££–£££
7–69 Botanic Avenue, Belfast
BT7 1JL
Tel. no 028 9023 9443 and
8–42 Upper Arthur
Street, Belfast BT1 4GJ
Tel 028 9024 9009
www.ampmbelfast.com
info@ampmbelfast.com

2 courses + half a bottle of wine

£ under £20
££ £20–£35
£££ over £35

Whether in Queen's Quarter or the city centre, AM:PM has your needs covered with great menus at both locations. Sample live jazz at Botanic Ave or cool DJs at Arthur Street on Saturday nights.

Cafe Vaudeville ££
25–39 Arthur Street, Belfast BT1 4GQ
Tel. no 028 9043 9160
www.cafevaudeville.com
info@cafevaudeville.com
Open: 11.30am–1am (bar); 12pm–3pm and 5pm–9pm (restaurant)

With a burlesque music hall theme, this 'luxe bar and dining establishment' is truly a showstopper on a grand scale. At the city centre end of the Golden Mile, this is a popular haunt with hen and stag parties. The food is a clever mix of French with Irish/American. Wash it down with plenty of Champagne – tres bien!

Irene & Nan's ££
12 Brunswick Street, Belfast BT2 7GG
Tel. no 028 9023 9123
www.ireneandnans.com
info@ireneandnans.com
Open: 11am–1am (bar); 12pm–9pm (restaurant)

This retro-kitsch brasserie is slap bang in the middle of the famed Golden Mile. A bar as well as a bistro, there's a good selection of bar food, a lunch menu and a dinner menu. If you choose it for the main event, start off with the mussels and follow it with an 8oz Irish Rib Eye Steak for a taste of the Emerald Isle.

Metro Brasserie ££
13 Lower Crescent, Belfast BT7 1NR
Tel. no 028 9032 3349

www.crescenttownhouse.com
info@crescenttownhouse.com
If you love your food, the Metro serves up an excellent choice of dishes all using locally sourced ingredients. Also has a very good vegetarian menu.

RBG ££
4 Clarence Street West,
Belfast BT2 7GP
Tel. no 028 9067 7700
www.belfast.parkinn.com
info.belfast@rezidorparkinn.com
Open: from 6.30am (last orders 9pm–10pm)

This New York style bar and grill in the Park Inn Hotel won't disappoint when it comes to steaks and classic burgers. The laid back atmosphere is perfect for a chilled start to your hen night, sample a few cocktails mixed by their well trained and experienced bar staff and you're set up for a great night on the town.

Tedfords Restaurant ££
5 Donegall Quay, Belfast BT1 3EF
Tel. no 02890 434000
www.tedfordsrestaurant.com
info@tedfordsrestaurant.com
Close to The Odyssey complex, come and sample the gorgeous local seafood (and stunning desserts) in its fabulous dining room and bar with views of the River Lagan.

RGB Grill and Steak House at the Park Inn.

where to party

Music is central to Irish culture so, not surprisingly, there is a plethora of live music venues and clubs of all descriptions to be found in Northern Ireland's first city.

The bar at Bambu Beach Club.

Bambu Beach Club
Unit 3, Odyssey Pavilion, 2 Queen's Quay, Belfast BT3 9QQ
Tel. no 028 9046 0011
www.bambubeachclub.com
bbclub@ultimateleisure.com

This is the ultimate fun party venue. With the bar staff in shorts or bikinis and sexy dancers on stage every half hour, the surf is most definitely up here!

Club Mono
96–100 Ann Street, Belfast BT1 3HH
Tel. no 028 9027 8886
www.monobelfast.co.uk
clubmono@btinternet.com

Close to the city centre, Mono is a favourtie for dance music fans playing great funky house tunes. The stylish interior is cool and trendy and the place attracts some seriously big name DJs.

Club Thompson's
3 Patterson's Place, Belfast BT1 4HW
Tel. no 028 9032 3762
www.clubthompsons.com
info@clubthompsons.com

A Belfast clubbing institution, Thompsons hosts numerous nights catering for the various styles from hip hop to house. On Saturdays you'll find stunning club decor and funky, uplifting house music.

Stiff Kitten
1 Bankmore Square, Belfast BT7 1DH
Tel. no 028 9023 8700
www.thestiffkitten.com
enquiries@thestiffkitten.com

This funky contemporary club is one for the committed clubbers. Attracting some big name DJs, the dancefloor is always packed with a music conscious crowd. You're more than likely to bump into a stag party too.

For the ultimate girly night out, start the evening with a polercise party

With pole, burlesque or cheerleading parties on offer we guarantee you an evening to remember.

Welcoming you to the world of Burlesque. We invite you to shimmy into something less comfortable so we can show you how to pose, peel and strut like a pin-up. Flutter your eyelashes as you coax out your Sandra Dee side! Whip your inner Bettie Page into shape quick sharp! Put your new skills together in a cute routine with lots of laughs and surprises along the way!

A cheerleading party is the perfect way to celebrate a hen do. Experience your own high-energy, fun-filled cheerleading session. You will be taught a personalized hen party team chant for the bride, which you can later embarrass her with by screaming loudly down the street as you leave or the next bar you intend to hit. By the end of the session you will have a pom-pom dance routine, then it's off to the bars and clubs to show off your new moves on the dance floor.

Slip on your stilettos and bump and grind your way through a session of pole dance, you will be taught tricks and spins and will be shown how to link the moves together into a routine.

Party packages £20 per head, lasting approx 1½ hours, including wine reception and nibbles.

For more info check out our website www.polerciseltd.com or call 07545047988
Venues in Belfast, Derry, Letterkenny, Dundalk and Banbridge.

Party Hens or Party Stags – Have your last night of freedom at the dogs!

Excellent food, exciting thrills and a fantastic atmosphere - everything you need for a great celebration!

Your mate's getting hitched - you need to organise a night to remember. At Drumbo Park Greyhound Stadium we make sure everything goes to plan with pre-booking menu, special group rates starting from £16 per person and even the opportunity to get mentioned in our Race Programme or sponsor a race.

Call now on 028 9061 0070 to have an experience you and your friends will never forget.

Northern Ireland's New Night Out

57 Ballyskeagh Road, Co Antrim, BT27 5TE
T: 028 9061 0070 drumbopark.com

Drumbo Park
GREYHOUND STADIUM

The Bot (Botanic Inn)

23–27 Malone Road, Belfast
BT9 6RU
Tel. no 028 9050 9740
www.thebotanicinn.com
info@thebotanicinn.com

Belfast's top live entertainment venue and sports bar, this is top spot for action. With live sport on big plasma screens it's a bloke magnet. As night falls the DJs move in and turn this into a kicking club for all to enjoy.

The Empire

42 Botanic Avenue, Belfast BT7 1JQ
Tel. no 028 9024 9276
www.thebelfastempire.com
info@thebelfastempire.com

This old church has had new life breathed into it as a music hall with a full programme of live music and comedy. The underground bar is atmospheric and with three more floors of entertainment this place is legendary.

Union Street

8–14 Union Street, Belfast BT1 2JF
Tel. no 028 9031 6060
www.unionstreetpub.com
info@unionstreetpub.com

This trendy award-winning gay bar is a bar/restaurant/club all wrapped into one highly camp bundle. Here, deep in Cathedral Quarter, hens can enjoy a fun night out without the cattle market factor. Try the Saturday afternoon 'Sing or Die Karaoke' with Tina Leggs Tantrum, oozing with glitz and glamour, for new and seasoned singers alike starting at 4pm. From 8pm join Kenny K for the latest in chart, commercial and high camp.

A night out in Belfast can be full of glitz and glamour, so don't forget your lippy!

birmingham

'More canal mileage than Venice' – so say the guidebooks. Come on, there's much more to Birmingham than ducks and barges. It's our most culturally rich city, slap bang in the middle of the country, and it's got soul.

Council House (top), Brindley Place (middle), Broad Street (bottom).

what to do

Ask not what you can do in Birmingham, but what can Birmingham do for you. Retail therapy, a great club scene, waterside bars, fabulous restaurants, skiing...

t doesn't matter if you're a dyed in the cashmere Harvey Nicks gal or a stout-drinking quasar addict, Birmingham as got it all. That's because it's our glorious Second City and it's got a duty to compete bitchily with London.

While it can't quite muster the charm of our dear old capital, it's certainly easier to navigate, and that makes it ideal for a weekend break. Simply hop off the train at New Street and you're right in the fabulous shopping action of the New Bullring, the Markets and the Mailbox.

Then there's the very convenient situation of the most buzzing nightlife being around Broad Street. By the time you've got these essentials on your radar it's just a question of dropping in the details.

Brum is a town with atmosphere, and not just from the balti fumes. With a huge young, cosmopolitan population it's not surprising that the city's pulse can be clearly felt, day and night.

10 good reasons

1. Tamworth Snow Dome
2. Selfridges sans London
3. Cadbury World, mmmnn
4. dressed-to-kill club scene
5. The Glee Club for comedy
6. canal-side picnics
7. best curries in the UK
8. two local dog tracks
9. BYOB restaurants
10. Selfridges Food Hall

The iconic Selfridges store, the centrepiece of Birmingham's famous shopping centre – the Bullring.

sounds of the city

Relax The Living Room is a rather chic affair for Broad Street, but that doesn't mean it's not for your party. Or for the first bit of it, at least, before things get messy. There's a gorgeous private room with chandeliers, beautiful fabrics and great city views, where up to 16 can sit down to lunch or dinner. The modern British/European food and sophisticated cocktails are very serious matters at The Living Room, and the whole vibe is good if you're looking for a bit of wow factor and class for your party. You could also book an entertainer to come along – from a magician to a cabaret artist – and make full use of your VIP enclave. Once the cocktails have started to work their magic, you've only to totter out of the front door and you're on one of Birmingham's most vibrant streets.

Don't cha wish your girlfriend was hot like me? For those whose very selfless focus is on being a stunning sight for all to behold, Serenity Spa in the city centre buffs up your face for a night out, gives make up lessons for fretting brides-to-be and offers a wide range of therapeutic and beauty treatments. How divine, darling, after a morning's hard shopping at The Mailbox – home to the likes of Armani, Harvey Nicks and Jesire. And after all that effort, it can only be Liberty's in Hagley Road for dinner, champagne cocktails and dancing with the other beautiful people. Although obviously, you're the best. Mwa, mwa.

Dancing queen Hitting the dance floor with your mates and some cheesy old choons is hen party gold, and Birmingham caters for your needs with clubs such as Reflex (80s) and Flares (70s), both on Broad Street. Nearby, The Works has club classics and charty stuff on a Friday, and club anthems on a Saturday.

Killing me softly Cake and coffee stops are an all-important part of any decent trip round town, and we'd rather eschew chainstore swank for old-school charm any day. The Floating Coffee Company is a barge moored just off Bridleyplace that will serve up your hot chocolate and sweet or savoury pick-me-ups as the water gently rocks you. Artery clogging bliss.

Indulge yourself in a relaxing massage before your big night out.

There's mountains of fun to be had at Snow Dome in Tamworth.

We will rock you You're never too old for a natural high and Creation, the biggest indoor climbing arena in the Midlands, is the place to get one. If you're complete beginners, don't worry, you can book an hour and a half taster session for two–six people. And if that doesn't grab you, the fact that climbers consume mountains of cake between climbs will. Make sure you take plenty of the spongey sweet stuff along.

Lady ice Hen party skiing doesn't need to be confined to groups with more money and time off than the Queen. You can have real, guaranteed snow all year round at the Snow Dome at Leisure Island. The three slopes are set up for boarding, skiing, tobogganing or adrenalin tubing (high speed, spinning downhill descent on an inner tube). And once you're tired and soaked through you can stop and go to a funky city centre bar. You can't get that half way up a mountain now, can you?

Going underground An underground bar is great when you need to ignore the fact that it's still daylight outside as you order your first drink. An underground bar is particularly great if it's Bacchus. This is one gorgeous little

hideout, complete with ornate carved stonework, velvet drapes, art and pleasantly creaky antiques. Quirky rooms include a library and four poster bedroom which simply whisper to you, stay, stay my pretty. Resting happily in the seductive lap of the God of pleasure (that's Bacchus), sip a martini and just let all those daytime worries slide away. If you've managed to book rooms at the Burlington Hotel above, then the living is easy.

where to stay

From the original splendour of Victorian railway hotels to the modern and innovative chic of city centre accommodation, Brum has it all and in abundance.

hotels

Birmingham Central Backpackers £

The Eastside Tavern,
58 Coventry Street, Digbeth,
Birmingham B5 5NH
Tel. no 0121 643 0033
www.birminghamcentralbackpackers.com
info@birminghamcentralbackpackers.com

This family-run independent hostel is unique. From the warm welcome to the free nightly snack buffet, your hosts can't do enough to ensure you have a great time here. The usual range of single, twin and dorm rooms are all decorated in fun and funky colours.

Burlington Hotel £££

Burlington Arcade, 126
New Street, Birmingham B2
4JQ
Tel. no 0121 643 9191
www.macdonaldhotels.co.uk
reservations.burlington@
macdonaldhotels.co.uk

The historic Burlington hotel is situated close to the Mailbox, Selfridges and the Bullring for all your shopping needs, and Broad Street for nightlife and entertainment. The classic styling of the rooms suits the original Victorian splendour with all the facilities for a comfortable stay.

Eaton Hotel ££

279 Hagley Road, Edgbaston,
Birmingham B16 9NB
Tel. no 0121 454 3311
www.eatonhotel.co.uk
info@eatonhotel.co.uk

This beautifully styled independent hotel has all the modern facilities you need for a relaxing and luxurious stay in Brum. The hotel is located within 2 miles of the city centre so provides easy access to all the highligts. Why not have dinner in the top-class restaurant serving quality British fare?

shared room without breakfast

£ under £30
££ £30–£60
£££ over £60
pppn

NiteNite Birmingham £

18 Holliday Street,
Birmingham B1 1TB
Tel. no 0121 454 3311
www.nitenite.com
book@nitenite.com

This chic yet comfort-conscious hotel says 'no' to 'no frills' and gives you free Wi-Fi, blockbuster movies and bottled water all at a great price. The avant-garde design combined with the quality fittings makes this a cutting edge choice, complete with 42-inch plasma screens showing live views to the outside in lieu of a window. That's got to be a unique feature! This is a new take on affordable luxury.

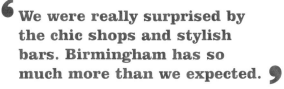

❛ We were really surprised by the chic shops and stylish bars. Birmingham has so much more than we expected. ❜

self-catering

Burne Jones House ££
11–12 Bennetts Hill, Birmingham
B2 5RS
Tel. no 0845 080 5104
www.cityquarters.co.uk

Burne Jones House is a development of 29 fully furnished serviced apartments in the shopping centre of Birmingham. The Grade II listed building has been converted into a range of unique apartments fully equipped with all mod cons including Wi-Fi. With a 24-hour check-in system you can just pick up the keys and chill out. The historic building even has a private roof terrace!

City-Nites £
Arena View, Edward Street, Birmingham
B1 2RX
Tel. no 0121 233 1155
www.city-nites.com
reservations@city-nites.com

A fabulous alternative to a hotel room. Situated directly opposite the NIA and Brindleyplace, these elegant apartments are ideally located for all the city's clubs, bars and restaurants. With a mixture of one- and two-bedroom apartments sleeping two–four adults, City-Nites is ideal for Hen Parties. If you're booking as a group then simply request adjacent apartments.

Postbox by Bridgestreet ££
120 Upper Marshall Street, Birmingham
B1 1LJ
Tel. no 0845 080 5104
www.bridgestreet.co.uk
info@bridgestreet.com

The PostBox is stylish city living at its most desirable. The complex offers 50 contemporary one- and two-bedroom apartments set right in the heart of Birmingham's most fashionable neighbourhood. A number of apartments offer balconies and the development provides the convenience of having a parking space right in the centre of the city. All apartments have freeview TV and DVD player.

* shared room without breakfast

£ under £30
££ £30–£60
£££ over £60
pppn

SACO @ Livingbase ££
3 Brunswick Square, Brindleyplace, Birmingham B1 2HR
Tel. no 0845 099 9092
www.birmingham.sacoapartments.co.uk
livingbase@sacoapartments.co.uk

Livingbase is home to 35 luxury serviced apartments, all with spectacular views over the city and are decorated to the highest standard. The accommodation ranges from studios through to double height duplex suites. Each apartment consists of fully fitted kitchen, spacious living/dining areas and bedrooms with separate bathroom. Each apartment features a range of Molton Brown toiletries – oooo!

Staying Cool @ Rotunda ££
The Rotunda, 150 New Street, Birmingham B2 4PA
Tel. no 0121 643 0815
www.stayingcool.com
hello@stayingcool.com

Hip hotel meets boutique serviced apartment. Stay in one of the exclusive apartments on the top two floors of the iconic and beautifully refurbished 60s Rotunda in Birmingham. Each Staying Cool apartment has floor-to-ceiling windows offering a breathtaking panorama of the city. Special features include free Wi-Fi, an Apple Mac entertainment system, a Bose iPod player and a Poggenpohl kitchen with cool appliances. Wow!

Sleep easy in this exquisite City-Nites bedroom.

where to eat and drink

It's the home of Balti, so you really have to try one while you're in Brum. There are plenty of places to get the Balti experience whatever the budget, so no excuses!

bars & pubs

Bacchus

Burlington Arcade, 126 New Street, Birmingham B2 4JQ
Tel. no 0121 632 5445
www.macdonaldhotels.co.uk

This quirky basement bar located under the Burlington Hotel is quite impressive. It has a sumptuous and elegant classical style – all velvet curtains, ornate plasterwork and antique furniture. It brings together the ancient civilisations of Rome, Egypt and Greece in one big orgy of excess!

The O Bar

264 Broad Street, Birmingham B1 2DS
Tel. no 0121 643 0712
www.obarbirmingham.com
trancef1@yahoo.co.uk

Slap bang in the middle of the nightlife is this super sexy 'style bar'. It serves some pretty fine cocktails and has a large selection of champagne. if you venture 'below' you'll find some lively beats down there and a great party atmosphere.

Malmaison

1 Wharfside Street, Birmingham B1 1RD
Tel. no 0121 246 5000
www.malmaison.com

Part of the Malmaison Hotel in The Mailbox, this light and airy, double-height bar and brasserie is stunning. With plenty of well selected wines and champagnes, chosen by their world class sommelier, and dangerously good cocktails, The Mal is a great place to kick off your evening in Birmingham.

Cocktails at Malmaison Bar.

Revolution

Five Ways, Broad Street, Birmingham B15 2HF
Tel. no 0121 665 6508
www.revolution-bars.co.uk/birmingham

Set right in the heart of Brum's nightlife, this atmospheric bar can take you from early evening cocktails in comfy leather chairs to cool club atmosphere with late night DJ and there's plenty of fun to be had in between. Why not find out about their cocktail masterclasses for a little taste of mixology. There are over ten private party areas, so cal to book one and discuss what other party packages they have on offer.

restaurants

Adil Balti and Tandoori £
148–150 Stoney Lane, Sparkbrook,
Birmingham B12 8AJ
Tel. no 0121 449 0335
www.adilbalti.co.uk

Renowned for some of the best curries in
Birmingham, Adil's still manages to keep the
price down. With a Bring Your Own (BYO)
policy and an off-licence next door, this is
guaranteed good value for money. They were
undergoing refurbishment and had moved
into temporary alternative premises as we
went to press, so call to check the address
and book beforehand.

Ha Ha Bar and Grill ££
178–180 Wharfside Street, Mailbox,
Birmingham B1 1RN
Tel. no 0121 632 1250
www.hahaonline.co.uk
haha.birmingham@
bayrestaurantgroup.com

With a fabulous view over the Gas Street
canal basin, Ha Ha has an enviable location.

'real life'

**We had lunch at The Floating
Coffee Company, a barge at
The Water's Edge in Brindley
Place, then shopping at The
Mailbox and dinner at Ha
Ha's. A real girlie day!**

Ha Ha Bar and Grill at The Mailbox.

**2 courses
+ half a bottle
of wine**

**£ under £20
££ £20–£35
£££ over £35**

A night of carousing requires serious sustenance.

And with a 90-seater terrace, there's no
better place to start your night off than with a
few cocktails in the early evening sunshine.
The food here is varied, but with a strong
focus on British-sourced produce.

Las Iguanas ££
Arcadian Centre, Hurst Street,
Birmingham B5 4TD
Tel. no 0121 622 4466
www.iguanas.co.uk

Famed for its Caipirinhas and its buzzing
funky Latino ambience, Las Iguanas is
perfect for a party. If you love Mexican,
Brazilian and Cuban flavours, you'll love it
here. Whether Fajitas are your fave or you
crave Chimichangas, you're going to find
something to tantalise your tastebuds and
tickle your fancy here. With cocktails served
by the pitcher, your party is definitely going
to swing.

Strada ££
109–111 Wharfside Street, The Mailbox,
Birmingham B1 1XL
Tel. no 0121 643 7279
www.strada.co.uk

If you love Italian food, you'll love Strada.
The cuisine is authentic and the surroundings
relaxed and contemporary. On the menu
you'll find hand-stretched pizzas, fresh
pastas, risottos as well as a selection of
grilled meat and fish.

where to party

Birmingham is literally brimming with canalside bars and restaurants together with city centre clubs and pubs. Going out here is...well, the new 'going out'.

If you need help, check out the 'fire officers' at the Pleasure Ladies Night at Oceana.

Flares
55 Broad Street, Birmingham B1 2HJ
Tel. no 0121 616 2957
www.flaresbars.co.uk
info@flaresbars.co.uk

No prizes for guessing this one...Flares is a 70s club and proud to be the grooviest disco around! If you love all those disco dancing floor fillers (and let's face who doesn't), Flares is the party destination for you. They will organise a personalised party package for you with your favourite funky 70s tracks, a free bottle of bubbly, 'Q Jump' tickets and a party pack with heaps of 70s bling. Groovy!

O2 Academy Birmingham
16–18 Horsefair, Bristol Street, B1 1DB
Tel. no 0121 622 8250
www.o2academybirmingham.co.uk
mail@o2academybirmingham.co.uk

The giant of the Birmingham music scene, this is where you'll find all the top gigs.

Current charting acts such as N-Dubz, Scouting for Girls and Paloma Faith are all featured in the line-up for 2010. With three separate venues rooms hosting different kinds of artists, this is *the* live music venue in Brum.

Oceana
1–5 Hurst Street, Birmingham B5 4EH
Tel. no 0845 4025390
www.oceanaclubs.com
birmingham@oceanaclubs.com

On the edge of Chinatown, this vast superclub has seven themed rooms to choose from. Book a private booth or suite, complete with champagne reception to add that extra layer of decadence to your nightclubbing experience. The resident DJs roll out a blend of dance music, commercial pop, R'n'B, hip hop and drum & bass mixed in with cheesy and party classics to lighten things up. Pleasure Ladies Nights male revue show is resident here on a Saturday night.

RƎVOLUTION
MASTERCLASS

GET BEHIND THE BAR AND BECOME A COCKTAIL MASTER IN THIS 90 MINUTE INTERACTIVE SESSION!

✪ COCKTAILS
✪ TASTING
✪ TOOLS
✪ SKILLS
✪ GAMES

HEN GOES FREE!
MINIMUM 8 PEOPLE

QUOTE PROMO CODE 'MARTINI' FOR FREE HEN OFFER
PACKAGES FROM ONLY £24.95 PER PERSON PLUS
NEW PARTY FOOD OPTIONS NOW AVAILABLE

TO BOOK...
ONLINE: REVOLUTION-BARS.CO.UK
PHONE: 0800 6300 860
ASK: A MEMBER OF STAFF

ANY OCCASION, ANY SIZE... REVOLUTION IS THE PERFECT PLACE TO EAT, DRINK & PARTY!

Revolution Vodka Bar, 5 Ways, Broad Street, Birmingham

Reflex

36–37 Broad Street, Birmingham B1 2DY
Tel. no 0121 643 0444
www.reflexbars.co.uk/reflexbroadstreet

If the cheesy choons of the 80s are more
your thang, then book yourselves a Reflex
party night. Whether it's Wham!, Duran Duran
or Spandau Ballet who float your boat, all the
classics will be pumping out here, so get that
New Romantic clobber on and backcomb
your hair within an inch of its life. Make sure
you book a party package here and get all
the necessary accessories to make your 80s
party rock.

Sence

70 Hurst Street, The Arcadian,
Birmingham B5 4TD
Tel. no 0121 622 4442
www.sencebirmingham.co.uk
info@sencebirmingham.co.uk

This self-confessed 'senceational' nightclub
experience has arrived in Birmingham. It has
the ambience of a glamorous bar, combined
with the edginess of a nightclub to create an
unbeatable atmosphere. At Sence the UK's
top DJs unleash themselves on the state-of-
the-art sound and lighting system. Book
yourself into the luxurious VIP area for a truly
memorable night. Don't worry, you won't
even have to queue at the bar as it's all
waitress service.

The Jam House

No.1 St. Pauls Square, Birmingham
Tel. no 0121 200 3030
www.thejamhouse.com
info@thejamhouse.com

A slightly more grown-up live music venue,
The Jam House welcomes over 21s only.
Located in the heart of the Jewellery Quarter
of Birmingham the venue occupies an
historic Georgian building. With seating
spread over three stylish floors, the
atmosphere is relaxed and infomal. Opened
by R'n'B maestro, Mr Jools Holland, The Jam
House has a similarly cool vibe. For dinner
book a table on the top floor and sample
some of the freshly cooked international
cuisine, alternatively for a larger group you
can arrange a buffet.

The Works

182 Broad Street, Birmingham B15 1DA
Tel. no 0121 633 1520
www.fivewaysleisure.com/the-works.htm

If you love your club classics and dance
anthems with a few chart favourites thrown in
for good measure, then head to The Works
for a monster mash up. There are three
rooms each with a different musical 'flava',
so get dressed fresh and funky and check
out the sounds.

The 'senceational' Sence nightclub.

blackpool

England's answer to Las Vegas is a dizzying and rather delightful feast of fairground thrills, beach, clubs, arcades and illuminations, and she's ready to welcome you with wide-open arms. And a tequila slammer.

Beach and Tower (top), carousel (middle), trams (bottom).

what to do

As soon as you tell your mates that Blackpool is your destination *de* hen, you've set the tone for the weekend. It's going to be full-on fun. Scream for the ride to go faster...

As we're pretty sure you must know the kind of thing that goes on in Blackpool, maybe we should tell you what doesn't go on? Snobbery, long faces, low-key tastefulness, early rising, boredom and work are all pretty low down the agenda. Sounds like a pretty good set up for a few days of mayhem with your best mates, doesn't it?

So how did one town on the north-west coast gain such a distinctive culture? Well, leisure isn't just an optional extra in Blackpool. The city was established as somewhere to 'take the cure' – that is bathe in the sea – in the 18th century, and bowling greens, archery ranges and holiday cottages were soon built. By 1893 the three piers (OTT and proud) were in place and hosting 19th century rave ups, such as tea dances and vaudeville theatre. The place was built for partying, day and night, and that has to be a good reason to go, doesn't it?

It's soooo tacky, you say? Well, maybe. But imagine a tasteful Blackpool. Zzzzzz...

We say, sort out some fancy dress, organise an itinerary and paint the town the loudest shade of red you can.

Thrill-seekers' paradise.

10 good reasons

1. **sandy beaches**
2. **candy floss highs**
3. **winning Daytona races**
4. **party atmosphere**
5. **the illuminations...ahhh**
6. **the rides**
7. **cheap accommodation**
8. **good value clubs and bars**
9. **compulsory fun 24:7**
10. **cycling along the prom**

sounds of the city

Killer queen Murder mystery nights and weekends have been popular in the UK for a good 20 years now. You turn up and get to dress up, eat, drink and be entertained by actors and a dubious, but usually hilarious, plot. You'll know your character and what to wear from an invite sent to you beforehand. It's brilliant fun and it's going on in Blackpool. Lots of party organisers offer sleuthing nights, but we suggest you check out ukgirlthing.com for more details.

Crazy Book in with sudden-impact.co.uk for MAD – multi activity days, that is. Here, you can wreak revenge on that cow who's beaten you to be chief bridesmaid by pumping paint bullets into her. If you fear such attacks from others, make it laser tag, which doesn't hurt but still involves running around shrieking a lot. Team that up with relatively relaxing archery, quad biking or air rifle shooting. Call the team, who are based on a farm just outside Blackpool, on 01253 767279.

You make it easy Contact blackpoolhenparties.co.uk and get a two night package wrapped up by people in the know. You can choose from a list of activities including paintballing, burlesque cabaret dancin and pampering. In the evening you'll b hitting The Syndicate nightclub or enjoying a little risqué cabaret, as well as getting free entry to various bars. Hotel B&B is arranged, and you can tag all sorts of extras on. Weekend prices start from just £59 per person.

I want to ride my bicycle Calling all fitness freaks – step away from the candyfloss and get on your bikes to explore the coastal areas, such as the pleasant nine-miler from Blackpool North Pier to Fleetwood. You can hire bikes to get around Blackpool itself, it being a leader of the national push to get people cycling, or escape into the mercifully flat lands of Fylde and Wyre. Here, miles of safe country roads are punctuated with teashops and pubs. Visitlancashire.com has a useful list of timed/ability rated cycle routes in the beautiful county of Lancashire, so you can get out and cycle 'til you're worn out, rest up in a country pub, then head back to the bright lights later on.

Blackpool Pier.

summer dining
for friends, families and colleagues

A la carte menu and tapas now being served from 5pm till late*

OPEN FROM 9AM TILL VERY LATE

Join us for afternoon tea 3pm to 5.30pm*

Cafe Menu from 9am until late

Great food prepared by some of the Fylde's best chefs

Fully Licensed Bar

Drink or Dine in our al fresco area

*subject to change

TOAST
CAFÉ · BAR · GRILL

28 Corporation Street, Blackpool (near Grand Theatre)
Book your table now on 01253 749777

Taste LANCASHIRE QUALITY ASSURED

For more information visit our website www.toast-cafe-bar.co.uk email: info@toast-cafe-bar.co.uk

WANT A HEN PARTY WITH A DIFFERENCE?

Why are we different?
The hen gets to enjoy her fabulous hen party for FREE!

With hen events available across the UK and Europe, let us take away the hassle and stress of organising an amazing hen experience!

Contact us on **0203 151 7824** or
email **sales@hen4free.com** for more information

HEN 4 FREE
www.hen4free.com

You spin me round Pleasure Beach Blackpool is Britain's most popular theme park, with 6.5m visitors per year. It was originally conceived as a place to 'make adults feel like children again and to inspire gaiety of a primarily innocent character'. Bless.

Sing when you're winning Take a ride on the 32m-high ferris wheel on Central Pier to warm up your vocal cords. Then, make some real noise at Nellie Dean's karaoke bar on the Promenade.

Meanwhile, at Club Sanuk, there's something altogether easier on the senses, with the Adonis Cabaret Show. The club itself is a party haven, with seven bars, five rooms and four music styles. Your hen party package will include friendly hospitality, a buffet and cocktail, games, prizes and comedy.

You're so vain If you think you'll need an afternoon away from the bright lights and partying, seek out the loveliness of the Imperial. This stunning Barcelo hotel on North Promenade is a city landmark and, more importantly, has a gorgeous pool and leisure suite, with spa and beauty therapists just dying to meet you and make you feel amazing.

Later, as you're looking so fine, maybe you should head for Rumours – one of Blackpool's newest and most sophisticated clubs. Drinks promotions ensure that it's still pretty good value for money, so you can dance and drink the night away without blowing your hen party budget.

Book into a leather-clad VIP booth, with private dance floor and reserved area of the bar, if you fancy upgrading yourself. Honey, you're so worth it.

Fairground rides are plentiful in Blackpool.

'been there...'

My hen party was in July, so I wanted to head for the beach. It was hot and sunny, so we got loads of time on the beach and drinking al fresco! The club was a bit naff, but you go for the holiday atmosphere – loads of people having a brilliant time. On the Saturday we spent the afternoon doing laser tag and quad bikes at Whyndyke Farm, which was a laugh.

❛ **We spent a day at the Pleasure Beach reliving our childhood, which was such a blast. We all screamed like banshees on the Infusion ride – what a laugh!** ❜

where to stay

As Britain's most popular seaside destination, there are plenty of places to stay in Blackpool. Just make sure the accommodation you choose suits your party.

b&bs & hotels

Ash Lodge £
131 Hornby Road, Blackpool FY1 4JG
Tel. no 01253 627637
www.ashlodgehotel.co.uk
admin@ashlodgehotel.co.uk

This cosy B&B is set in a residential area just a short walk from the Hounds Hill Shopping Centre, Blackpool Tower, the beach and the promenade. Proprietors Mary and Margaret will give you a warm welcome and there's even free parking.

Barceló Blackpool Imperial Hotel £££
North Promenade,
Blackpool FY12HB
Tel. no 01253 623971
www.barcelo-hotels.co.uk
stay@barcelo-hotels.co.uk

Victorian grandeur at its most impressive, the Imperial is a landmark on the North Promenade. You can walk to all the attractions from here or hop on the tram that stops across the road. All the facilities you'd expect from a four-star hotel, including a health club with swimming pool, are here.

Chequers Plaza Hotel ££
24 Queens Promenade, North Shore
Blackpool FY2 9RN
Tel. no 0800 0273107
www.chequersplaza.com
enquiries@chequersplaza.com

Having recently undergone a major facelift, this three-star hotel is the perfect place for peace and quiet. Set a little way away from the nightlife, but with fabulous views of the Irish Sea, it's a relaxing haven. Yet it's only ten minutes walk to the town centre.

✳ shared room without breakfast

£ under £30
££ £30–£60
£££ over £60
pppn

Number One St Luke's ££
1 St Lukes Road, Blackpool FY4 2EL
Tel. no 01253 343901
www.numberoneblackpool.com
info@numberoneblackpool.com

Voted Britain's best B&B in 2007, this is no ordinary B&B. With elegantly styled rooms and luxury fittings it is more of a small boutique hotel. Even the beautifully appointed bathrooms have LCD TVs and speakers! You can have a continental breakfast brought to your room or indulge downstairs.

Party Inn £
The Lark Inn, 41–43 Banks Street, Blackpool FY1 2AR
Tel. no 0845 2575025 (local rate)
www.partyinn.co.uk

As the name suggests, this B&B accommodation welcomes party groups and offers several packages with VIP entry to all of Blackpool's top nightspots. Located in the centre of town, Party Inn is close to all the clubs, as well as the beach and train station.

Elegant bedrooms at Number One St Luke's.

The Lawton ££

58–66 Charnley Road,
Blackpool FY1 4PF
Tel. no 01253 753471
www.thelawtonhotel.co.uk
thelawtonhotel@gmail.com

The Lawton is dedicated to helping you have
a great time in Blackpool. There's a large well
stocked bar with wide screen TV to help you
relax and prepare for the night ahead and
multiple occupancy rooms to choose from.

Fantastic bathrooms at Number One St Luke's.

self-catering

Berkswell Holiday Apartments £

10 Withnell Road, Blackpool FY4 1HF
Tel. no 01253 342434
www.berkswellflats.co.uk
sheila.reception@tiscali.co.uk

With five apartments sleeping
two–four people, the Berkswell
can accommodate a group
of up to eighteen. The
apartments are well furnished
with everything you need for
a comfortable stay and your
hosts, Jim and Sheila, will
ensure you have a fantastic
stay.

✳ shared room without breakfast

£ under £30
££ £30–£60
£££ over £60
pppn

Jade Holiday Apartments ££

10 Clifton Drive, Blackpool FY4 1NX
Tel. no 01253 341500
www.jadeapartments.com
jade-southshore@hotmail.co.uk

Overlooking the Pleasure Beach and just 1
minute's walk to South Promenade, these
well appointed apartments are very well
located. They're also close to transport links.
The apartments are all one- or two-
bedroomed and fully furnished.

Marton Mere Holiday Park ££

Mythop Road, Blackpool FY4 4XN
Tel. no 0871 4680494
www.caravancamping.co.uk

If you want to get away from the nightlife and
enjoy the absolutely beautiful scenery and
coastline just outside Blackpool, then
camping is a great option. This Haven park is
close to Midgland Riding School, where you
can enjoy wonderful hacks, or you can rent
bikes at the Park and discover the true
Lancashire yourselves.

The Beach House £

204 Queens Promenade, Blackpool
FY2 9JS
Tel. no 01253 352699
www.thebeachhouseblackpool.co.uk

These luxurious five-star apartments
were regional best self-catering
winners in 2008/9 and you can
see why. With an gorgeous
views over sea and sandy
beaches, the seaside theme
continues inside with a cool
contemporary feel. The seven
apartments in the complex sleep
between two and five people, so
you can all be together. Each
apartment has a dedicated parking bay
and the trams stop just across the road.

Blackpool Tower.

COCKTAIL MAKING EXPERIENCE
£22.50 per person

HEN PARTY MENUS
from £12.95 per person

FOR MORE DETAILS CALL US ON
01253 749 777

28 Corporation Street, Blackpool. FY1 1EJ.

In the heart of Blackpool,
close to the bars and clubs

TOAST
CAFÉ - BAR - GRILL
www.toast-cafe-bar.co.uk

New! Foreplay Lessons...
for hens who love men

2 hours of fun and sexy entertainment... but no nudity or undressing – sorry!

Learn the techniques every bride-to-be should know in the private areas of our nationwide wine bars, your home or your own venue

For group bookings and ticket events, mention 'The Hen Party Handbook' and the hen goes FREE*

Info Pack info@milkymoments.co.uk; www.milkymoments.co.uk

As featured in Cosmopolitan, TimeOut, Channels 4 and 5

'The most fun I've had in my sensible knickers' Sam from London

*Groups of 9 or more

where to eat and drink

From fish and chips to fine dining, Blackpool has it all and plenty of it. However, you can't come to Blackpool and not try a big stick of fluffy pink candy floss – it's the law!

bars & pubs

Brannigans

35 Market Street, Blackpool FY1 1EZ
Tel. no 01253 752277
www.brannigansbars.com

With cocktails, shooters and drinks promos galore, Brannigans offer the best party night in Blackpool. On a Saturday, DJ Damo plays all the latest chart and party tunes from 8pm guaranteed to get you dancing. You can book your hen party here on the website.

Flagship Bar

Coral Island, Promenade, Blackpool FY1 5DW
Tel. no 01253 627250
www.theflagshipbar.com
info@theflagshipbar.com

There's always a party at the 'Flaggie' and it's alway free. So why pay to go anywhere else? During the day, sports are showing on eight giant plasma TVs and by night resident DJ Ian Bradshaw plays party choons, runs party games and gives away loads of stuff. Friday night is theme night so find out what's on and get dressed up!

Nellie Dean's Karaoke Bar

150–152 Promenade, Blackpool FY1 1RE
Tel. no 01253 623737

If you fancy yourselves as X factor stars and you want the microphone in your hand on your hen night, then Nellie Dean's Karaoke Bar is the place for you. Even if you just want to sit back and let the others make fools of themselves, this is a very entertaining night out. Open 'til 4am the atmosphere here is pumping all night long with all the best cheesy tunes.

Brannigans in Market Street.

Roxy's Fun Bar

23 Queen Street, Blackpool FY1 1NL
Tel. no 01253 622573
www.roxysonline.co.uk

In true Chicago style Roxy Hart and her friends will entertain you with fabulous drag acts. As well as the main stage, there's Velma Kelly's bar, Billy Flynn's bar and Mama Morton's. If you love Chicago, you'll love Roxy's. DJ Matty keeps the party going with cheesy choons 'til the small hours.

Walkabout

1–9 Queen Street, Blackpool FY1 1NL
Tel. no 01253 749132
www.walkabout.eu.com

The classic Aussie bar brings the spirit of Australia, through awesome food, beer and authentic Aussie staff. The atmosphere is second to none. With permanent amazing drinks promotions and hen and stag party packages, they'll make your party one to remember Aussie style. Check out the free Bucking Bronco on Saturday afternoons for the 2010 season. Try and beat your mates, you may even win a prize.

cafés & restaurants

Baci £

7–39 Talbot Road, Blackpool FY1 1LL
Tel. no 01253 296688
www.baciitalianrestaurant.co.uk
info@baciitalianrestaurant.co.uk

Just round the corner from the famous Funny Girls is this funky Italian restaurant serving delicious pasta, mouthwatering steaks and fresh fish. Italian for 'kisses', Baci offers a great hen party option – the Italian Feast, where you can enjoy a selection of starters and main course dishes hand-picked for you by the chef.

Seniors £

106 Normoss Road, Blackpool FY3 8QP
Tel. no 01253 393529
www.thinkseniors.com
normoss@thinkseniors.com

A traditional fish and chip shop, but with a contemporary twist. The restaurant is modern and vibrant and fish comes fresh from Fleetwood each day. There's always something a bit different on the 'catch of the day' board, so why not give it a whirl?

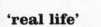

'real life'

We had a real laugh at Nellie Dean's Karaoke Bar. It's a totally unpretentious place, you can just let your hair down and have a good time without any worries.

X factor hopefuls apply here.

West Coast Rock Cafe.

Toast ££

28 Corporation Street, Blackpool FY1 1EJ
Tel. no 01253 749777
www.toast-cafe-bar.co.uk
info@toast-cafe-bar.co.uk

New on the scene in Blackpool, Toast is dedicated to serving fresh locally sourced produce presented beautifully. Inside the double-height ceiling with mezzanine level gives it a feeling of city chic. Tapas is served all day and there's a great value early bird menu, but for the day-after-the-night-before we recommend the traditional Sunday Roast.

West Coast Rock Cafe ££

5–7 Abingdon Street, Blackpool FY1 1DG
Tel. no 01253 751283
www.westcoastrock.co.uk
westcoastrock@blueyonder.co.uk

A legend in Blackpool eateries, the West Coast has been serving Mexican food for 20 years and won the local Best Restaurant of the Year in 2009. You can also get juicy 100% beef burgers, the best steaks in town, succulent Barbecued Ribs, Chicken, Pizza, Pasta and loads more. Big parties are their speciality and you can party 'til late in the 'Club Above' upstairs.

where to party

In the season, Blackpool is totally buzzing with a party vibe. If you're thinking of heading here in the winter, check with venues for opening information first.

Club Sanuk

168–170, North Promenade, Blackpool
FY1 1RE
Tel. no 01253 292900
www.clubsanuk.co.uk
info@clubsanuk.co.uk

With six different rooms of pure entertainment, Sanuk is a great place for your hen night. They have a fab hen party package that can be booked online including free entry before midnight, Q Jump and a free bottle of bubbly to start your night.

Flares

124–130 Promenade, Blackpool FY1 1RA
Tel. no 01253 299688
www.flaresbars.co.uk

No prizes for guessing this one...Flares is a 70s club and proud to be the grooviest disco around! If you love all those disco dancing floor fillers (and let's face who doesn't?), Flares is the party destination for you. They will organise a personalised party package for you with your favourite funky 70s tracks, a free bottle of bubbly, Q Jump tickets and a party pack with heaps of 70s bling. Groovy!

Fun at Flares – the grooviest disco around.

Betty Legs Diamond puts on a spectacular show at the Green Parrot Bar.

Funny Girls

5 Dickson Rd, Blackpool FY1 2AX
Tel. no 0844 2473866
www.funnygirlsonline.co.uk
funnygirls@itpleisure.com

Funny Girls isn't just a club night it's more of a Blackpool institution. Now housed in the old Odeon cinema this is an utterly unique night of top quality live transvestite acts.

Green Parrot

22–28 Clifton Street, Blackpool FY1 1JP
Tel. no 01253 620906
www.greenparrotblackpool.co.uk
info@greenparrotleisure.com

During the day you can relax and chat over coffee and cake or a glass of wine and light lunch with background music and clips of iconic movies and dances for you to enjoy. At night the mood slowly changes to create a party atmosphere. Now with the infamous Betty Legs Diamond Cabaret Show nightly Wednesday to Sunday.

Funny Girls

Celebrating 16 years

THE STAGE IS SET ....FOR AN EVENING TO REMEMBER!

" The biggest thing to hit **Blackpool** since the Tower"
The Stage

"Funny Girls is beyond genius"
Elle Magazine

" The most **talked about** venue in **Blackpool**"
Daily Mirror

Funny Girls, 5 Dickson Road, Blackpool, FY1 2AX
Tel: 0870 350 2665 www.funnygirlsonline.co.uk www.facebook.com/funnygirlsonline

Rumours

Talbot Square, Blackpool FY1 1NG
Tel. no 01253 293204
www.rumoursandhush.co.uk
rumoursandhush@btinternet.com

This sophisticated night spot is a wine bar, a nightclub and a party venue all in one. A recent refurbishment has brought a fresh look and an atmosphere that caters for a chic, diverse crowd of more discerning clubbers. Together with its funky counterpart Hush, they're redefining the club scene in Blackpool.

The Alabama

Liberty's Hotel, 1 Cocker Square, Blackpool FY1 1RX
Tel. no 01253 291155
www.thealabama.co.uk
info@thealabama.co.uk

A multi award winning cabaret venue hosted by the outrageous Leye D Johns. Featuring fun floor shows, with the beautiful Liberty Dancers and the best singers in the North West. When the show finishes at midnight the party keeps on going with a disco.

The Syndicate Superclub

130–140 Church Street, Blackpool FY1 3PR
Tel. no 01253 753222
www.thesyndicate.com
info@thesyndicate.com

The Syndicate claims to be the biggest party in the UK, and with a capacity of 5000 over three floors they must be right! Whatever your taste in music you'll find something to please whilst you strut your stuff on the biggest revolving dancefloor in Europe. So get on your glad rags and your slap and get down there for some serious partying.

Level two at The Syndicate Superclub.

This is Stag & Hen Party Heaven!

S Syndicate
Blackpool

Blackpool...
The UK's No.1
Hen & Stag party destination

For details of what's on visit our website
www.thesyndicate.com

Party hotline:
01253 753 222

bournemouth

Buckets and spades at the ready – we're digging for UK gold. If you love long, sandy beaches, a dynamic holiday vibe and the sight of sun-drenched surfer boys wandering around, Bournemouth is an absolute treasure. With seven miles of award-winning beaches, it's time to don that bikini, girls!

Sailing (top), beach huts (middle), the Pier (bottom).

what to do

This city by the sea boasts soft, sandy beaches, great clubs, a vibrant young population and a real holiday atmosphere. It's Britain's no. 1 staycation resort.

In 2007, a certain bank surveyed the country and discovered that Bournemouth was the happiest place in the UK. Furthermore, we can reveal that it's not because they're all over 90, mad and living off the state, oh no. In fact, Bournemouth has a massive young population, thanks to the university, thousands of language students, the bay's increasing popularity with surfers and a growing media industry. That's not to say that you can't still get a nice cup of tea and a slice of cake.

Bournemouth started life as a health resort and it's still good for the soul, having well below average rainfall and a generally sunny climate.

All in all, if your hen do is to take place in the summer, it seems a pity not to go to Bournemouth. Some of the UK's finest sandy beaches, the pleasure gardens, the pier, a thriving club scene and thousands of people milling around looking for fun, is bound to make for a fantastic few days.

10 good reasons

1. sand, sea and surf
2. watersports
3. holiday atmosphere
4. Boscombe surf reef
5. the Italianate Gardens
6. hiring a beach hut
7. kayak racing
8. riding in the New Forest
9. mini golf
10. spa hotels

There's plenty of surfer eye candy, thanks to the new Boscombe surf reef.

sounds of the city

Hyper music The O2, formerly the Opera House, should definitely be able to provide a highlight night for your hen party. Acts that have graced the stage include the Yeah Yeah Yeahs, Ian Brown and Tinchy Stryder, and it's a stop on the NME Shockwaves tour. The venue is beautiful, with royal boxes, proscenium arch and art deco features still intact.

Deep honey The desire to meet surfers will be strong once you see those buff blondies wandering around, and one way to make it happen is to book yourselves in for a surfing lesson. It's hard work but superb fun, and while body boarding and getting a dunking might be the general standard, some of you are guaranteed to be able to stand up at the end of the day. Which is probably more than you'll be able to say at the end of the night. Surf Steps will tailor the lesson to your needs.

Slide show Polestars offer masses of brilliant hen party ideas for venues all over the country. Those that catch our eye in Bournemouth are cheerleading and the cocktail-mixing masterclass.

Both are great value and a real giggle, and who knows when cocktail making expertise could come in handy…later in your hotel room with a couple of tooth mugs and the mini bar, probably. As to the cheerleading, what with all that jumping around and shouting, we can't think of a better way to get the laughter flowing for a fantastic hen night.

She's like the wind Poole Harbour is one of the best places to learn to windsurf – like most men, it's shallow and windy! Book in for two three-hour lessons and you've got a full beginner's course and two fantastic afternoons to look forward to. You'll quickly progress from hardly being able to climb onto the board to cruising across the bay at speed with a big grin on your face. Contact Poole Windsurfing for info.

Salt water If you feel like pushing the boat out for your one and only hen party, keep it literal with a private luxury boat charter from Principal Power. You'll be sipping champagne on comfortable white leather seats and feeling posh until the skipper opens up the throttle,

If you feel the need for speed, hire a Zapcat with exhilaration.co.uk and zoom across the bay Bond girl style.

at which point it's time to down your drinks and enjoy slicing through the waves at top speed – there's nothing like it for making you want to scream whooooo hooooooooo! There's a selection of sleek power boats for charter, but we recommend the elegant Princess V48, with two seating areas, a bar, an electric barbeque and sun deck. And that's how you make dear old Bournemouth feel like St Tropez.

Twist and shout How better to admire Thomas Hardy country than by viewing it from every angle, over and over again? True, your mind may be on other things as you career down a steep Dorset incline in a giant bouncy ball – especially if they've shoved a mate and a bucket of water in with you. At £15 per ride for a group of ten+, Zorbing is one cheap thrill you'll never forget. Call Zorb South on 01929 426595.

Hellbound We've seen some sights, but Saturday night debauchery in a church? Jesus! Ladies, if you're looking for Bournemouth's best, most opulent nightclub, it has to be V. This is a fairly new arrival on Bournemouth's scene, and has an impressive events diary including parties from Hed Kandi. You can book a VIP package where you'll queue jump and have a private booth with platters of sushi, or just get glammed up and mingle in with your very party-minded fellow heathens. Shame on you all.

Space cowboy Laserquest is one of the best hen activities going. It's the perfect icebreaker – if some of your friends don't know each other, this will get rid of any shyness! By the time you've hunted each other through swirling fog, flashing lights and pitch blackness, mercilessly zapped each other with lasers and had your winner and loser certificates presented, you'll all be ready for a great night out.

18 with a bullet If you want something a bit more hardcore then try paintballing, either outdoor in authentic woodland just outside Dorcheseter, or indoors in the Bournemouth arena. MegaPaintball provide all you need for an unforgettable experience, just look them up at megapaintball.co.uk.

Heaven Bournemouth used to be a health resort – a perfect excuse for a pamper while you're there. Try the Hallmark on the West Cliff – lovely stuff

Zorb South is the place for thrillseekers.

where to stay

A popular tourist destination since the Victorians brought the railway to Bournemouth, it's a town with plenty of choice from seaside chic to rural charm.

hotels

Cremona B&B ££

1 St Michael's Road, West Cliff, Bournemouth BH2 5DP
Tel. no 01202 290035
www.cremona.co.uk
enquiries@cremona.co.uk

Situated in the centre of Bournemouth, close to the beach, shopping and nightlife, you'll always get a warm welcome here. The rooms are clean and comfortable with ensuite facilities, and the breakfasts are legendary.

* shared room without breakfast

£ under £30
££ £30–£60
£££ over £60
pppn

Hallmark Hotel and Spa £££

Durley Chine Road, Bournemouth BH2 5JS
Tel. no 01202 751000
www.hallmarkhotels.co.uk/bournemouth
bournemouth.sales@hallmarkhotels.co.uk

This four-star hotel has recently been transformed at a cost of £1.8million into one of the finest boutique-style hotels in Bournemouth. It offers everything a group of girls needs on a pre-wedding celebration: light and airy relaxing rooms, health spa and gym, stylish brasserie serving fine wine, champagne and carefully prepared meals.

Mory House ££

31 Grand Avenue, Southbourne, Bournemouth BH6 3SY
Tel. no 01202 433553
www.moryhouse.co.uk
stay@moryhouse.co.uk

The modern spacious bedrooms at Mory House have a real seaside feel. They are all ensuite and feature TVs, DVD players and hairdryers in every room.

Premier Inn Bournemouth Central £

Westover Road, Bournemouth BH1 2BZ
Tel. no 0870 423 6462
www.premierinn.com

With over 500 hotels in their group, the people at Premier know how to run a hotel! Bournemouth Central is close to 7 glorious miles of sandy beaches, the town centre and all the nightlife. Many of the rooms have balconies and a sea view and they all have a comfy bed.

The Cumberland Hotel ££

27 East Overcliff Drive, Bournemouth BH1 3AF
Tel. no 01202 290722
www.cumberlandbournemouth.co.uk

This 1930s iconic Art Deco hotel is full of character. The many original features are complemented with modern twists since a refurb in 2006. Well located, it's a great place to stay.

Relax in pure comfort at Hallmark Hotel Bournemouth.

self-catering

Bournecoast ££
26 Southbourne Grove, Bournemouth
BH6 3RA
Tel. no 01202 437 888
www.bournecoast.co.uk
info@bournecoast.co.uk

This local family-run holiday letting agent will
fix you up with the perfect accommodation
for your group. They have a huge range of
properties in the Bournemouth area in
a wide variety of sizes so they are
perfectly placed to find you the
ideal self-catering
accommodation.

Poole Harbour Rental ££
Suite 44, Poole BH15 2BA
Tel. no 07778 586710
www.pooleharbourrental.com

Elegant and stylishly decorated,
serviced self-catering rental accommodation,
with individual character. The rooms are
spacious, airy, light, warm and welcoming
with all the essential luxury of a top-quality
serviced apartment. The various properties
are located around Poole Harbour.

shared room without breakfast
£ under £30
££ £30–£60
£££ over £60
pppn

Riviera Holiday Apartments ££
Studland Road, Alum Chine,
Bournemouth BH4 8HZ
Tel. no 01202 763653
www.rivierabournemouth.co.uk
reservations@rivierabournemouth.co.uk

With indoor and outdoors pools, spa bath
and sauna, these apartments offer a relaxing
break and they're just 2km from the beach.
Each apartment sleeps from
two–seven people in simply
furnished and well-equipped
surroundings.

St George's Holiday Flats £
4 Cecil Road, Boscombe,
Bournemouth BH5 1DU
Tel. no 01202 303066

In a highly sought-after location, just a
short walk to golden sandy beaches and the
shopping area, these are well suited to those
wanting to catch some rays on the beach.
Parking is available and there is free Wi-Fi.

Wootton Mews Apartments ££
3 Wootton Gardens, Bournemouth
BH1 1PW
Tel. no 01202 556432

Wootton Mews Holiday Apartments are
situated in the heart of the town, meaning
that you will be within minutes of all the fun
and exciting facilities that Bournemouth has
to offer. You have a range of different sized
apartments within a converted Victorian
property. Parking permits are available to
guests on request.

The spa at Hallmark Hotel and Spa.

6 **We had a fabulous apartment in Bournemouth with a sea view. It was great waking up in the morning to the sound of waves.** 9

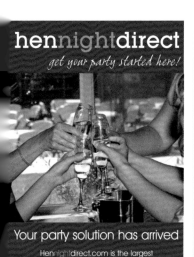

where to eat and drink

There are more than 250 restaurants in Bournemouth and just as many pubs and bars. Spoilt for choice, your only problem is deciding which to choose.

bars & pubs

Aruba

Pier Approach, Bournemouth BH2 5AA
Tel. no 01202 554211
www.aruba-bournemouth.co.uk
info@aruba-bournemouth.co.uk

This exotic world bar brings a touch of the tropics to the Southern English coast. There is an extensive list of wines, beers and champagne sourced from every corner of the globe and both their innovative and classic cocktails are to die for.

At Bar So they don't just mix cocktails, they 'flair' them

Bazaar

103 Commerical Road, The Triangle, Bournemouth BH2 5RT
Tel. no 01202 241998
www.bazaarbar.co.uk
info@bazaarbar.co.uk

This intimate lounge bar is set over two floors. Downstairs has a pool table and outside deck. Upstairs you can expect to hear everything from breaks and dub reggae through to soulful house, US garage and hip hop, nu soul, funk and disco. Live singers and acoustic sessions are lined up for 2010.

Bar So

Exeter Road, Bournemouth BH2 5AG
Tel. no 01202 203050
www.bar-so.com
barso@royalexeterhotel.com

This stylish bar is the place to see and be seen in Bournemouth. With two levels and an extensive terrace, it has something to suit every mood. This place is serious about cocktails, even holding their own 'flair' and mixology competition in 2009, bringing bar tenders from around the world.

Bliss

1–15 St Peter's Road, Bournemouth BH1 2JZ
Tel. no 01202 318693
www.bliss-bar.co.uk
bliss.bournemouth@yellowhammerbars.com

Situated in the very heart of the town centre this is Bournemouth's premier style bar and clubroom. Chill out in the luxurious bar area where you can reserve a booth or VIP area or head downstairs to bump and grind the night away to the latest R'n'B, hip hop and Urban Music. What about cocktail masterclasses? Bliss has it all.

The Lounge

30 Exeter Road, Bournemouth BH2 5AR
Tel. no 01202 296394
www.theloungebournemouth.co.uk
info@theloungebournemouth.co.uk

The Lounge is a sleek and shiny bar with a chic clientele. There are plenty of drinks offers here to get your party started and resident DJ Sleek Ray plays a selection of classic and upfront party jams on Saturdays.

restaurants

Indian Lounge £
148 Christchurch Road, Bournemouth
BH1 1NL
Tel. no 01202 293355
www.indian-lounge.com
info@indian-lounge.com

Widely complimented for its delicious Indian
food and attentive staff, you can't do better
that Indian Lounge if you love a good curry.
Unless of course you try Indian Ocean on
West Cliff Road.

La Stalla Restaurant £
270 Wallisdown Road, Bournemouth
BH10 4HZ
Tel. no 01202 535642
www.lastalla.co.uk
enquiries@lastalla.co.uk

Everyone loves Italian and this restaurant
welcomes groups of all sizes. Whatever your
favourite, from the traditional pizzas and
pasta dishes to steaks, poultry and fish, you'll
find it all on the extensive menu here.

'real life'

**Me and my friends went to
Westpoint in West Cliff Road
because we all love seafood.
We weren't disappointed – the
food was great and the wine
even better!**

Locally caught shellfish.

**2 courses
+ half a bottle
of wine**

**£ under £20
££ £20–£35
£££ over £35**

Bournemouth has plenty of places for fine dining.

Nippon Inn £
124 Charminster Road
Bournemouth BH8 8UT
Tel. no 01202 258859
www.nipponinn.co.uk

If you like noodles or sushi washed down with
a cold Kirin beer, this is the place for you.

Salsa Latin Bar Restaurant ££
82 Charminster Road, Bournemouth
BH8 8US
Tel. no 01202 789696
www.salsabar.co.uk

There's always a lively atmosphere in this
warm and inviting Spanish tapas bar. Choose
from a wide selection of classic tapas dishes
or try something from the Mexican menu, if
that's not your thing there's pizza and pasta
too. Wash it all down with jugfuls of Sangria!

The Lazy Shark £–££
682 Christchurch Road, Bournemouth
BH7 6BT
Tel. no 01202 303417

This lively eatery in Boscombe is just a little
bit different. It has a restaurant and separate
sports bar. The modern European food is
stunning and the service friendly and helpful.
It's the ideal venue close to the new surf reef.

where to party

Bournemouth has a steamy nightlife scene.

Bumbles

45 Poole Hill, Bournemouth BH2 5PW
Tel. no 01202 557006
www.bumblesnightclub.co.uk

A Bournemouth institution, Bumbles is hen party heaven. With Dreamboys International, self confessed 'sexiest boys on the planet', performing their sizzling routine there every Saturday night, it must be high up on your list. Choose from the Red Room (RnB) and the Blue Room (Cheesy party tracks).

DNA

224–226 Old Christchurch Road,
Bournemouth BH1 1PE
Tel. no 01202 319362
www.dnabournemouth.co.uk
info@dnabournemouth.co.uk

DNA, or Daytime Nightime Anytime, is the town's top RnB club.partying through the night until 5am. If you've got some serious stamina then DNA is the club for you.

Dusk till Dawn

205 Old Christchurch Road,
Bournemouth BH1 1JU
Tel. no 01202 551681
www.dusktilldawnclub.com
dusk@dusktilldawnclub.com

The club offers two floors of alternative Dance Music with a state of the art sound system. Dusk till Dawn's underground music policy, quality sounds and opening hours make it an exclusive club for serious music heads on the South Coast. Don't expect cheesy or charty stuff here, but do expect plenty of drinks promos and a great atmosphere.

The up-for-it crowd at The Old Fire Station.

Klute Lounge

20 Exeter Road, Bournemouth
BH2 5AQ
Tel. no 01202 252533

A restaurant, a bar and a club all wrapped up in one neat package of entertainment. You can book a VIP booth for your group or even a room if you have a lot of friends.

The Old Fire Station

36 Holdenhurst Road, Bournemouth
BH8 8AD
Tel. no 01202 963888
www.oldfirestation.co.uk

Half commercial club, half student union for Bournemouth University, The Old FireStation has been rocking Bournemouth for over 15 years. With guest DJs and live events there's plenty of noise in this listed ex-firestation.

❝**The club scene in Bournemouth is great. Everyone is really up for it and having fun.**❞

Toko Nightclub

33–39 St Peters Road, Bournemouth
BH1 2JZ
Tel. no 01202 318 952
www.toko-bar.co.uk
toko.bournemouth@yellowhammerbars.com

With room for over 1000 people, this is the place to make friends! Famous for its huge fish tanks and awesome party atmosphere it is a must see for any Bournemouth visitor. There are two floors offering very different experiences. The main room is dedicated to party, whereas the basement offers a more intimate clubbing experience for those who love to dance.

V Club

The Church, Exeter Road,
Bournemouth BH2 5AQ
www.vbournemouthrocks.com
promotions@vbournemouth.com

This is a truly opulent venue in a converted church with a fantastic balcony overlooking the dancefloor. With a fabulous sound and light show to match, a great line up of events and permanent drinks offers, this is a guaranteed good night out.

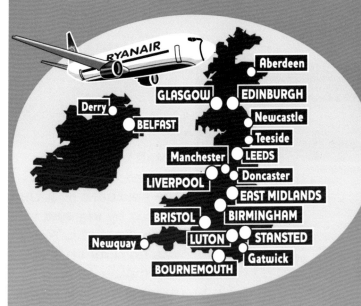

brighton

Small but perfectly formed, Brighton is the southern gem that shines by day and rocks by night. You can do it all on foot – depending on how many cocktails you've had of course – and the place is geared up for 24:7 fun.

Sign (top), the Pier (middle), the Royal Pavillion (bottom).

what to do

Since the Prince Regent established the mad Pavilion Palace as his den of debauchery in the 1820s, Brighton has been a byword for a good time.

So just what is it about this stretch of pebbly coast that makes it so different to Blackpool and other seaside towns around the UK?

The question needed proper research. And, frankly, we needed no second bidding to head down there. For your sake, dear reader, we spent a long, arduous weekend, shopping in the funky North Laine area, walking on the downs, drinking heavily in beachside bars and proper old pubs, wandering through the Lanes boutiques and eating in superb restaurants all over town, trying to work out what gives it that *je ne sais quoi*.

A few shots later, perched on the kitchen worktop of the random party we'd somehow ended up in, we came up with an unshakeable hypothesis. 'It's just an amazing town.'

Since Brighton aint cheap and brain cells are irreplaceable at our age, we hope you use this research wisely.

All the fun of the fair!

10 good reasons

1. loads of undie boutique
2. veggie restaurants
3. picnics on the Downs
4. beachside clubs
5. the buzz
6. straight-friendly gay scene
7. UK's longest orbing run
8. Tuaca (Italian liquer)
9. posh boutique hotels
10. cheap, central hostels

sounds of the city

Shake your tail feather You know what a bride needs to really take her mind off dresses, spray tans, mother-in-laws and caterers? 'Orbing', that's what. Replace petty worries with genuine fear for your life! Throwing yourself down a very steep hill inside a bouncy ball is both therapeutic and proof that you need therapy. It also gives you the chance to head to the lovely South Downs for a day of walks, picnics and craziness at orb360.co.uk. Later on, you could follow up with cocktail making lessons at Roger Dodger the Fish (RDF), Preston Street. And if that little lot won't shake things up a bit, we don't know what will.

Underwater love If you find the English Channel an acceptable receptacle for a dip, then book a full day of watersports, including kayaking, windsurfing, ringo rides behind a speed boat and waterskiing, and finish with a BBQ dinner on the beach. Visit ViewBrighton.co.uk to find out more.

Rubberband girl The trampolines on the Palace Pier are fun, but Jumpzone bungy trampoline on the beach is, in our opinion, one of the most ridiculous things you can do. Therefore, it should not be missed. If you want something a bit edgier, the UK Bungee Club has several 'events' on Hove Lawns throughout the year. Book in and jump off. And since you're wearing a grin of hilarity already, a night at the excellent Komedia stand-up comedy club might round the day off nicely.

Welcome to the House of Fun
Wandering up the Palace Pier with a face full of unhealthy food is always lovely, as is the obligatory stop for pics of your mates faces grinning through the bawdy cut-outs next to the arcade. Seaside magic. And, when the man with the money belt shouted in bored tones, 'It's fun! It's exciting!', it was certainly enough to get our bums on seats at the Dolphin Derby for half an hour. It is fun and exciting, in case you're wondering. But not as fun as the dodgems, and not as exciting as the Crazy Mouse rollercoaster, which looks innocent but dangles you out over the sea in a most alarming manner. Eek, eek! The House of Horror is good for some girly screaming, too.

Roll down Europe's longest orbing course at Orb360 set atop Devil's Dyke.

Truffalicious
A Chocoholic's fantasy!

• Fun n frolics in a great atmosphere creating your own Belgian chocolate truffles

• Involves plenty of hands on experience working with warm melted Belgian chocolate!

• Eat as much chocolate as you desire throughout, plus chocolate fountain provided!

• Around 2 hours of yummy fun!

• 7 days a week all year round

After all that chocolatiering why not make use of our luxurious facilities: showers, covered jacuzzi and BBQ and sauna. Bring your own food and wine and relax in our picturesque courtyard and surrounds.

Accommodation available.

MUDMANIA
DOWN & DIRTY OFF ROAD RACING!
for dirty girls only!

Experience our down 'n' dirty off road racing near the party town of Brighton.

• 4 buggies race each other round out purpose built muddy track

• each driver gets practice laps & 4 races in our fun, safe, automatic buggies

• 4 drivers with most points get into our final for the podium presentation of medals, MudMania t-shirt and fizz!

• around 2 hours of fun

• 7 days a week, all year round

BOOK NOW

www.mudmania.co.uk

To book a naughty session of indulgence or a mucky muddy thrill, or why not combine the two, call Caroline on: 0780 317 3117

Girls! Can it be so easy to book a Heavenly Hen Do?

Imagine hen party hell

● **hours traipsing round in the cold looking for bars!** 'NIGHTMARE'

● **losing half your group waiting for unreliable and expensive taxis!** 'NIGHTMARE'

● **trying to organise a great night out in a town you don't know!** 'NIGHTMARE'

Now imagine everything being taken care of... from venues to music! No Fuss. No Stress. No hassle. One phone call and it's all done.

Book now and get FREE nightclub tickets for the Friday

Great Venues! • Q Jump! • Free Shots! • VIP entry!

HIGHWAY 69
BRIGHTON PUB CRAWL

07816 230510
sales@highway69.co.uk
www.highway69.co.uk

The wind beneath my wings

Getting your thermals on gets sexy when you're talking paragliding. Airworks of Glynde will enable you to 'soar like a bird' with tandem or taster flights. You sit securely on the lap of an instructor while he flies you around on a thermal breeze above Sussex.

Driving along in my automobile

Don't leave the driving to the stags. Getting kitted up and driving like a loon is what we ladies love best. Karting Nation's 800 metre track has a lap time and position display as well as tunnels and a split level track.

If you really want to get dirty, Adventure Connections does off-road 400cc buggies to have you bounding around at high speed on a mudslick. In total control and looking fab, naturally.

Luck be a lady Hove has one of the UK's best dog tracks, and the Saturday action starts at 5pm. If you want a more dressed-up do, perhaps a days' horseracing might be the thing. For later on, one of the Marina's swanky attractions is the Rendezvous Casino – high on glitz and the perfect opportunity to ditch the jeans and slink around in a sexy dress.

I bet you look good on the dancefloor

Well if you don't now you will after a few hours with the very friendly professional dancers from Madame Peaches. Wiggle and wobble, bump and grind, shimmy and shake with a 90-minute burlesque lesson building up to a full routine incoporating props, such as riding crops, fans and nipple tassels – don't worry these can fi on top of your clothes! Or not...

'been there...'

The first night we booked ourselves a karaoke party at Gars, which does fab Chinese food. You get a private room so things got pretty loud. Anyway, as you can imagine we were a big fragile next day so we just used the hotel pool and had a chill. Saturday night it was off to club Oceana for the Adonis Cabaret, which was soo cheesy but really good fun!

Become Burlesque Babes for a day and learn to shake and shimmy with MadamePeaches.com.

where to stay

If you want somewhere stylish, luxe or chic to stay, Brighton's the place. From boutique B&B to super cool self-catering, this funky town has it all...at a price!

hotels

Holiday Inn Brighton Seafront ££

137 Kings Road, Brighton BN1 2JF
Tel. no 01273 828250
www.hibrighton.com
reservations@hibrighton.com

As the name suggests, this hotel is well located opposite the beach. It has everything you would expect in a 4-star international hotel chain, including Wi-Fi and air conditioning. There are several lounges and bars to relax in and two restaurants. Check the website for special offers on room rates.

shared room without breakfast
£ under £30
££ £30–£60
£££ over £60
pppn

Jurys Inn £

101 Stroudley Road, Brighton BN1 4DJ
Tel. no 01273 862121
http://brightonhotels.jurysinns.com

Join ranks with other hen and stag parties at this central hotel located near the train station. It's also walking distance to the centre and the seafront. With comfy rooms equipped with Wi-Fi, it's a good choice.

Brighton beachfront.

Kings Hotel ££

139–141 Kings Rd, Brighton BN1 2NA
Tel. no 01273 820854
www.kingshotelbrighton.co.uk
info@kingshotelbrighton.co.uk

Located right in the heart of Brighton and very close to the beach, the Kings Hotel is a magnificent Regency hotel converted from three former private residencies. The modern boutique style is clean and fresh; and the K bar, overlooking the sea, is a great place to start off your evening.

New Madeira Hotel ££

19–23 Marine Parade, Brighton BN2 1TL
Tel. no 01273 698331/0800 970 7634(free)
www.newmadeirahotel.com
info@newmadeirahotel.com

This seafront guesthouse offers a variety of rooms from budget to boutique (some with a jacuzzi bath) to suit your wallet. The period building has been fully modernised and the friendly staff will make your stay truly memorable.

West Beach Hotel ££

135 Kings Road, Brighton BN1 2HX
Tel. no 01273 323161
www.westbeachhotel.co.uk
rooms@westbeachhotel.co.uk

This hotel offers a little individuality. It boasts five quad rooms featuring four single beds perfect for a group booking. Twins and triples are also available, many with a sea view so make sure you put in your request.

self-catering

Best of Brighton Cottages £–£££
4 Laureens Walk, Nevill Road,
Rottingdean, Brighton BN2 7HG
Tel. no 01273 308779
www.bestofbrighton.co.uk
www.apartmentsinbrighton.com
enquiries@bestofbrighton.co.uk

Offering about 100 fully furnished
apartments, houses and cottages in
Brighton & Hove and the
surrounding countryside. Letting
periods start at three days and
properties are available in all
price ranges and sleep from
2–20 people.

Crown Gardens £–££
7 Gloucester Yard, 121–123
Gloucester Road, Brighton BN1 4AF
Tel. no 01273 608378
www.crown-gardens.co.uk
enquiries@crown-gardens.co.uk

The Brighton experts in finding
accommodation for groups, Crown Gardens'
friendly staff will provide you with the perfect
base for your party. They specialise in
centrally located apartments and cottages
close to Brighton's buzzing centre, ideal for
short lets.

Florence House Garden Annexe £
18 Florence Road, Brighton BN1 6DJ
Tel. no 01273 506624
www.brightonlets.net

This tranquil cottage is set in the garden of a
Victorian House just a mile from the seafront.
Sleeping up to nine people in five bedrooms,
it's ideal for a medium-sized group.

My Holiday Let £–££
6 Brunswick Place, Hove BN3 1EB
Tel. no 07976 923733
www.brightonholiday.com
catherine@myholidaylet.com

These luxury apartments are the self-catering
alternative to a boutique hotel. Just a stone's
throw from the beach, these gorgeous bow-
fronted regency apartments have a 5-star
rating and a Gold Award. Simply furnished,
they ooze understated style.

Palms Properties ££
25 Waterfront, Brighton Marina,
Brighton BN2 5WA
Tel. no 01273 626000
www.palmsproperties.co.uk
booking@palmsproperties.co.uk

Palms offer a wide range of accommodation
in Brighton Marina from waterside
studios to luxury penthouse
apartments. The four
apartments range from a
studio to three bedrooms,
all furnished to a high
standard.

✳ shared room without breakfast

£ under £30
££ £30–£60
£££ over £60
pppn

Queensbury Mews ££
15 Queensbury Mews
Brighton BN1 2FE
Tel. no 01273 270636
www.queensburycottage.co.uk
info@queensburycottage.co.uk.

This luxury townhouse is set right in the city
centre and close to the seafront, perfect for a
night on the town. Recently modernised and
refurbished, it is bright and airy with stylish
neutral decor.

Vida Retreats ££
5 Somerhill Rd, Hove BN3 1RP
Tel. no 01273 220358
www.vidaretreats.com

This is the ultimate luxury accommodation for
large groups. Lansdowne Regency Villa and
Somerhill Edwardian Mansion are 5 minutes
apart and sleep 22–30 in sumptuous style.

Brighton Marina.

where to eat and drink

Eat and drink from the global village in Brighton. There are food and beverages from all over the world here, all you need to do is find the time to try them.

bars & cafés

Browns Bar & Brasserie
3–4 Duke Street, Brighton BN1 1AH
Tel no. 01273 323501
www.browns-restaurants.co.uk

In the 40 years since Browns started it has become synomous with good food served in stylish surroundings. Here in Brighton that is as true as ever. Come for brunch, lunch, drinks, dinner or even afternoon tea.

Carluccio's
Unit 1 Jubilee Street, Brighton BN1 1GE
Tel. no 01273 690493
www.carluccios.com

For serious coffee aficionados Carluccio's has to be on the list. Pop in for a latte and biscotti while shopping, browse the gorgeous deli foods, or go for a blow-out lunch. You won't be disappointed, this is the art of eating Italian.

Koba
135 Western Road Brighton BN1 2LA
Tel no. 01273 720059
www.kobauk.com
info@kobauk.com

A little off the beaten track, you'll find this gem of a place. Its intimate and mysterious atmosphere draws you in and the cocktails make you stay! Enquire about mixology here.

Leo's Lounge
54–55 Meeting House Lane, Brighton BN1 1HB
Tel no. 01273 207040

This leopard print lined bar set in Brighon's trendy Lanes is the perfect place to start your evening off with cocktails or champagne.

Carluccio's Café.

Oxygen
63–65 West Street, Brighton BN1 2RA
Tel no. 01273 727378
www.oxygenbrighton.co.uk

This trendy bar has a 'shot-tail' (shooter cocktails) menu of over 40 concoctions plus regular cocktails on promotion in the early evening. The saloon bar theme makes this a wild card, but it will come up trumps.

Roger Dodger the Fish (RDF)
76 Preston Street, Brighton BN1 2HG
Tel no. 07761 166 300
www.rogerdodgerthefish.com
iinfo@rogerdodgerthefish.com

This place is legendary in Brighton for hen and stag parties. Claiming to be 'the sexiest bar in Brighton if not the world', the bar is split into a girls' area and a boys' area. The girls' area has sexy barmen, a princess and a pole (for dancing on...). You can arrange burlesque dance classes here, have a big screen movie showing and learn to make cocktails, or all three. There's nothing they won't do to entertain you on your hen night.

restaurants

**2 courses
+ half a bottle
of wine**

**£ under £20
££ £20–£35
£££ over £35**

El Mexicano £

7 New Road, Brighton BN1 1UF
Tel. no 01273 727766
www.elmexicano.co.uk
info@elmexicano.co.uk

Delicious authentic Mexican food and
Spanish tapas all freshly prepared on the
premises. Set in Brighton's 'theatreland' it's
handy for pre- or post-theatre dining. A
deposit is required for groups of eight or
more and the maximum on Saturday is 14.

Gars ££

19 Prince Albert Street, Brighton BN1 1HF
Tel. no 01273 321321
www.gars.co.uk
info@gars.co.uk

In the heart of the Lanes, Gars offers a wide
range of traditional Chinese food with a
smattering of Thai and Japanese dishes for
a taste of the Far East. The food is nicely
complemented by the modern Asian decor
featuring bamboo flooring and silk shades.

'real life'

**Me and my chicks all went
down to Brighton from
London and had a great time
wandering around the Lanes,
just stopping for lunch at
Jamie's Italian.**

Retail therapy.

Old Orleans is hen party paradise.

Havana ££

32 Duke Street, Brighton BN1 1AG
Tel. no 01273 773 388
www.havana.uk.com
info@havana.uk.com

The laid back colonial style of this former
theatre evokes the ambience of the
Caribbean times past. An international menu,
accompanied by fine wines and moody jazz,
creates a leisurely evening out.

Jamie's Italian £££

11 Black Lion Street, Brighton BN1 1ND
Tel. no 01273 915480
www.jamieoliver.com

Jamie Oliver's passion for food is at the
forefront of this new chain of restaurants.
Simple, rustic Italian dishes all prepared with
the best local and seasonal ingredients will
make your mouth water. The all-Italian wine
list offers something a bit different, too.

Old Orleans ££

13 Prince Albert Street, Brighton BN1 1HE
Tel. no 01273 747000
www.oldorleans.com
oldorleans.brighton@intertainuk.com

Experts in hosting hen and stag parties, Old
Orleans can cater for any size of group. It's
no surprise that the menu is mainly American
incorporating favourites such as wings and
nachos. You can also reserve an area in the
bar at no cost.

where to party

The club scene in Brighton is buzzing with a unique vibe that people regularly travel miles for every weekend. For a truly memorable hen party Brighton's the place.

Audio

10 Marine Parade, Brighton BN2 1TL
Tel. no 01273 697775
www.audiobrighton.com

Set on two levels you have a choice of the downstairs bar or the Above Audio cocktail bar. There is also a terrace, which they bill as 'the classiest smoking area in Brighton'! This chilled out venue plays a mix of chart music and funky house downstairs and when the action wraps up about 2am, you can carry on partying in the upstairs club until 4am. There are no pretentions here, just honest fun.

Casablanca

3 Middle Street, Brighton BN1 1AL
Tel. no 01273 321817
www.casablancajazzclub.com
info@casablancajazzclub.com

Going since 1980, Casablanca is a mainstay of the Brighton scene. It prides itself on being a fun, independent environment, just a little bit different to the rest. On offer here are two floors with two different sounds: one playing live music, the other featuring a DJ. Saturday nights see a blend of live latino and the finest funk bands around playing to an up-for-it crowd who are there to enjoy the music.

Digital

187–193 Kings Rd Arches, Brighton, BN1 1NB
Tel. no 01273 227767
www.yourfutureisdigital.com
steve.joyce@yourfutureisdigital.com

This club is serious about music boasting some top-quality sound and light gear. On Saturday nights they feature 'Playroom', with sounds of house and electro along with an adult bouncy castle, ball pit, space hoppers, inflatables and giant games. This could be your last opportunity to revisit your childhood so revel in it.

It's always cocktail time in Brighton's lively scene.

Funky Buddha Lounge

169–170 Kings Rd Arches, Brighton
BN1 1NB
Tel. no 01273 725541
www.funkybuddhalounge.co.uk
info@funkybuddhalounge.co.uk

Housed in the subterranean arches of the
seafront, the Funky Buddha Lounge is the
city's premier style venue. Open till 4am this
venue won't sting you on the door or the bar.

Komedia

44–47 Gardner Street, Brighton BN1 1UN
Tel. no 0845 293 8480
www.komedia.co.uk
info@komedia.co.uk

Located in the trendy North Laine area of
Brighton, Komedia is famed for its award-
winning formula of great shows, fab food,
excellent drinks choice and welcoming
atmosphere. Whether you fancy laughing at
stand-up comedy, grooving with sultry
cabaret, kooky club nights...or all three...it's
the perfect venue for any Hen party!

Lucky Voice

8 Black Lion Street, Brighton BN1 1ND
Tel. no 01273 715770
www.luckyvoice.com
brighton@luckyvoice.com

If you're seeking a different yet classy hen
night idea, Lucky Voice has all you need.
They'll organise everything for you, give you a
private karaoke room, a dressing up box, ply
you with cocktails, teach you how to make
them and then let you sing your hearts out.
Sounds like fun!

Oceana

West Street, Brighton BN1 2RE
Tel. no 0845 296 8590
www.oceanaclubs.com/brighton
oceana-brighton@luminar.co.uk

This multi-million pound venue has seven
themed rooms and two VIP suites to choose
from. Chill in the Aspen Ski Lodge, dance
your heart out in the Icehouse, party the night
away in the New York Disco or relax in the
Parisian Boudoir. Who knows where you'll
end up?

Rendezvous Casino

Park Square, Brighton Marina, Brighton
BN2 5UF
Tel. no 01273 605602
www.rendezvouscasino.com

If you want some thrills on your last night of
freedom, head to the tables at Rendezvous.
There's a wide range of games on two floors
including roulette, blackjack, texas hold'em,
three card poker and let it ride.

Spend a night at the tables at Rendezvous Casino.

The Honey Club

214 Kings Rd Arches, Brighton BN1 1NB
Tel. no 01273 202807
www.thehoneyclub.co.uk
info@thehoneyclub.co.uk

Another vast multi-room venue including two
beachfront terraces. With a different music
genre in every room, there's something for
every musical taste here.

bristol

Way out West it's Bristol – the funky, friendly city that's buzzing every weekend. The locals can't get enough of the relaxed party vibes, great shopping, dockside eateries and fantastic pubs. And if this is your chosen hen party destination, you'll love it too.

Georgian Terrace (top), The Harbour (middle), Clifton Suspension Bridge (bottom).

what to do

Sandwiched between swanked-up docks and Georgian terraces is Bristol's heart – boats, boutiques, rowdy bars, gigs, street art, smart restaurants...it's one hell of a 'sanger'.

Bristol's got all the lively nightlife, big name shopping, harbourside bars, pack 'em in cheap eateries and top restaurants you could possibly want from a modern cosmopolitan city. On top of all that is a liberal sprinkling of that arty, funky pixie dust that makes people come back again and again. Locals and visitors alike love the particular brand of laid-back cool that oozes from every nook and cranny of this historic city.

Perhaps you'll start your weekend off by gathering at the Avon Gorge Hotel – it overlooks the suspension bridge and gorge, and has a big outdoor deck where you'll enjoy superb burgers with your first couple of drinks.

Take a ramble to the downs, stroll around in classy Clifton for shopping and lovely little pubs and cafes, or head down to the harbourside clubs, where you'll find lots of people wearing fancy dress and getting very, very loud. If that's not your scene, how about a gig? The O2 Academy books some great big name acts.

Quieter local pursuits include stunningly scenic hot air balloon flights, cycling the canal path to Bath, the luxurious new cinema at Cabot Circus (with its superb shopping, from Harvey Nicks to Top Shop), taking in bit of street theatre, swimming, spa and lunch at the Lido...'arr, it's gurt lush, is Brizzle'.

Visit Brunel's SS Great Britain at Bristol Dock.

✳ 10 good reasons

1. **harbourside drinks**
2. **funky pubs**
3. **floating eateries**
4. **St Werburgh's farm**
5. **art and museums**
6. **tea and cake in Clifton**
7. **views of the gorge**
8. **great gigs and clubs**
9. **ancient, creaky pubs**
10. **fab shopping**

sounds of the city

I've got a lovely bunch of coconuts
The Lido in Bristol doesn't look much from outside, and your guests might think it's a bit odd to have a swimming pool party at your age, but don't let that stop you. The pool and beach hut-style changing rooms ooze Victorian seaside charm, and the attractive restaurant overlooking them serves good, modern food with a smile. Aside from the pool there's a sauna, steam room and hot tub. You can get some blissful body treatments, including the Ananda face massage, bio-energising body wrap and other sciencey sounding stuff, and retox with a nice drink at the poolside bar. Total winner.

God Save the Queen Thornbury Castle in South Gloucestershire was the marital home of Henry VIII and Ann Boleyn, but don't dwell on the matricidal detail. Book the group into the Tudor Hall for fabulous food in the company of suits of armour, creepy family portraits and decapitated animals for an authentic castle vibe. The Boyling House and Great Oven rooms next door can be turned into a casino and a bar for your event. Great for a big group of ladies who like to get off the beaten track and do something a bit quirky and truly unique.

You can leave your hat on Fancy the idea of making your own fascinators? 'What's that?' you cry. A fascinator is a very chic little cocktail hat, perfect to set off a wedding outfit. So, book your hens in for a workshop at Clara Bows Millinery, where you'll be guided step-by-step into making your own wearable works of art. Not only that, but you can team it up with a fabulous afternoon tea all laid out on beautiful vintage china. This is a classy and indulgent hen party *par excellence*!

Smash it up Flying Saucers in Clifton is a mellow few hours if there's nothing you like more than making stuff, having a chat with your mates and eating biscuits. You'll paint pottery, perhaps producing a set of bespoke tableware for the bride and groom to lovingly tuck away for best. There's never an occasion special enough for some items, is there? Call 0117 927 3666.

Make your own stunning 'fascinator' with the experts at Clara Bows Millinery.

HELP! Did you know that getting married is one of THE most stressful things you can do? What you need is a little divine intervention. The Stress Angels will waft into your Bristol hen party HQ and massage all your stress away. Browse a list of holistic or beauty treatments, from spray tan to Indian head massage, then kick back with your mates and a glass of fizz while the miracles take place. These loveable Angels of Mercy are well known in the city for saving local workers from death by stress, and their pamper parties combine expertise with lots of fun to keep you smiling. To be pummelled into peacefulness, visit bathstressangels.co.uk.

Hoop dreams Go loopy with Emma at Hooping Mad; she'll teach you how to tame the unruly hula in a fun and unique couple of hours that should have you all giggling and gyrating your socks off. Many's the hula hoop that's been languishing in the primary school PE shed since the dawn of the computer age, but it's back and, like all simple things, it's brilliant. Hula's an activity that few will be expecting, and surprise is the key to a memorable hen party. It's catching on in the West, with courses and classes popping up all over – be warned, you may become addicted. Find Hooping Mad on Facebook or visit hoopingmad.co.uk.

Rock and Roll Star OMG, you know you want a piece of this action...a glass of bubbly, a tour of the recording studio and then – yes – a recording of you and your mates performing two songs together! It's X-factor without the X, it's Britain's got Talent without the Talent...it's a right laugh anyway. You could actually take this seriously – it's a professional outfit and who knows, Simon Cowell might be lurking in the shadows – but most people just get the fancy dress on and give it some welly. You'll take away a souvenir CD, and they will even ferry you back into the centre of Bristol. Visit popstarparty.biz.

Do the hand jive baby Grease, Thriller, Mamma Mia, Chicago, Lady Gaga, Moulin Rouge...just some of the themes to choose from at the divine Diva Dance Academy. Once you arrive (suitably dressed, of course), you'll get two hours of expert tuition, put together a routine and have a mini photoshoot. While it may sound intimidating, the emphasis is on fun, not skills – so get those day-glo leg warmers/fishnets on and give it the old razzle dazzle.
Or plug into the ancient art of flaunting your assets with the meowwsome Pink Kitten Dance School. Burlesque lessons start with a gentle warm up and some sultry posing, then you'll learn how to put a wiggle into your walk, á la Marilyn Monroe. You'll then be ready to put together a sexy routine, complete with feather boas.

All hands on deck For an original night out in Bristol, we recommend The Thekla – a club boat moored on the lively Mud Dock. Some of the city's best nights happen aboard this much-loved vessel. Keep it simple (but good) by booking your group in for food and drinks on the top deck before the party gets going down below.

'been there...'

We had a couple of hours at Bristol Climbing Centre inside St Werburgh's church, then tea and cake at the City Farm, then back to the apartment for a bit. Saw Beth Ditto at the Academy later on – she rocked! Obviously, we had a few so woke up late next day. We all went for milkshake and burgers at GBK on Sunday, then did a bit of shopping – it's great for vintage, so I was in heaven.

where to stay

For big city lights and the big chain hotels, where you know exactly what to expect, Bristol's your bag. There are plenty of budget places as well as blow the budget ones.

hotels & hostels

Cabot Circus Hotel £
Bond Street South, Bristol BS1 3EN
Tel. no 0845 094 5588
www.futureinns.co.uk
reservations.bristol@futureinns.co.uk

Belonging to Future Inns, a small chain of three hotels, the Bristol outlet is attached to the shiny new shopping centre – Cabot Circus. With 149 ensuite rooms and Chophouse Restaurant and Bar, it has all the facilities you need in a central location.

City Inn ££
Temple Circus House,
Temple Way, Bristol BS1 6BF
Tel no. 0117 925 1001
www.cityinn.com
bristol.reservations@cityinn.com

Just a few minutes walk from Temple Meads station, this is the ideal place to book for a hen party. All rooms feature iMac computers, free Wi-Fi and Sky TV, but you won't be spending much time there. Instead why not have an alfresco meal on the terrace overlooking the beautiful Temple Gardens. Alternatively, if the weather's a bit parky unwind in the soft-styled surroundings of the award-winning restaurant.

Hotel Ibis Bristol Centre ££
Explore Lane, Harbourside,
Bristol BS1 5TY
Tel. no 0117 989 7200
www.ibishotel.com

This international chain offers all the services and facilities you need to get a good night's sleep after some serious partying – comfy beds, ensuite shower rooms and more. There's also another branch of the hotel near Temple Meads station.

**shared room
without
breakfast**

£ under £30
££ £30–£60
£££ over £60
pppn

Ramada Bristol City ££
Redcliffe Way, Bristol BS1 6NJ
Tel. no 0844 879 9106
www.ramadajarvis.co.uk

This hotel offers four-star luxury and is conveniently located in the city centre. Swim in the pool and dine beside a 17th century kiln. And it's just five minutes walk from Temple Meads station and the lively waterfront.

The Bristol Hotel £££
Prince Street, Bristol BS1 4QF
Tel no. 0117 923 0333
www.doylecollection.com
bristol@doylecollection.com

The Bristol Hotel offers luxury and style with a great atmosphere. In a fabulous quayside setting, just a stone's throw from the SS Great Britain, it's a great place to spend your hen weekend!

self-catering

Bristol Serviced Lets ££

The Refinery, Jacob Street,
Bristol BS2 0HS
Tel. no 0871 226 1902
www.servicedlets.com

Serviced Lets Design Apartments has chosen the pick of the crop of Bristol's most stunning modern apartment developments both in the city centre and trendy Clifton. So whether you want Georgian splendour in Clifton or contemporary design near the harbour, this company has it all.

Geometric Serviced Apartments ££

Braggs Lane, Old Market, Bristol BS2 0BE
Tel. no 0117 954 7490
www.geometricapartments.com
info@geometricapartments.com

These stylish contemporary apartments are furnished to the highest standards, featuring Bamboo teak flooring, designer bathrooms and chic Italian furniture. These one- and two-bedroomed apartments are the ultimate in boutique self-catering.

Portland Apartments ££

c/o 64 Archfield Rd, Bristol BS6 6BQ
Tel. no 0117 924 9111
www.portlandapartments.co.uk
reservations@portlandapartments.co.u

These spacious serviced apartments promis luxury and covenience. Superbly appointed and furnished with leather sofas, just kick off you shoes and relax with a personalised service to ensure you will have an unsurpassable stay.

shared room without breakfast
£ under £30
££ £30–£60
£££ over £60
pppn

Premier Apartments ££

30–38 St Thomas Place, S Thomas Street, Redcliffe, Bristol BS1 6JZ
Tel. no 0117 954 4800
www.premierapartmentsbristol.com
info@premierapartmentsbristol.com

Located in Redcliffe, these apartments are 5 minutes walk from Temple Meads train station and the trendy Cabot Circus shoppin centre. The 64 one- and two-bedroomed apartments are located within one building. Wi-Fi and LCD TVs are available in all apartments.

Premier Apartments, Bristol.

where to eat and drink

In the summer you'll find hordes of people eating and drinking alfresco in the popular Harbourside area, winter sees a shift to the cosy pubs and smart bars of Clifton.

bars & pubs

Bijou

135 Whiteladies Road, Clifton, Bristol
Tel. no 0117 970 6589
www.barbijou.co.uk
mark@barbijou.co.uk

One of a kind, this fancy cocktail bar offers free hire of the venue and you can bring your own DJ or hire the bars at a small cost. Or try one of their cocktail courses and learn to design your own cocktail.

Joe Public's

Beacon House, 3 Queen's Avenue, Clifton, Bristol BS8 1QU
Tel. no 0117 973 1249
www.joepublics.com
info@joepublics.com

This underground bar, live music venue and nightclub is one of Bristol's most unique offerings. And you can book an area for your hens for free here. From the funky retro styling to the cool beats played by the hottest local DJs, Joe Public's is just a little bit different.

Revolution

Old Fish Market, St Nicholas St, Bristol BS1 1UA
Tel. no 0117 930 4335
www.revolution-bars.co.uk/bristol

Set in the impressive Old Fish Market building, close to the Harbour area, Revolution Bristol offers the tried and tested winning formula of fun party atmosphere in stylish surroundings. They offer a personal service for hen parties, providing you with invites, reserved area, bespoke menu personalised with photos of the bride-to-be and messages from her hens.

The White Lion Bar

Avon Gorge Hotel, Sion Hill, Clifton, Bristol BS8 4LD
Tel. no 0117 973 8955
www.theavongorge.com
events@theavongorge.com

The panoramic views of Clifton Suspension bridge and the Avon Gorge from the terrace at The White Lion are truly stunning. It's a great place for a long lunch on a sunny day; order a chilled glass of wine and a tasty dish from the varied menu, sit back and take in the view. The Avon Gorge Hotel, the setting of The White Lion, is also an option for accommodation if you want to base your hen night in Clifton.

The terrace of The White Lion Bar.

cafés & restaurants

Aqua Italia ££
Welsh Back, Bristol BS1 4RR
Tel. no 0117 915 6060
www.aqua-restaurant.com
bristol@aqua-restaurant.com

With two outlets in Bristol and one in Bath, Aqua has perfected its formula of healthy, tasty and beautifully presented Italian cuisine. Enjoy Italian wines and cocktails here, as well as aperitivos, grappas and the best espresso coffees. Choose from the newly refurbished interior with marble bar and cosy corners or the waterfront terrace.

Cosmo ££
The Pavillion, Triangle West, Clifton, Bristol BS8 1ET
Tel. no 0117 934 0999
www.cosmo-restaurants.co.uk
bristol@cosmo-restaurants.co.uk

The Pan Asian menu and exceptional value for money makes Cosmo a popular hen party destination. With six live cooking stations, including a freshly prepared sushi area, you can watch chefs turn your chosen raw ingredients into mouth-watering sizzling dishes before your eyes.

2 courses + half a bottle of wine

£ under £20
££ £20–£35
£££ over £35

Gourmet Burger Kitchen ££
74 Park Street, Bristol BS1 5JX
Tel. no 0117 316 9162
www.gbk.co.uk
info@gbk.co.uk

These are no ordinary burgers! Using only the freshest ingredients, GBK have created a large menu of classic combos and innovative taste combinations. Whether you're after a sustaining bite on Saturday night before you hit the town or a restorative lunch on Sunday, GBK will hit the spot.

Riverstation £££
The Grove, Harbourside, Bristol BS1 4RB
Tel. no 0117 914 4434
www.riverstation.co.uk
relax@riverstation.co.uk

This light and airy open-plan restaurant and bar-kitchen serves modern European food using carefully sourced, local, fresh ingredients. Enjoy a fanastic meal on one of the two open-air terraces overlooking water with stunning view of the harbour.

Severnshed ££
The Grove, Harbourside, Bristol BS1 4RB
Tel. no 0117 925 1212
www.shedrestaurants.co.uk
severnshed@shed-restaurants.com

This former boathouse on the banks of the floating harbour offers a laid back yet luxurious dining experience. On Saturday nights DJs create a lively club atmosphere.

Watershed Café Bar £
1 Canon's Road, Harbourside, Bristol BS1 5TX
Tel. no 0117 927 5100
www.watershed.co.uk
info@watershed.co.uk

This trendy arts centre and cinema on the harbour has a buzzing café bar popular with locals and visitors alike. Open from early in the morning to late at night, you can come here for breakfast, lunch or dinner. Grab a table on the balcony and enjoy watching the world go by on Bristol's bustling waterfront. Bright and airy, this café-bar is the perfect place to start off your weekend.

Shaken not stirred.

where to party

Clubbing in Bristol is high on the list of reasons to choose this Westcountry city for your hen do. There's everything from huge warehouse clubs to intimate jazz bars.

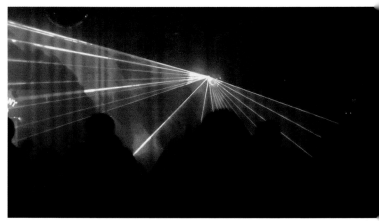

You most certainly won't be short of places to party in Bristol – the possibilities are endless.

Avon River Cruises

37 Colthurst Drive, Hanham, Bristol
BS15 3SG
Tel. no 0117 904 3671
www.avonrivercruises.co.uk
avonrivercruises@blueyonder.co.uk

The Silver Salmon is the most stylish cruiser on the River Avon and operates throughout the year. It's the ideal way to spend your hen party either in Bath from May to September or Bristol from October to April. You can charter the boat for dancing, live music or a sit down meal.

O2 Academy

Frogmore St, Bristol BS1 5NA
Tel. no 0117 927 9227
www.o2academybristol.co.uk
mail@o2academybristol.co.uk

The O2 Academy Bristol welcomes the hottest UK and international acts. Book tickets for your fave and enjoy a memorable hen do with the thrill of a big gig.

Oceana

Harbourside, Bristol BS1 5UH
Tel. no 0845 293 2860
www.oceanaclubs.com
oceana-bristol@luminar.co.uk

The Oceana concept of seven themed rooms, including five bars and two unique clubs can be found in many cities across the UK. The Bristol superclub offers private booths and VIP areas plus Q-jump packs for for a hassle-free fun hen night.

Panache

All Saints Street, Bristol BS1 2LZ
Tel. no 0845 241 7185
www.panachebars.com
info@panachebars.com

Voted Bristol's No.1 club by bristolnightlife.com, Panache is host to a wide range of music playing the latest commercial tracks in the main room and R'n'b classics in the second room. Join the guestlist online for reduced price entry.

Rɘvolution
MASTERCLASS

GET BEHIND THE BAR AND BECOME A COCKTAIL MASTER IN THIS 90 MINUTE INTERACTIVE SESSION!

☆ **COCKTAILS**
☆ **TASTING**
☆ **TOOLS**
☆ **SKILLS**
☆ **GAMES**

HEN GOES FREE!
MINIMUM 8 PEOPLE

QUOTE PROMO CODE 'MARTINI' FOR FREE HEN OFFER
PACKAGES FROM ONLY £24.95 PER PERSON PLUS
NEW PARTY FOOD OPTIONS NOW AVAILABLE

TO BOOK...
ONLINE: REVOLUTION-BARS.CO.UK
PHONE: 0800 6300 860
ASK: A MEMBER OF STAFF

ANY OCCASION, ANY SIZE... REVOLUTION IS THE PERFECT PLACE TO EAT, DRINK & PARTY!

Revolution Vodka Bar, Old Fishmarket, St Nicholas St, Bristol

Pero's Bridge taking you across the harbour into Bristol's humming nightlife scene.

Platform 1

Platform 1, Clifton Down Station,
Whiteladies Road, Clifton,
Bristol BS8 2PH
Tel. no 0117 973 4388
www.platform1club.com
info@platform1club.com

The club's event planners can organize your hen party so you can put your feet up and count down the days until the biggest party Bristol has ever seen!

Prive

13–15 King Street, Bristol BS1 4EF
Tel. no 0117 929 3220
www.privebristol.com
info@privebristol.com

A chic and elegant nightclub, this is the perfect place for a hen do. With a beautifully decorated interior and five star service, Prive is the place to be. Reserve a table in the champagne bar for a classy evening.

Shake Rattle & Bowl at The Lanes

22 Nelson Street, Bristol BS1 2LD
Tel. no 0117 929 4861
www.shakerattleandbowl.com
letsdance@shakerattleandbowl.com

It's a club, a cinema, a bowling alley, a karaoke bar and a diner all wrapped into one exciting venue with a retro 50s theme. This is a monthly night so check the website for details. Bowling is available every night.

The Big Chill

15 Small Street, Bristol BS1 1DE
Tel. no 0117 930 4217
www.bigchill.net
sadie.f@bigchill.net

The ultimate laid back festival now has two bars to its name – Bristol and London. In the Bristol venue you can expect to find cool live music and resident DJs playing the best of the global music scene.

The Syndicate

15 Nelson Street, Bristol BS1 2JY
Tel. no 0117 945 0325
bristol.thesyndicate.com
bristol@thesyndicate.com

Bristol's biggest club features a variety of events on Saturdays from Foam Parties to Skool Discos. They also offer a variety of party packages with Q Jump entry and champagne that can be booked in advance. Check the website for details.

The Thekla

The Grove, Bristol BS1 4RB
Tel. no 0117 929 3301
www.theklabristol.co.uk
office@theklabristol.co.uk

A live music venue, a club and a bar all on board this boat moored at Mud Dock. Open seven nights a week the Thekla offers various nights featuring all music types from house to contemporary indie.

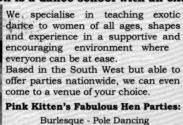

cardiff

*Millenium Stadium (top), Mermaid Quay (middle),
Cardiff Bay at night (bottom).*

Cardiff has been busy. While the English have been smugly thinking they've got the British thing all sewn up, she's emerged as Europe's newest city beauty, with a fresh look and some surprisingly chic accessories.

what to do

It's official...the Welsh capital rocks!
Whether you want coastal cool, urban
sprawl, rural rambles or small town charm,
they've got it all in this bite-size city.

The English often neglect Wales due to its inconvenient position on that rocky outcrop in the west. Location, location, location – somebody should have told them. Still, as it's there it seems churlish not to explore. And that's just what adventurous hens are doing. You're not far over the Severn Bridge before you hit the Welsh capital city, which just might have everything you need for a classic hen weekend.

Cardiff is full of surprises. OK, we know about the Millennium Stadium and rugby, but how about the Millennium Centre and the rather chic

Cardiff Bay? The club scene has earned nationwide recognition, but the shopping and live entertainment is growing up to be rather fabulous too.

Also, it's near some lovely beaches. But did you realise it practically backs on to the fabulous Brecon Beacons national park (breconbeacons.org)? You'll be hard pushed to find a city with so much to do on its doorstep, be it riding, surfing, quad biking or crazier things you won't find in many other UK spots, such as white-water rafting, gorge jumping and caving. It's worth the toll, honest.

Riding in the Brecon Beacons, near Llanthony Priory.

10 good reasons

1. friendly locals
2. good shopping
3. top gigs at The Point
4. club scene
5. it's near the sea
6. lots of outdoorsy stuff
7. up and coming eateries
8. it's practically abroad
9. The Live Lounge
10. Chapter Arts Centre

sounds of the city

Sittin' on the dock of the bay
Cardiff's dockers may be turning in their graves, but since the demise of the coal shipping trade, the kind of work that goes on around the old docklands is more along the lines of serving cappuccino to airy-fairy rich types like you and me. Hurrah! Cardiff Bay is now an impressive freshwater lake two miles from the city centre, and is fringed with an array of eateries, drinkeries, shopperies and ponceries.

Jump on the Baycar bendy-bus or the water bus from the city centre for an evening of culture at the Wales Millennium Centre (wmc.org.uk), where you can catch the likes of Jimmy Carr or Al Murray for comedy and shows such as Chicago and Strictly Come Dancing, as well as opera, ballet, contemporary dance and music, for the high browed. Just arriving at the WMC has a certain wowness, and the location is perfect for bayside chilling before the show.

Opportunities for adrenalin thrills in said bay include rowing, sailing, kayaking and power boating. A canoe slalom centre is also due to open in 2010. Visit adventurecardiff.com – this company can arrange a two-day multi-activity course for you, with water- and land-based thrills aplenty.

We're on a road to nowhere If you yearn to get off the beaten track, take your mates for a weekend's camping in the picture-postcard Taff Valley, where you can choose from activities including gorge walking, quad biking, clay pigeon shooting, archery and raft building. It's hen party gold, farm-style – great fun as long as you like getting very, very muddy. A little further off the track, try shaggysheepwales.co.uk for action-packed weekends in Pembrokeshire. If you're a horsey type then head to Downs Side Riding Centre in Penarth. What better way to take in the scenery than from the saddle?

I will survive What you need before a girl's night out is a salt scrub, a mineral soak and a good buffing – AKA coasteering. You'll climb around a cliff at sea level, leaping, swimming and clinging to dear life as the waves crash around you. Although you're safe in the hands of speciality organisers such as adventureswales.co.uk, it's still a challenge that feels like real survival. If that only whets your appetite, get the company to organise a full weekend of mayhem. They'll drop you into Cardiff for recovery drinks (and dancing if you've got the energy) in the evening.

Wales Millenium Centre dominates the skyline at the beautiful Cardiff Bay.

Calling all Chocoholics...

Chocs Away have the perfect solution to your hen party dilemma

Tel: 01495 790790 www.chocsawayparty.co.uk
Email: chocsawayparty@googlemail.com
Located just 25 mins drive from the M4!

A fun-filled activity that everyone will enjoy, guaranteed not to give you a headache!

At the end of the day take away a box of beautifully presented chocolates made by you.

Starters:
Enjoy a chocolate fountain with plenty of strawberries and marshmallows to satisfy your craving.

Main course:
Try out your creative skills with moulds (naughty or otherwise), pipe out delicious vanilla creams and whip up some creamy fudge.

Dessert:
Compete in the 'Chocs Away Party Game'.

Even complete beginners will create professional looking chocolates, which are all boxed up for you to take home.

Go on, indulge yourselves!

Here come the girls Alright, if you really want the marine hydro massage, not an Atlantic dunking, check out the 'Here come the girls' package at the swoon-inducing St David's Hotel and Spa. Accommodation, Welsh brekky and lunch in this hotel with views over Cardiff Bay would be good enough, but they throw in champagne, a juice bar, two treatments and use of the fabulous health suite. There's lovely!

Ooh la la la Shop, drink, eat, club. Exhausting, being 'It'. Still, if you think you're up to such Paris Hiltonesque action, how's about a nice amble around the famous arcades to shop for nick-nacks, accessories and…stuff. Lunch on Italian favourites at Zizzi, which is a little more glamorous than it's chain rivals but won't break the bank. Follow that with some proper

shopping in Queen Street, and then it's time for a little drinky in elegant 33 Windsor Place. Later, keep things at the artier end of partying with a trip to trendy Boudoir – all interior decor and beautiful people.

Murder on the dancefloor Cardiff's club scene is one good reason to go there. The city has some fantastic clubs and caters for all of you, from the giggly gaggle who don't get out much to the relentless fun bunnies who are out every weekend. Or, horror, a blend of both. Good news, Evolution has a room for cheesy pop and another for proper choons. Events at the club bring in world-class DJs such as Lisa Lashes.

If you don't want the big club vibe, then Clwb Ifor Bach might be the friendly crush of live music, decent DJs and fun-lovin' locals you're after.

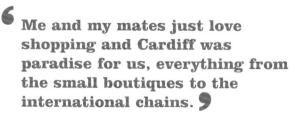

Cardiff's arcades are great for boutique shops.

'been there…'

I had a group of 13 mates, all based around the South West. It was too much for me, so I got Wales Activity Breaks to sort it out. We did mad stuff like gorge walking as well as drinking a lot at night. The Glee comedy night was the best. Cardiff's fun at night but you should definitely get out and do activities in the Brecon Beacons in the day. It's gorgeous.

❛ **Me and my mates just love shopping and Cardiff was paradise for us, everything from the small boutiques to the international chains.** ❜

where to stay

With a massive amount of regeneration around Cardiff Bay in recent years, the Welsh capital has been firmly put on the map and has the accommodation to suit.

hotels

Cardiff Bay Hotel £
Hemingway Road, Cardiff CF10 4AU
Tel. no 0845 094 5487
www.futureinns.co.uk/cardiff.htm
reservations.cardiff@futureinns.co.uk

Owned by the small West Country chain, Future Inns, this large hotel is just a few steps away from the vibrant nightlife of Cardiff Bay and is near the city centre. The ensuite bedrooms are comfortable and spacious with free internet access and local phone calls. There's also free parking which is a real bonus; all in all exceptional value for money.

shared room without breakfast

£ under £30
££ £30–£60
£££ over £60
pppn

Mercure Cardiff Lodge Hotel ££
Wharf Road, East Tyndall Street, Cardiff CF10 4BB
Tel. no 02920 894000
www.mercure.com
h6623@accor.com

This economy hotel is just minutes from the city centre and the waterfront. With contemporary styling throughout the 100 ensuite bedrooms, complete with power showers, this makes a good option.

NosDa @ The Riverbank £
53–59 Despenser Street, Riverside, Cardiff CF11 6AG
Tel. no 02920 378866
www.nosda.co.uk
info@nosda.co.uk

Uniquely situated on the banks of the River Taff and in the shadow of the Millennium Stadium, NosDa provides budget accommodation with ensuite private rooms and dormitory beds. Breakfast is included and there is a restaurant and late bar here.

Park Inn City Centre £–££
Mary Ann Street, Cardiff CF10 2JH
Tel. no 02920 341441
www.cardiff-city.parkinn.co.uk
info.cardiff-city@rezidorparkinn.com

Set right in the heart of the city, Park Inn has all the comforts you'd expect of an international chain. The funky RGB restaurant and bar serves modern food and great cocktails.

The St David's Hotel and Spa £££
Havannah Street, Cardiff CF10 5SD
Tel. no 02920 454045
www.thestdavidshotel.com
stdavids.reservations@principal-hayley.com

If you've got cash to splash, why not blow it here at the world famous luxury hotel and spa overlooking Cardiff Bay.

The River House Backpackers £
59 Fitzhamon, Embankment, Riverside, Cardiff CF11 6AN
Tel. no 02920 399810
www.riverhousebackpackers.com
info@riverhousebackpackers.com

Recently ranked as one of the top ten hostels in the world at the annual 'Hoscars' awards, this family-run hostel is just a few minutes walk from the central train and bus stations. The spotless rooms here are a mix of twins, female and mixed dorms. Breakfast included.

self-catering

A Space in the City ££
18 Harrowby Lane, Cardiff Bay
CF10 5GN
Tel. no 08452 60 70 50
www.aspaceinthecity.co.uk/
cardiff-leisure
info@aspaceinthecity.co.uk

With serviced apartments in 16 locations across Cardiff city centre and Cardiff Bay, there is a wealth of choice with this company. The apartments feature all the luxuries you would expect from a four or five star hotel with top quality interior decor, broadband and housekeeping. All the apartments have a fully equipped kitchen, living area and separate bedrooms. This luxurious accommodation option offers greater flexibility than a hotel and fantastic value for money.

Canal Barn Bunkhouse £
Ty Camlas, Brecon LD3 7HH
Tel. no 01874 625361
bunkhouse-brecon-beacons-
wales.co.uk/index.htm
enq-us@canal-barn.co.uk

If you want a party full of outdoor adventure in the beautiful Brecon Beacons National Park, then this could be the perfect base for you. With canoeing, caving, rock climbing, abseiling, hang gliding, gorge walking, rafting, quad biking and paintball on the doorstep and six cosy bedrooms with bunks, this is great value group accommodation.

Wild Spirit Tipis £
8 Beech Road, Pont-yr-Rhyl,
Bridgend CF32 8AJ
Tel. no 01656 871592
www.wildspiritbushcraft.co.uk
info@bushcraftcourses.co.uk

shared room without breakfast
£ under £30
££ £30–£60
£££ over £60
pppn

For an accommodation option with a difference, how about a few nights under canvas in a traditional Tipi? Lie back on reindeer skins, with a chilled glass of champagne in your hand in front of a roaring log fire and look up at the stars. Situated in a beautiful location, 10 minutes from one of the most beautiful coastlines in Wales, with the mystical Merthyr Mawr Castle looming behind.

For a unique alternative to regular camping – try a traditional Tipi.

How about this?
A permanent memory of your hen night with no strings attached!

Just bring your gang along to the studio and record two of your favourite tracks. Then relax with nibbles and drinks while we work up some studio magic...
By the time you head off into town, you'll have cut your own CD.
That's more than Something Kinda Ooh... it's Something Kinda Aah!

10% discount when you mention Hen Party Handbook

Want to know more?
Visit www.spacestudios.co.uk/henparties
email info@spacestudios.co.uk
or phone 029 2046 2513

Life Drawing for Hens!

Contact us on
07830 381930
or email:
nude@a-muse.me
www.a-muse.me

Expect some requests for hen participation...

A great pre night out on the town session, an event for later in the evening, or perhaps on the Sunday morning...

We can come to your venue anywhere in Wales or the South West, or arrange a central Cardiff venue for you.
The model initially adopts some classic poses as you work through some fun drawing techniques. Often hilarious, especially if a secret to most of the party and a good deal more raunchy than a standard life drawing session.

where to eat and drink

The Welsh know how to have a good time and you'll find yourself singing along in the bars and restaurants with the best of them...after a couple of cocktails.

bars

33 Windsor Place

33 Windsor Place, Cardiff CF10 3BZ
Tel. no 02920 383762
www.33windsorplace.co.uk
33windsorplace@sabrain.com

This slick city centre bar and restaurant is a stylish place to drink and dine. They also offer free use of the Windsor Room for private dining for groups of eight or more, where you can order from the full menu or create your own tailormade menus.

Revolution

9–11 Castle Street, Cardiff CF10 1BS
Tel. no 02920 236689
www.revolution-bars.co.uk/cardiff

The Cardiff bar has many faces, from the opulent and intimate to the modern utilitarian, with different moods for different times of the day, there's bound to be an area that suits you. With plenty of ideas for your party, Revolution will do all they can to give you a great send off. We recommend their cocktail masterclasses and the giant Nintendo Wii for a bit of friendly rivalry. Have a look at their facebook page 'Revolution Cardiff' for events listings.

The Funky Buddha Lounge

48 Charles Street, Cardiff CF10 2GP
Tel. no 02920 644311
www.thefunkybuddhalounge.com
info@thefunkybuddhalounge.com

Claiming to be the funkiest little bar in Cardiff, the Funky Buddha features live music, the hottest DJs, delicious world cuisine from Italy to the Far East via the US, decadent cocktails, premium European beers and a hand-picked wine list. Does a storming Sunday lunch too.

Millenium Quay is buzzing at night.

The Live Lounge

9 The Friary, Cardiff Bay,
Cardiff CF10 3FA
Tel. no 02920 397967
www.theliveloungecardiff.co.uk

A stylish and sophisticated live music bar offering great music, an expansive drinks menu and a buzzing atmosphere. The Live Lounge is the perfect venue, whether you're looking for a fabulous dining experience, to chat and watch live music or party on through until 4am, they have it all!

Tiger Tiger

The Friary, Greyfriars Road, Cardiff CF10 3QB
Tel. no 02920 391944
www.tigertiger-cardiff.co.uk
info@tigertiger-cardiff.co.uk

Located right in the centre of Cardiff, near the Millenium Centre and set over two floors. Tiger Tiger boasts a stylish restaurant, four bars and club. Tiger Tiger has a place for everyone to relax, from the stylish Round Room to the Moroccan influenced Medina, to the comfortable Restaurant. They also host Lucky Voice Karaoke in private rooms with 6000 songs at the touch of a button.

restaurants

Henry's Café Bar ££
Park Chambers, Park Place, Cardiff
CF10 3DN
Tel. no 02920 224672
www.henryscafebar.co.uk

This smart and spacious bar and restaurant
serves a wide range of exciting cocktails, a
good selection of wines and champagne.
Choose from a wide range of grills, burgers
and pasta from the reasonably priced menu.
There's always a lively atmosphere here at
the weekend when Henry's is open until 1am.

Old Orleans ££
18–19 Church Street, Cardiff CF10 1BG
Tel. no 02920 222078
www.oldorleans.com
oldorleans.cardiff@intertainuk.com

Cardiff's original cocktail bar is still the place
to go for great cocktails and shooters, along
with an extensive menu of Cajun and
American food from the Deep South, cooked
fresh on the grill. Parties of 12 plus can also
be catered for in the private function room.

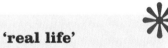

'real life'

**Cardiff is surprisingly good
for shopping. It has a really
great mix of modern malls,
like Capitol, and lovely
old-fashioned arcades with
independent shops.**

The Capitol shopping centre.

**2 courses
+ half a bottle
of wine
£ under £20
££ £20–£35
£££ over £35**

Champagne on ice – the essential hen night beverage.

Las Iguanas ££
8 Mill Lane, Cardiff CF10 1FL
Tel. no 02920 226 373
www.iguanas.co.uk/cardiff.asp
cardiff@iguanas.co.uk

The Latin American flavour of this well loved
chain spreads beyond the menu to buzzing
carnival atmosphere full of latino spirit. The
excellent cocktails here will get you in the
mood for partying and with happy hour until
7pm every day you may be tempted to have
more than one!

Zizzi ££
27 High St, Cardiff CF10 1PU
Tel. no 02920 645110
www.zizzi.co.uk
info@zizzi.co.uk

Situated just 5 minutes away from the
Millennium Stadium and Cardiff's shopping
malls and arcades, Zizzi Cardiff is a great
place to dine. The restaurant was once a
bank and has an impressive interior with high
ceilings, gentle lighting and plenty of space
to cater for large parties. Tuck in to some
excellent Italian food and wine in impressive
and welcoming surroundings.

where to party

Whether you want to party in the city centre or in The Bay, there are plenty of options in Cardiff. Clubs of all sizes and for all musical persuasions are ready and waiting.

Clwb Ifor Bach

11 Womanby Street, Cardiff CF10 1BR
Tel. no 02920 232199
www.clwb.net
info@clwb.net

AKA 'The Welsh Club', this is a great live music venue playing true Welsh Indie and Rock music. A down-to-earth club with soul, rather than fancy decor and lighting, it's set on three floors. On a Saturday night you'll find dirty pop on the ground floor, a funky soul, RnB, house party in the middle and the Vinyl Vendettas with their mix of indie, rock'n'roll and classic on top.

Exit Nightclub

48 Charles Street, Cardiff CF10 2GF
Tel. no 02920 640102
www.exitclubcardiff.com
info@exitclubcardiff.com

Cardiff's longest running gay club welcomes all with an open mind. Playing cheesy party favourites on two floors, you'll blend in well with your leg warmers and tutus.

Lava Lounge

The Old Brewery Quarter, St Mary's Street, Cardiff
Tel. no 02920 382313
www.lavaloungecardiff.co.uk
cardiff@lavaloungecardiff.co.uk

Popular for its retro nights and being the only Sunday nightspot in Cardiff, Lava Lounge is a fun and lively club. With plenty of party promotions on offer and two large plasma screens showing sport, this place is a magnet for hen and stag parties.

You only have one hen night – enjoy it!

 We loved partying in Cardiff, it was a real raucous night out. The Mill Lane and St Mary's Street end of the city has a great buzz going on.

Cardiff has some of the best clubs in Wales.

Liquid & Life

Imperial Gate, St Mary's Street,
Cardiff CF10 1FA
Tel. no 02920 645464
www.liquidclubs.com
cardiff@liquidnightclub.co.uk

Liquid is Cardiff's ultimate dance and event venue. Playing all the best in funky house, electro, R'n'B and dance and featuring some of the world's best DJs, with state of the art sound and lighting systems, amazing visuals and an excellent outdoor area, Liquid & Life presents an unrivalled clubbing experience.

Oceana

Greyfriars Road, Cardiff CF10 3DP
Tel. no 0845 296 8588
www.oceanaclubs.com/cardiff
oceana-cardiff@luminar.co.uk

At Oceana they're experts in hen and stag parties. Just contact the party planners through the website for a range of party offers. The resident DJs here play a good range of old skool party classics and anthems.

The Glee Club

Mermaid Quay, Cardiff Bay,
Cardiff CF10 5BZ
Tel. no 0871 472 0400
www.glee.co.uk
duncan@glee.co.uk

Offering the best stand-up comedy in Cardiff every weekend, The Glee on Mermaid Quay has hosted names such as Jimmy Carr, Jack Dee, Alan Carr and Lee Evans. There are also live music events here, check the website for a list of gigs; Cerys Matthews is billed for 2010. Food is served most nights and there's 10% off if you pre-order.

The Point

Mount Stuart Square, Cardiff CF10 5EE
Tel. no 02920 460873

This popular intimate live music venue has played host to some of the country's biggest acts: The Stereophonics and Funeral for a Friend to name but two. Housed in a beautiful converted church, The Point has great acoustics. Despite being a little rough around the edges this venue has an authenticity of its own.

RƎVOLUTION
MASTERCLASS

GET BEHIND THE BAR AND BECOME A COCKTAIL MASTER IN THIS 90 MINUTE INTERACTIVE SESSION!

- ✪ **COCKTAILS**
- ✪ **TASTING**
- ✪ **TOOLS**
- ✪ **SKILLS**
- ✪ **GAMES**

HEN GOES FREE!
MINIMUM 8 PEOPLE

QUOTE PROMO CODE 'MARTINI' FOR FREE HEN OFFER
PACKAGES FROM ONLY £24.95 PER PERSON PLUS
NEW PARTY FOOD OPTIONS NOW AVAILABLE

TO BOOK...
ONLINE: REVOLUTION-BARS.CO.UK
PHONE: 0800 6300 860
ASK: A MEMBER OF STAFF

ANY OCCASION, ANY SIZE... REVOLUTION IS THE PERFECT PLACE TO EAT, DRINK & PARTY!

Revolution Vodka Bar, 9-11 Castle Street, Cardiff, CF10 1BS

dublin

If Dublin doesn't manage to get you smiling, then nowhere will. The city's famed for hospitality, music and lots and lots of booze, so where better to spend your last few days of freedom? In the daytimes you'll love the history, arty stuff and new café culture, not to mention mad sports of all sorts in the emerald-green countryside.

Trinity College (top), Ha'penny Bridge (middle), Canal and docks (bottom).

what to do

Welcome to the city of song, ceilidh, literary genius and piss artistry – throw those up-tight English ways into the river Liffey and celebrate, Irish style, in Dublin.

It's a capital city, it's got different money and you have to travel there on a plane. Now that's exotic. While the climate may be, in local parlance, 'shite', we love Dublin so much that it's impossible to imagine a better place for a weekend away – and what better excuse than your hen do?

Set between coastal and rural scenery that'll take your breath away, Dublin's also got all the cosmopolitan charms and culture you could ask for from a city break. It's all here, from arty cafés, the Guinness brewery tour, superb shopping, seafood restaurants and spa, to the nation's favourite, horseracing – you never know, the luck of the Irish might rub off as well.

To cut to the chase, though, the real 'craic' is to be had after dark. The tradition of live music in pubs is thriving – even if you've no set plans, you'll have a great night going between the old pubs and dancing to ceilidh bands. Experience tells us that you'll meet some real randoms and it won't be pretty, but that's half the fun of it.

For those seeking a big night out rather than pub culture, there are masses of clubs to choose from thanks to Dublin's fun and lively young population and tourists aplenty. If you can't pick, just hand it all over to a hen party organiser so that when you step off the plane, someone else has taken care of all the details, from where you're staying to what music you're dancing to later on. The Irish hospitality isn't world famous for nothing – just relax and enjoy.

You can't go to Dublin without trying the black stuff.

10 good reasons

1. pub ceilidhs
2. beautiful countryside
3. bags of character
4. fun and friendly locals
5. the Guinness brewery tour
6. riding in the Liffey Valley
7. lunch on the MV Cill Airne
8. cockles and mussels
9. art and culture
10. docklands

sounds of the city

I gotta feeling If tonight's got to be a good, good night – but you've no clue as to how to make that happen – then tap into the rich vein of Dublin party knowhow that is Create Your Night. Whether you'd like entry at the chic, over-25s-only Sycamore Club, or mayhem at mega club Sin, CYN will package up your perfect night out. They organise entry, the odd free drink and a nice place to sleep it off. You won't even need to navigate, as you'll have a guide with you at all times to make sure you get there, get in and have a great time. Have a look at createyournight.com

The young ones As every good student knows, it would be a crime to let the cost of accommodation cut into your beer money. If yours is a summer hols hen do, just contact the university. Forget all those nightmare halls of residence you may have haunted in your youth – these are rather swish, clean and civilised. A mere 50 Euros gets you your own comfy room and a full Irish breakfast. There's even a fitness suite, sports hall complete with climbing wall and squash courts, spa and pool. The kids of today, eh? Don't know they're born. Contact linda.m.murphy@dcu.ie or visit summeraccommodation.dcu.ie.

Choose a theme and Create Your Night will do the rest.

Bus song If a bus load of you are hitting Dublin, first warn the locals, then visit partybus.ie. Their travelling venues offer varying levels of clubness, with tiered seating, on-board musicians or DJs, dancefloor, hostess service and even karaoke. The driver (brave or mad, you decide) will pick you up from your hotel and transport you, in unique style, to clubs or bars around the city. What easier way to organise your rowdy rabble of chickens?

Send in the clowns For those who are worried about doing the same old stuff everyone else does for their hen party, here's something a little weirder. Team Circus will show you how to juggle, ride a unicycle, walk on stilts, hula hoop or do 'hat tricks'. Imagine how impressed your other half will be when you start juggling the plates at the wedding reception! Visit discoverdublin.ie/circus.

Putting on the Ritz If you are a small group on a big budget, then find an excuse to blow your cash at Mount Juliet, just outside Dublin. Here, you can act like royalty, indulging in queenly pursuits such as horse riding in the gorgeous countryside, clay pigeon shooting, archery, golf, fishing, spa and fine dining. La dee daa! Tucked away down a winding driveway in the midst of a 1500-acre, walled estate, it doesn't get much better than this, ma'am. Visit mountjuliet.ie for more details.

Food, glorious food Eating is essential. You probably haven't really factored it into your top five priorities (club, bar, dress, shoes, hair), but how about learning some sharp kitchen skills, then starting your evening off with your own four-course feast? Loads of fun, and food, glorious food for all you budding Nigellas out there. Just visit cooksacademy.com.

Get off your high horse Ireland has long be known as the land of the horse and you could hear stories about Dublin's kids keeping feral ponies in their backyards, houses or even flats, not so long ago. The best riding's to be had out of town, however. Gorgeous Wicklow is home to Bel-Air, a beautiful country house hotel and equestrian centre. If you're all confident in the saddle, you can brush up your cross-country, show jumping or dressage skills, alternatively just go on a leisurely hack and enjoy the sights of the Emerald Isle. For more information go to belairhotelequestrian.com.

Fight for this love Don't let the lads have all the fun, ladies! Paintball at Combatzone is shamelessly touting its wares to stags and forgetting that there are plenty of feisty women out there who'd like nothing better than a few hours of paint-pellet wafare. 75 Euros gets you the full SWAT package, with semi-automatic guns, camouflage, goggles and three gruelling hours of pelting each other in scary woodland terrain. Fight for your rights at combatzonepaintballing.ie.

Tradition As we all know, cockles and mussels are something of a custom in Dublin. If you love seafood, head to Davy Byrne's, where you'll still find some of the city's best. This fashionable pub, once frequented by James Joyce, retains it's oldy worldy charm but is swankily modern, too. Also, it's just off the main shopping area, Grafton Street – what more can you ask?

'been there...'

Four of us booked cheap flights and a budget hostel and went to Dublin for two nights of the Irish craic. I was totally surprised how beautiful the city is, and we did cram in a bit of culture. But let's face it, it's all about pub crawls and jigging with God knows who to live ceilidh music all night...you just can't beat it for a hen weekend.

Learn traditional Irish dances in a music pub environment with Irish Dance Party.

where to stay

Arranging accommodation near the fun is essential and easy to do in Dublin. From basic to bling, you'll find good rooms a walk or cab ride from the clubs and pubs.

hotels & hostels

Ballsbridge Inn £
Pembroke Road, Ballsbridge, Dublin, Ireland
Tel. no +353 1 437 3444
www.d4hotels.ie/ballsbridge-inn.html
reservations@d4hotels.ie

With cheap rates available, and being just an easy bus ride to the airport, this large hotel is a well connected choice that has all you need for a weekend break. A leisurely 10 minute stroll will take you straight into the city centre where you can spend all the money you've saved on accommodation.

Harding Hotel ££
Copper Alley, Fishamble Street, Christchurch, Dublin 2, Ireland
Tel. no +353 1 679 6500
www.hardinghotel.ie
info@hardinghotel.ie

✳ shared room without breakfast
£ under £30
££ £30–£60
£££ over £60
pppn

Located in Temple Bar – one of Dublin's hot spots – the Harding Hotel is brilliant for a short break. You'll be right in the heart of the city with no need to worry about booking cabs or getting on buses – just do it all on foot. Beware, there's a karaoke in the pub downstairs on a Friday night – not everyone's cup of tea, but could be a good start to the weekend.

Kilronan House ££
70 Adelaide Road, Dublin 2, Ireland
Tel. no +353 1 475 5266
www.kilronanhouse.com

A safe 15 minutes walk from the joys of Grafton Street and a stones throw from St Stephen's Green, you'll find this charming guesthouse. Situated in the Georgian Quarter of the city, Kilronan House oozes atmosphere and quality. A smallish group of hens would be welcomed here, as long as you're all house-trained, and you'll love the old fashioned hospitality, fab Irish breakfasts and top location.

O'Callaghan Stephen's Green Hotel ££
Stephen's Green, Dublin 2, Ireland
Tel. no +353 1 607 3600
www.ocallaghanhotels.com
info@ocallaghanhotels.com

A calm atmosphere awaits you at this boutiquey establishment on the quiet south-west corner of Stephen's Green, which is slap bang where you want to be on your Dublin mini-break. Comfy beds, a reasonable breakfast (if you can haul yourself up in time) and a close proximity to theatres, pubs, shops and historic sights...what more could you want?

Radisson Blu Royal £££
Golden Lane, Dublin 8, Ireland
Tel. no +353 1 898 2900
www.radissonblu.ie/royalhotel-dublin
info.royal.dublin@radissonblu.com

Just a short stagger from Temple Bar and Grafton Street is the Radisson Blu Royal...the kind of place where you know what you're going to get and how it's going to be packaged. It's clean, modern and very comfortable, with friendly staff and a rather splendid breakfast. If you've got the cash to splash this is the hotel for you.

self-catering

Amberley House £
34 Lower Gardiner Street,
Dublin 1, Ireand
Tel. no +353 1 874 6979
www.amberleyhousedublin.com
info@amberleyhousedublin.com

Near the shops, Henry Street and the main
train and bus stations is the brilliantly priced
Amberley House. These apartments are
clean and basic with stripped floors and
decent furnishings and enough kit to ensure
you can prepare basic meals, but you're not
going to need that are you? B&B rooms are
available, too.

Augustine Apartments ££
42–76 Saint Augustine Street,
Dublin 8, Ireland
Tel. no +353 1 677 6600
www.augustineapartments.com
augustine@staydublin.com

These apartments are brilliantly located for
getting around Dublin on foot. With 21
spacious one-bed apartments, each
sleeping two or three people, this is an
impressive self-catering option. Services
include LCD TV, free Internet access,
well-equipped kitchen, stylish furnishings,
and a 24-hour reception.

Herbertons Apartments ££
St. Anthony's Road, Dublin 8,
Ireland
Tel. no +353 1 416 9587
www.herbertonapartments.com
info@herbertonapartments.com

Herbertons is a fantastic choice for location,
but the real draw here has to be the
swanky leisure facilities. You can use the
sauna, hydrotherapy pool, normal pool,
steam room and jacuzzi. There are also
fitness classes and gym facilities if you
want them! The apartments, with wooden
floors and a modern feel, sleep from one
to six people and have good cooking
facilities. There's also car parking; handy if
you're hiring a car to get out into the
countryside.

Imagine Ireland Holiday Cottages
£–£££
c/o Embsay Mills, Embsay, Skipton
BD23 6QF
Tel. no 01756 707 773
www.imagineireland.com

For a range of holiday cottages, from city
centre abodes to charming coastal
hideaways, this agency is an easy-to-use
option.

Latchfords Self-catering Apartments ££
99–100 Lower Baggot Street,
Dublin 2, Ireland
Tel. no +353 1 676 0784
www.latchfords.ie
info@latchfords.ie

Inside a lovely Georgian house, in a quiet yet
accessible corner of Dublin, these
apartments have independent access to
allow you to come and go freely, ensuite
facilities, kitchenettes, tv, wireless broadband
and basics like an iron
and phone that will
make you feel at
home. These
quality flats and
studios have
recently been
refurbished.

shared room without breakfast

£ under £30
££ £30–£60
£££ over £60
pppn

Dublin has a good choice of modern apartments.

where to eat and drink

Famous throughout the world, Dublin pubs are worthy of the reputation. So, whilst in Dublin on your hen party it's vital to plot a visit to one or two while you're there.

bars & pubs

4 Dame Lane

4 Dame Lane, Dublin 2, Ireland
Tel. no +353 1 679 0291
www.4damelane.ie
hello@4damelane.ie

A cool and trendy bar over several floors with a The Beat Suite club on the top floor. This is one of *the* places to be seen and fills up quickly. So get there early, if you want to get a stamp allowing you club entry, as numbers are limited. Several DJs play over the course of the night and it's a grat venue if your hens want to chat and drink as well as have a bop.

Buskers

Fleet Street, Temple Bar, Dublin 2, Ireland
Tel. no +353 1 612 9246
www.buskersbar.com
buskers@tbh.ie

Buskers, one of Dublin's top end bars offers a tantalising food menu served from noon until 9pm. Celebrate in style and choose cocktails from the extensive cocktail list. From a Mai Tai to Singapore Sling you are in for a treat. Or why not have a go at concocting your own!

Café en Seine

39 Dawson St, Dublin 2, Ireland
Tel. no +353 1 677 4567/677 4549
www.cafeenseine.ie
info@cafeenseine.ie

Set over three floors Café en Seine is a stylish venue and does not fail to please. The stunning Art Nouveau decor is complemented by an amazing three storey atrium. Providing great entertainment, the bar is open until 2.30am Wednesday to Saturday, so plenty of time to get the drinks in!

Davy Byrne's

21 Duke Street, Dublin 2, Ireland
Tel. no +353 1 677 5217
www.davybyrnes.com

Situated just off Grafton Street, Davy Byrne's was immortalised by the writer James Joyce. Nowadays it's famous for its fabulous food, and in particular seafood: fresh salmon, smoked salmon and crab. The ultimate Dublin seafood supper served here is oysters and Guiness. Try it for the real taste of the Emerald Isle.

Samsara

35 Dawson Street, Dublin 2, Ireland
Tel. no +353 1 677 4444
www.lastampahotel.ie/samsara-facilities

Located in the heart of Dublin's city centre attached to the La Stampa boutique hotel, Samsara is winner of Best Late Night Bar 2010. Open until 2.30am with DJs spinning tunes on Friday and Saturday nights until late. The venue is ideal for group bookings and can accommodate parties of up to 150.

The Church

Junction of Mary Street & Jervis Street, Dublin 1, Ireland
Tel. no +353 1 828 0102
www.thechurch.ie
reservations@thechurch.ie

Being a hotspot with tourists, The Church, is unique in every sense. Located at the heart of Dublin's shopping district, once you step into the venue you'll understand why it is so popular. With its beautifully decorated interior, this is the prefect setting for a hen do and you can even reserve part of the main bar for private parties.

cafés & restaurants

FXB Grill@Ryan's ££
Parkgate Street, Dublin,
Ireland
Tel. no +353 1 677 6097
www.fxbrestaurants.com
ryans@fxbrestaurants.com

The steaks are to die for at
this Steak and Seafood
restaurant, the Aberdeen
Angus beef coming direct
from the owner's farm. Dining
is upstairs at Ryan's pub in a
cosy warm environment with a
great atmosphere.

Il Vicoletto ££
5 Crow Street, Temple Bar, Dublin,
Ireland
Tel. no +353 1 670 8633

This authentic little Italian rarely
disappoints. It's as close an
experience as you can get to real
Italian cooking outside of Italy.
Dishes range from the essential
pasta served with well known
favourite sauces to the less
predictable, but no less authentic,
fish and meat mains, all featuring
quality ingredients. The three-course
set menu offers plenty of choice and is
great value for money. The staff are
particularly helpful without being pushy or
annoying. A great choice for a small group of
discerning hens.

Olesya's Wine Bar ££–£££
18 Exchequer Street, Dublin 2, Ireland
Tel. no +353 1 672 4087
www.olesyaswinebar.com
info@olesyaswinebar.com

At Olesya's it's all about wine. With a cellar of
over 400 varieties from all over the world and
at least 100 of those available by the glass,
it's *the* place in Dublin to enjoy a glass or
two. The eclectic menu is carefully designed
to complement the extensive wine list and
there will definitely be something perfect for
you on there. Food is served all day long,
whether you want a civilised lunch stop or a
leisurely meal with your hens.

**2 courses
+ half a bottle
of wine**

**£ under £20
££ £20–£35
£££ over £35**

Solas Bar & Restaurant £
31 Wexford Street, Dublin 2, Ireland
Tel. no +353 1 478 0583
www.solasbars.com
info@solasbars.com

Awarded best cocktail bar
in Ireland and featured in
the New York Times review
section the excellent
ratings say it all. Enjoy a
refreshing cocktail made to
order with the best
ingredients. On their food
menu they offer two courses from
€12.50 seven days a week excluding
lunch hours between 1pm and 2pm which
makes Solas Bar perfect for eating out on
your hen night.

The Pig's Ear ££
4 Nassau Street, Dublin 2, Ireland
Tel. no +353 1 670 3865
www.thepigsear.ie
info@thepigsear.ie

Sample some good honest Irish fare with a
modern twist at this bright and airy,
contemporary restaurant. The quality of the
food here is top class and value for money is
exceptional. Dishes come served in quirky
pans and jars for a unique feel. All in all a
relaxed and fun eating experience. Try the
Potted Crab, Brawn Puree, Sea Trout or
Braised Beef Cheek and finish up with the
Cheesecake – delish.

where to party

Clubbing in Dublin is everything you expect from a capital city, but in a compact area.

Dandelion Cafe Bar

St Stephen's Green West, Dublin 2, Ireland
Tel. no +353 1 476 0870
www.welovedandelion.com
info@welovedandelion.com

At the heart of Dublin's city centre this bar, eatery and nightclub provides a full programme of entertainment and plays host to the hottest DJs and performers from across the globe. Recent appearances include Alexandra Burke and Beyonce! There's a special 'bachelorette' party package on offer including a three-course meal, nightclub entry with a reserved table in the VIP area and complimentary bottles of champagne, see website for prices.

NV Nightclub

27 Leeson Street, Dublin 2, Ireland
Tel.no +353 1 676 3380
www.nvnightclub.ie
info@nvnightclub.ie

NV is a chic, modern city centre nightclub situated on Dublin's historic Lower Leeson Street. It offers a relaxed atmosphere with top DJs playing the very latest chart, mainstream and old school classics. Aside from the sleek and luxurious main room, there is the Onyx Room and Dublin's best equipped 'Beer Garden'. The Onyx Room is a permanently covered outdoor venue with comfy seating and plasma screens. The Beer Garden features a full bar and outdoor cinema!

Sin

17–19 Sycamore Street, Temple Bar, Dublin 2, Ireland
Tel.no +353 1 633 4232
www.sinbar.ie
info@sinbar.ie

Totally tempting – Sin does what it says on the tin! Bounce on a Saturday is one of the most sexy and sintilating club nights in Dublin. Attracting a lively and friendly crowd each week, Bounce is the perfect way to spend your hen night.

Lights, music, dancing – it's how every good hen night should end!

The Sugar Club

8 Lower Leeson Street, Dublin 2, Ireland
Tel.no +353 1 678 7188
www.thesugarclub.com
info@thesugarclub.com

Soak up the atmosphere at The Sugar Club Arts Centre with its beautifully decorated interior and state-of-the-art sound and lighting. This former cinema plays host to bands, comedians, club nights as well as film screenings. Check the website for the latest information on upcoming events. The cocktail bar is ideal if you want to book a private venue for a party of up to 80 hens.

The Twisted Pepper

54 Middle Abbey Street, Dublin 2, Ireland
Tel. no +353 1 873 4038
www.bodytonicmusic.com/
thetwistedpepper/

The Twisted Pepper is a cafe, music, art and all round entertainment space. Split into six different areas, the venue plays host to live gigs, club nights, AV shows, multimedia events, exhibitions and more. You can book The Box – a cosy basement space – for a private party of 30–40 hens and bring in your own entertainment from DJs to Butlers.

Great city– Dublin does not disappoint.

The Village Venue

26 Wexford Street, Dublin 2, Ireland
Tel. no +353 1 475 8555
www.thevillagevenue.com
neil@thevillagevenue.com

Open seven nights a week this club offers a friendly and welcoming atmosphere and whatever your musical taste The Village caters to all! Friday night is party night and reputed to be 'the most fun Friday in Dublin' with regular appearances by dancers, singers, MCs and top DJs. On a Saturday the emphasis is on dancefloor tunes brought to you by Mix Master Fionn. Check the website for playlists and special events.

Twentyone (XXI) Club & Lounge

21 D'Olier Street, Dublin 2, Ireland
Tel. no +353 1 671 2089
www.twentyone.ie
info@twentyone.ie

Tastefully decorated XXI offers a unique setting for a hen party. Special features include seven plasma screens, eight bed booths, VIP area for private parties and functions, and an amazing new dancefloor with dance podiums. This is Ireland's only club with fully live DVD video mixing VJ's. Book up in advance and receive free entry for the whole party, get an area reserved for the night, a complimentary bottle of champagne on arrival and a free Hummer ride to the club (subject to availability). Sounds a pretty good deal to us.

edinburgh

Ross Fountain (top), Fringe Festival (middle), Princes Street (bottom).

Famed for hogmanay and its Fringe Festival, Edinburgh is a city that knows how to put on a party. For hens, it's a brilliant short break choice – culture, clubs and capital city vibes all rolled into one beautiful package.

what to do

She's a stunning city with a 1000-year-old heritage, sparkling cultural life and feisty character – so Scotland's capital is high on our list of top cities for your hen party.

Preparing for your trip to Edinburgh should probably involve a steadily rising drinking curve and an increase in stodge, because it would be criminal to wimp out on ceilidh dancing and whisky tots, not to mention the rib sticking puddings and hearty savouries that stay the effects of the occasional cool breeze around these parts.

It's also essential to gen up on events – check who's playing, where you can find a ceilidh and the opening hours of the Castle, Costume Haha fancy dress shop and other cultural essentials.

If you're going to hit town in August be prepared to get swept into the torrent of festival goers rushing through the city streets 24:7. It's fun but it's full on, and most pubs and hotels seriously inflate their prices. You'll need to book rooms well in advance if you want to do the Festival for your hen.

But Edinburgh is far from sleepy the rest of the year. Superb hen activities, nightclubs, shopping, bars, eateries and more await you.

10 good reasons

1. views over the city
2. mini highland games
3. capital city vibes
4. locally-sourced food
5. whisky tasting
6. the architecture
7. dancing at a pub ceilidh
8. watching the fireworks
9. shopping
10. Coco's chocolatier

Edinburgh Castle by night.

sounds of the city

All time love For views that make you catch your breath, head for Edinburgh Castle. Don't worry about naff displays and dusty pamphlets here, it's a genuinely interesting trip for about a tenner, and will give you that smug feeling that you've done something civilised. The rest of your historic tour will involve walking on the Royal Mile, which runs from the Castle in the west to the 15th-century Palace of Holyroodhouse in the east. En route you'll find various blue-plaque houses, churches and curiosities, so give yourselves time for a good old poke around. This is real, old Edinburgh. The controversial new parliament building will bring you back to the present with a slap, and then it will be time for a skinny latte and a double choc muffin or a slice of Dundee Cake, no doubt. Replenished and ready for a climb, head up to Arthur's Seat, the volcanic rock formation that towers over this end of the city. It's not for those with vertigo.

Feel so high There is another way to enjoy the stunning views of Edinburgh without ruining your Jimmy Choos and that's the Harvey Nicks Forth Floor Brasserie, from which you can take in gorgeous views of the Firth of Forth and the urban skyscape while you sip and nibble your way through suitably expensive refreshments.

Dream a little dream of me
Boobytrap Boutique is just one of many wallet-lightening retail gems in the classy West End area just off Princes Street. But it's not only shopping for curve-enhancing lingerie that's on offer here. Boobytrap does a fabulous champagne tea combined with burlesque dancing lessons from Edinburgh's own very fabulous Miss Lily White. Burlesque dance is all about embracing your feminine power and sexiness as a woman. Expressing these inner instincts with flirtatious moves using a feather boa, killer heels and satin gloves may almost be enough to take your mind off the spread of cakery laid out on linen cloths – just. That's correct ladies: champagne, sex and cake in a shop...and not a whingeing, innuendo-punting bloke in sight. It's the stuff that dreams are made of.

Harvey Nichols store, check out the 'Forth' floor.

'been there...'

Five of us got invited to stay in a mate's flat for the Fringe Festival, so I thought, perfect for the hen do. It was mental in Edinburgh – crowded, expensive and full-on! The shows we saw were mainly really good and I loved the city, but I wish I'd saved the hen do for another time – it felt a bit like having your birthday at Christmas! Climb up Arthur's Seat for the view!

Putting on the ritz More glamour's to be had with 'Vegas', a night that lounges in a few choice Edinburgh venues, including Ego and The Voodoo Rooms, and asks you to dress up in 40s rat pack and Hollywood style for big band sounds, showgirls, funk and burlesque. It attracts a great, diverse crowd of clubbers and is a perfect excuse to really big up the vintage satin, costume jewellery and bouncy curls for a night of all-out flirting. Why not brush up your moves beforehand with a burlesque dance class with Madame Peaches, find them at madamepeaches.com.

Scotland the brave It's time to stop fannying around and get your hands dirty. With caber tossing, farmer racing, haggis rolling and tug-o-war on the menu, the mini highland games, as organised by gobananas.co.uk, are a true test of your ladies' Celt spirit. Make sure you have Irn Bru with your porridge that morning – you could well meet another hen or stag party on the field, so competition is likely to get fierce. If that's not enough action, you can team it with quad biking, archery or high ropes and make a day of it. All overseen by men in kilts, which is why you want to visit Scotland, isn't it?

Food. glorious food Edinburgh's rather splendid boutique hotels and fine restaurants have made the city a snuggly romantic breaks favourite. But if you need somewhere that's good fun for a group to eat, drink and be merry, try the ornate Voodoo Rooms on West Register Street. There's a crowd-pleasing menu we can only describe as American-Italian-Scottish with an Asian zing. The cocktails are lush.

Meanwhile, when only Italian carbs will do after some arduous Princes Street shopping, it's got to be nearby Bar Roma. They take group bookings and serve up an extensive, fresh Italian menu as well as good pizzas, risottos and pasta dishes.

I'd like to teach the world to sing Why not have a Pop Party at Groove Tunnel recording studio. Lay down professionally mixed tracks, and get your very own CD complete with a photo of your group on the front. Accessories are all provided and you can even have dance lessons with a professional choreographer, if you want the full X Factor experience. A package complete with bubbly and snacks, a copy of the CD and photograph each starts from £20 per pop star.

Have a Pop Party: the ultimate in karaoke, plus you get your own CD to take home with you.

where to stay

Thanks to the needs of The Fringe Festival, Edinburgh has more than a few places to rest your weary bones: from uni halls and apartments to five-star boutique hotels.

hotels

Cowgate Tourist Hotel £
96–112 Cowgate,
Edinburgh EH1 1JN
Tel. no 0131 226 2153
www.cowgatehostel.com
info@cowgatehostel.com

❋ shared room without breakfast
£ under £30
££ £30–£60
£££ over £60
pppn

This hostel is clean and brightly painted, giving it a friendly, informal feeling that's perfect for a relaxed and slightly hedonistic few days in Edinburgh. Apartments have twin, four- or six-bedded rooms with a communal kitchen and TV area. Around you is the lovely Old Town, and the castle is just 2 minutes walk away.

Malmaison £££
1 Tower Place, Leith, Edinburgh EH6 7BZ
Tel. no 0131 468 5000
www.malmaison-edinburgh.com
edinburgh@malmaison.com

The original Malmaison is an impressive boutique hotel on the banks of the Forth in Leith. Complete with a turreted clock tower, it makes you feel like royalty when you check in. The suites are pretty fabulous: every one of the 100 rooms is individually styled. The Mal Bar has a reputation for serving up some of the best wine, cocktails and coffee in the city. There's also a great brasserie and private dining rooms.

Hotel Ceilidh-Donia ££
14–16 Marchhall Crescent,
Edinburgh EH16 5HL
Tel. no 0131 667 2743
www.hotelceilidh-donia.co.uk
reservations@hotelceilidh-donia.co.uk

This three-star Victorian hotel a mile from the centre has 17 comfortable, homely rooms with ensuite facilities. The bar and restaurant are smart and welcoming, and there is a lovely landscaped garden for sunny weather. A cosy, welcoming place and a popular choice.

Mercure Edinburgh Point Hotel ££
34 Bread Street, Edinburgh EH3 9AF
Tel. no 0131 221 5555
www.mercure.com
H6989@accor.com

This big, stylish hotel almost spans the gap between the great-value giant chain and the boutique, and has a fabulous view of the castle. Rooms are large and nicely styled with lovely ensuite bathrooms. The bar and restaurant are also suitably swish – all round, you get the feeling that you've got a bit of a bargain. The location is good too – you're in walking distance of all the major sights and attractions.

Travelodge £
33 St Mary's Street, Edinburgh EH1 1TA
Tel. no 0131 221 5555
Tel. no 0871 984 6137
www.travelodge.co.uk

It may be a big chain, but Travelodge Central is near everything and great value for money. There are several sister lodges available in Edinburgh if this one's booked up. Rooms are clean, smart and spacious, with plenty of facilities. Parking is available at a reasonable rate.

self-catering

Albany Street Apartments £
35b & 37b Albany Street, Edinburgh
EH1 3QN
Tel. no 0131 558 9007/07780 923 711
www.albanystreetedinburgh.com
clare@topparkapartments.com

There are plenty of stunning self-catering apartments in Edinburgh, and these are no exception. Beautifully spacious and light, with polished wood floors and crisp linen, the apartments are in a fabulous, safe location near Princes Street. They make a great place to relax after a big night out or a day's shopping – and the city centre shops, eateries and bars are all within easy reach.

shared room without breakfast

£ under £30
££ £30–£60
£££ over £60
pppn

Edinburgh Festival Apartments £–£££
127 Rose Street, South Lane,
Edinburgh EH2 4BB
Tel. no 0131 220 7950
www.festivalapartments.com
info@festivalapartments.com

Apartments of all shapes and sizes are offered in central areas including Holyrood, The Royal Mile, Old Town and New Town. Hen and stag parties are welcome, and groups can be catered for all year round. The apartments tend to have wow factor, but if you're on a budget enquire about a hostel. The rooms are spacious, you still get your own kitchen area and there's a staffed bar and restaurant.

Edlets ££
14 Albany Street, Edinburgh EH1 3QB
Tel. no 0131 510 0020
www.edlets.com

If you're worried about having too much choice when you've seen the long list of accommodation on the Edlets website, don't fret. You need only fill in the online enquiry form or make a call and you'll soon have one of the team seeking out your ideal accommodation. The flats are of a high standard and towels and linen are provided. Most have home comforts such as DVD player, Wi-Fi, flatscreen TV and dishwasher.

No. 19 the apartment ££
19 Queen Street EH2 1JX
Tel. no 07762 229379/01334 828 697
www.no19theapartment.co.uk
belinda@no19theapartmentedinburgh.co.uk

Enquire about the flat or No. 32 the town house, both of which have the interior design and location that will secure wow factor for your hen party. Gorgeous, feminine and funky, the venues have the perfect atmosphere and creature comforts to allow a group of ten or more to chill out and enjoy each other's company. And the city centre's attractions are right outside your front door.

Queen Margaret University ££
Edinburgh EH21 6UU
Tel. no 0131 474 0000
www.qmu.ac.uk
capitalcampus@qmu.ac.uk

In Uni holidays you can book into halls of residence to enjoy the cushy ensuite rooms with shared living rooms and kitchens. You'll stay in the lush green surrounds of Musselburgh, a short train trip or 30 minute bus ride from central Edinburgh. If it's too much to contemplate getting up and making eggs and bacon after a night on the town, you can arrange to have breakfast included.

Festival Apartments offers some stylish choices.

where to eat and drink

From the glamourous, glittering Tigerlily's to the down-to-earth Monster Mash, Edinburgh caters for all your needs. But we love Rick's for the Scottish menu.

bars

Belushi's
9–13 Market Street, Edinburgh EH1 1DE
Tel. no 0131 226 1446
www.belushis.com
mark.glover@belushis.com

If you're looking for a big night of drinks, dancing and laughs, Belushi's is a great city-centre choice. This chain has bars in most of the UK's major party towns and knows how to make you feel welcome, whether you want to eat huge burgers and have a few casual drinks or hire the private room for your party.

Cargo
129 Fountainbridge, Edinburgh EH3 9QG
Tel. no 0131 659 7880
www.festival-inns.co.uk/bars
cargo@festival-inns.co.uk

A cavernous waterside bar with funky lighting, a vibrant ambience and matching multi-coloured cocktails.

Dragonfly
52 West Port, Edinburgh EH1 2LD
Tel. no 0131 228 4543
www.dragonflycocktailbar.com
info@dragonflycocktailbar.com

You can get a cocktail masterclass or just drink colourful concoctions in this popular and very stylish venue. Food is snacky, not substantial. Larger groups of hens may want a private room – ask about the Parlour Bar, where you can party in private and have canapés and drinks brought to you. Music goes on until 1am on the weekend.

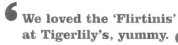
We loved the 'Flirtinis' at Tigerlily's, yummy.

The cosy atmosphere at The Living Room.

The Living Room
113–115 George Street,
Edinburgh EH2 4JN
Tel. no 0131 226 0880
www.thelivingroom.co.uk

A classy bar any time of day, The Living Room's chocolate leather sofas and classic decor just beg you to relax for a few hours over a well chilled glass of wine or two. On weekdays you're likely to catch a talented pianist tinkling on the ivories, whilst on weekends the atmosphere gets more lively with DJs playing funky house. The odd touring live act also make an appearance. The menu is a good quality British and European crowd pleaser. The perfect place to spend a few hours.

Tigerlily's
125 George Street, Edinburgh EH2 4JN
Tel. no 0131 225 5005
www.tigerlilyedinburgh.co.uk

You could spend a lot of time in this chic boutique hotel bar. Glittering disco balls, cute little booths, fabulous original and classic cocktails and a champagne bar all make you feel like the kittens bits, and there's a restaurant and Lulu's nightclub attached too.

restaurants

Khublai Khans ££
43 Assembly Street, Leith, Edinburgh
EH6 7BQ
Tel. no 0131 555 0005
www.khublaikhans.co.uk
edinburgh@khublaikhans.co.uk

You'll still be talking about Khublai Khan's
long after the wedding! They offer an evening
of exotic food and delicious cocktails in a
friendly, fun atmosphere. The Hen even gets
to dress up in traditional Mongolian garb and
sit on her very own throne for the evening!

La Favorita ££
325–331 Leith Walk
Edinburgh EH6 8SA
Tel. no 0131 554 2430
www.la-favorita.com

Not only is this Edinburgh's best pizza, it's
also good value and does delivery.

L'Amore ££
97/101 Fountainbridge, Edinburgh
EH3 9QG
Tel. no 0131 228 5069
www.lamoreditalia.co.uk

For food and laughs before you
head off to one of the nearby
clubs, this unpretentious
Italian also offers karaoke.

**2 courses
+ half a bottle
of wine**

**£ under £20
££ £20–£35
£££ over £35**

Go Mongolian at Khublai Khans.

Monster Mash Café £
4a Forrest Road, Edinburgh EH1 2QN
Tel. no 0131 260 9806
www.monstermashcafe.co.uk

The city's top spot for retro British favourites
such as bangers and mash.

Rick's Boutique Hotel £££
55a Frederick Street, Edinburgh EH2 1HL
www.ricksedinburgh.co.uk

This gem of a boutique hotel is just a step
away from the main shopping areas and the
perfect place to show off some of your
designer purchases. The Scottish food is
fresh and beautifully executed at this very
stylish and chic restaurant.

Stac Polly ££
38 St Marys Street, Edinburgh EH1 1SX
Tel. no 0131 557 5754
www.stacpolly.com
bookings@stacpolly.com

For fabulous modern Scottish food, try one of
three Stac Polly restaurants in Edinburgh. Fine
seasonal food, reasonably priced is served in
relaxed, unpretentious surroundings.
Private dining rooms are available.

Tex Mex II ££
64 Thistle Street, Edinburgh
Tel. no 0131 260 9699
www.texmex2.com
fatdonny@texmex2.com

The interior is as fresh and
colourful as the Tex Mex food and
the cocktails look pretty good too. A
restaurant with very high quality food served
in a laid back atmosphere.

The Cambridge Bar £
20 Young Street, Edinburgh EH2 4JB
Tel. no 0131 226 2120
www.thecambridgebar.co.uk
info@thecambridgebar.co.uk

With a huge burger menu, including veggie
options, low carb options and quite a few full
monty diet busters, this is a great place for
an informal lunch. Located close to all the
New Town and West End attractions.

where to party

Whether you want live entertainment, clubbing or comedy, you'll find plenty to whet your appetite in Edinburgh. Have yourselves a good old highland fling!

Cabaret Voltaire

36 Blair Street, Edinburgh EH1 1QR
Tel. no 0131 220 6176
www.thecabaretvoltaire.com
speakeasy@thecabaretvoltaire.com

This venue under the streets of Cowgate has an amazing events diary, from indie night, Sicknote, every Thursday to dance at Killer Kitsch on Sundays – both of which are free. On Saturdays you'll find the likes of house and techno night Ultragroove or the eclectic Dare! and some big name DJs. Additionally, this twin-roomed club hosts up to 30 live gigs per month.

City

1a Market Street, Edinburgh EH1 1DE
Tel. no 0131 226 9560
www.cityedinburgh.co.uk
edinburgh@citypeople.info

Offering free entry to hens and stags and various promotion nights including text for queue jump and the fabulous Broke! With cheap entry and drinks on Fridays, City has a lot going for it. The venue is very stylish, with swanky booths and seating areas as well as great lighting and a top sound system.

Club Ego

14 Picardy Place, Edinburgh EH1 3JT
Tel. no 0131 478 7434
www.clubego.co.uk

Nights at Ego include the decadent Burlesque 'Vegas' night, acts such as Mr Scruff, Judge Jules and Gil Scott Heron, popular gay night 'Vibe' and more. The venue started out as a dance hall and the main dancefloor still has the look of a huge, sparkly, ornate ballroom. So put your dancing shoes on and get the sequins out for a night at Club Ego.

Mata Hari club (top) and Kasbar (above), Espionage.

Espionage

4 India Buildings, Victoria Street, Edinburgh EH1 2EX
Tel. no 0131 477 7007
www.espionage007.co.uk
edinburgh@espionage007.co.uk

Make your way through the labyrinth of rooms at Espionage to discover five floors' worth of dancefloors, chill-out areas and bars including the Kasbar cocktail bar, the Pravda club on the mid level and the Mata Hari club in the basement. The events diary is full at this massively popular Edinburgh venue, so check out their website for more details.

There's more to the Edinburgh club scene than the Highland Fling.

Po Na Na

43b Frederick Street,
Edinburgh EH2 1EP
Tel. no 0131 226 2224
www.ponana.com
edinburghpnn@ponana.com

The Moroccan-themed Po Na Na remains a good-looking but relaxed little venue for a dance to good music, a vibrant atmosphere and rather nice chill-out areas where you can have a chat.

The Stand

4 India Buildings, Victoria Street,
Edinburgh EH1 2EX
Tel. no 0131 477 7007
www.thestand.co.uk
admin@thestand.co.uk

Scotland's homegrown stand-up comedy venue has acts on every night of the week – from total beginners to big names. On Sunday there's also a free lunchtime show to help you laugh your hangover into history. Food and drink are reasonably priced.

The Voodoo Rooms

19a West Register Street,
Edinburgh EH2 2AA
Tel. no 0131 556 7060
www.thevoodoorooms.com
info@thevoodoorooms.com

Fridays see a great line up, with comedy stand up until 9pm, then dancing to live music until 1am. Other nights see casino, bands and more, taking centre stage at this beautiful venue where you can enjoy a full menu, well stocked bar and the odd cocktail. Group bookings are welcome and may get a discount.

Why Not

14 George Street, Edinburgh EH2 2PF
Tel. no 0131 6248633

This little venue offers good value on drinks and entry, a mixed clientele, chart, dance and house music and the perfect location, under the famous Dome Bar in George Street, making it a popular place with hens who want to let their hair down.

glasgow

Away from the shortcake and tartan heritage, Glasgow is the real Scotland. Don't expect anything less than real partying, real humour and a really good time in Scotland's most vibrant and most up-and-coming city.

Mitchell Library (top), Kelvingrove Art Gallery (middle), Doulton Fountain (bottom).

what to do

Fast-paced, hard as nails, dry-humoured and partying like it's Armageddon, Glasgow is a city with personality, history, culture, the arts...and the most fabulous shopping.

If Edinburgh is Scotland's jewel, Glasgow's the rest of the outfit. The city has such a vibrant atmosphere and so much going on that a weekend can feel way too short. But with a little planning, Glasgow's a great short break city.

Although it has a long, rollercoaster of a history, much of that isn't really tourist fodder. Indeed, the city has done a great job over the past 20 years to smooth over its cracks and become a cultural hub rather than a troubled industrial town. So when you hit Glasgow, you won't so much be viewing historic buildings (although the architecture is lovely) as soaking up the here and now – the shops and galleries in the day and the clubs, live music venues, comedy and pubs at night.

And don't expect the cheesy tourist welcome in Glasgow. If you're out partying, you'll be included, but the red carpet won't get rolled out. The locals are famously intolerant of bullshit. So if you want to party hard, just do it.

Glasgow may not be the most obvious choice, but it's one of the best.

There's always a great party atmosphere in Glasgow.

10 good reasons

1. shopping
2. exploring Lomond's isles
3. the club scene
4. fun, feisty locals
5. picnics in the parks
6. handsome city centre
7. buzzing at night
8. good value bars
9. moseying in the West End
10. shopping

sounds of the city

Money can't buy it The shopping is amazing, but if you've not got the heart to dangle your cash in front of Calvin Klein, Jo Malone and the gang before remembering about the rent and making a hasty exit, then swerve Buchanon Street and head for the West End via the 'clockwork orange' subway. Here you'll find retail loveliness that amounts to something like Camden market meets Carnaby Street. With lots of boho charm and cobbledy streets, you'll be happy browsing.

Gay bar Scrub that, we mean day spa (day spa, day spa) Spa in the City on Vincent Street does a Luxury Beauty Experience with an aromatherapy facial, makeover, manicure and Toni & Guy blow dry, all washed down with a couple of glasses of bubbly. Perhaps the perfect end to a few hours' retail therapy in Buchanon Street and Princes Square, darling.

Cool scene If you do want to go to a gay bar, you're in the right town. The club and bar scene in Glasgow is kicking, Bennet's and Cafe Delmonica hailed as the best fun gay venues.

Groups with partying hard at the top of their night's agenda should head for The Tunnel – two big rooms and about 1000 people dancing in them every Friday and Saturday night. This club's about having fun, but the quality's there too with top resident and guest DJs.

Sub Club on Jamaica Street is hailed as one of the best clubs in the world. As it's full of cool meedja type people, you need to blend in or you won't get in, so leave the whistles and tiaras at home for Sub Club. This is the place to go if you're a small band of regular clubbers who are looking for Glasgow's best club scene.

Showdown Poledancing parties are hilarious – especially if you feign injury and watch from the bench! Complete failure to look remotely sexy is part of the fun: you won't and that's OK. At Heavenly Pole at the Play bar in Renfield Street you'll be shown how it's done then taught a lap dance and a few pole tricks. That should make Monday mornings on the Routemaster much more fun. A male stripper can be booked, if you want to give the bride-to-be a few blushes.

Get yourself scrubbed up, chilled out and feeling gorgeous at Spa in the City in Vincent Street.

Underneath the arches A venue you shouldn't miss, The Arches is a massive multi-arts venue that's best known as a clubber's paradise, with regular nights from Mr Scruff, Hed Kandi, Octopussy and more, and massive parties. The Arches showcases new and groundbreaking theatre and art and the venue is also becoming renowned for putting on some fantastic gigs. Check the listings at thearches.co.uk because this place could provide your hen party highlight. It's an awesome night out.

Where's your head at? This and many other questions such as 'why do I always do this to myself?' may well be popping into your befuddled minds on Sunday morning. But Glasgow isn't known as the Dear Green Place for nothing. It's got no less than 70 parks in which to rest and recover. If the sun's shining, there's nothing better than lounging in the gorgeous botanical gardens on Great Western Road with a bag of deli goodies. If it's peeing down, head for the Willow Tea Rooms on Sauchiehall Street designed by Charles Rennie Mackintosh for fabulous brekky and culture in one tasty hit.

Gold One way to explore a city is to contact huntfun.co.uk and get them to send you on a treasure hunt. The hen party package can be personalised and the hunt will take you a couple of hours unless people get lost, get a raging need to stop for a glass of wine or get distracted by the joys of shopping…. Let's call it four hours then.

'been there…'

I have to admit that I couldn't understand the accent until the very last day, but the Glaswegians seemed like really nice people anyway! The city centre's totally beautiful and people are right about the shops. We didn't budget for that though, so most of us stuck to eating and drinking a lot! We went dancing at The Arches and did mini highland games for daytime laughs – real quality.

A Huntfun treasure hunt is a great way to see the city and have a great laugh at the same time.

where to stay

If you must sleep when you're in Glasgow, it's easy to find central, stylish digs to match any budget in this up-and-coming destination for tourists.

hotels

Alamo Guest House ££
46 Gray Street, Kelvingrove Park,
Glasgow G3 7SE
Tel. no 0141 339 2395
www.alamoguesthouse.com
reservations@alamoguesthouse.com

This great value, family-run guesthouse looks over Kelvingrove Park and is an easy walk from all the attractions of the West End, City Centre and riverside. Just 2 minutes away are some of Glasgow's best bars and restaurants. Rooms are very smart and elegant, with excellent facilities and attention to detail.

Argyll Guest House £
Sauchiehall Street,
Glasgow G3 7TH
Tel. no 0141 357 5155
www.argyllguesthouseglasgow.co.uk
info@argyllguesthouseglasgow.co.uk

Just a few minutes' walk from the IMAX cinema and the vibrant night scene of Byres Road is this homely budget guesthouse. Rooms are ensuite and have Wi-Fi and TVs. A Scottish buffet breakfast is available at a small additional cost.

Devoncove Hotel £-££
931 Sauchiehall Street,
Glasgow G3 7TQ
Tel. no 0141 334 4000
www.devoncovehotel.com
info@devoncovehotel.com

A nicely decorated, smart hotel offering reasonable room rates and a complementary fitness suite. All rooms are ensuite and have

✳ shared room without breakfast

£ under £30
££ £30–£60
£££ over £60
pppn

freeview TV and Wi-Fi access. Last minute deals may be available online. Parking is free, subject to availability.

Saint Judes Boutique Hotel £££
190 Bath Street, Glasgow
Tel. no 0141 352 8000
www.saintjudes.com
info@saintjudes.com

Saint Judes is rather proud of its mixology skills, and offers cocktail masterclasses. In your individually designed room is a private martini bar with cocktail kit and recipe book, an iPod docking station, Hi-Fi, 24-hour room service and oodles of space and luxury. Why bother leaving the room? Well, if you do feel the need, Mama San Bar is one of the city's smoothest clubs, it's open until 3am and it's just downstairs.

The Sherbrooke Castle Hotel ££-£££
1 Sherbrooke Avenue, Pollokshields,
Glasgow G41 4PG
Tel. no 0141 427 4227
www.sherbrooke.co.uk
enquiries@sherbrooke.co.uk

This beautiful red sandstone 'castle' sits in its own landscaped grounds in a leafy suburb of Glasgow's southside. The city centre's attractions are just 10 minutes away, as is the Hampden Park stadium. You may be able to get a good deal on a few smart twin rooms, which hopefully will give you free reign to discover the delights of the Morrison's restaurant before you cosy up by an open fire in the lounge and have a few drinks.

self-catering

38 Bath Street £££
38 Bath Street, Glasgow G2 1HG
Tel. no 0845 222 38 38
www.38bathst.co.uk

At £80 each per night you can grab some two-bedroom apartments in this beautiful building and enjoy a seriously luxurious stay in Glasgow. Although the decor and opulence seem hotel-like (as do the maid service, reception and concierge), each flat has its own separate living room and well-equipped kitchen so the experience is actually very relaxed and homely – perfect if you're planning a night in.

✳ shared room without breakfast

£ under £30
££ £30–£60
£££ over £60
pppn

Bankell Farm Camping and Caravan Site £
Strathblane Road, Milngavie, Glasgow
G62 8LE
Tel. no 0141 956 1733
www.bankellfarm.co.uk
info@bankellfarm.co.uk

This family-run campsite is in the perfect spot to explore Glasgow, Loch Lomond and the West Highland Way, so if you're a walker and the sun's shining it could be a great choice.

Ben Lomond Lodge £
Rowardennan, Loch Lomond
Tel. no 07721 638091
www.benlomondlodge.co.uk

This lovely, modern lodge sleeps six and is perched on the bonnie banks of Loch Lomond – one of the UK's most beautiful spots. It's only 45 minutes' drive from Glasgow, but you'll feel like you're in the middle of nowhere when you're enjoying a few sunset drinks together on the deck. Boat hire, walking and golf are on tap and if you need to take the kids with you, what could be better than the wide open spaces?

City Apartments £
401 North Woodside Road, Glasgow
G20 6NN
Tel. no 0141 342 4060
www.mcquadehotels.com
city@mcquadehotels.com

The Scottish Tourist Board has awarded these apartments four stars, and when you arrive at your west end address and see the facilities on offer (including that hen party essential, the trouser press) you'll be surprised that this is actually a very budget-friendly option. The apartments are maintained as part of the Albion Hotel next door, so it's all clean and up together.

Drumboy Holiday Cottage £
Drumclog Strathaven, South Lanarkshire ML10 6QJ
Tel. no 01357 440544/07766 347 896
www.drumboy-lodge.com
gillian@drumboy-lodge.com

Surround yourself and eight of your friends with beautiful countryside on a peaceful working farm in the Clyde Valley. The ideal spot for walking, horse riding or golf, the lodge is also within a 15-minute drive of retail centres, theme parks and boat trips to the Isles of Arran and Millport. Glasgow is about 27 miles away.

Unique Cottages £–£££
Monksford Road, Newtown St Boswells
TD6 0SB
Tel. no 01835 822277
www.unique-cottages.co.uk

Unique country holiday cottages in stunning locations all over Scotland can be found and booked through this company. Each property has been carefully selected to offer the best cottage holidays available in bonny Scotland.

Get ready for the biggest day of your life!

THE ULTIMATE
STAG
AND HEN
DESTINATION

Head to the ultimate party destination with food, drink and a whole host of activities including our real snow slope, climbing, adventure golf, bowling, laser games and cinema.

PLAY EAT SHOP
AT THE ULTIMATE ENTERTAINMENT DESTINATION

xscape.co.uk/braehead 0141 885 7082 / 7083 / 7085 / 7088 corpbh@xscape.co.uk

where to eat and drink

There are so many good bars in Glasgow that it's tempting to say, just hit the streets and see where you end up. But here are a few to get you started.

bars

Bar Soba
11 Mitchell Lane, Glasgow G1 3NU
Tel. no 0141 204 2404
www.barsoba.co.uk

If you like to try something a little different, you might enjoy Soba's Thailand-inspired cocktails, flavoured with chilli, lemongrass and other fragrant treats. Live music and DJs ensure the vibe is cool and upbeat, while the two-floor venue is perfectly designed to let groups party in style.

Cocktail time at The Sports Cafe Glasgow.

Madness Theatre of Fun
30 Bothwell Street, Glasgow G2 7EN
Tel. no 0141 204 5999
www.madnesstof.com
madnesstof@aol.com

If you want to get thrown into party mode this is the place to go drinking. Live shows of all descriptions, with tributes to Moulin Rouge, Roy Chubby Brown, Michael Bublé and many more acts, as well as Boogie Nights, Glasgow's Got Talent and other regular events mean that the place is far from being dull.

The Bunker Bar
193–199 Bath Street, Glasgow G2 4HU
Tel. no 0141 229 1427
www.thebunkerbar.com
info@thebunkerbar.com

Dodge under the radar and head for the Bunker Bar if you're looking for a pre-club bar with atmosphere, cheap drinks, food promos (largely it's pizza and pasta), regular DJs and passes to the club next door. It makes life sooo easy – and if you can't be bothered to move after a few Woo Woos, Manhattans or other cocktaily delights, book your own cosy booth and stay put until 2am.

The Loft
Ashton Lane, Hillhead,
Glasgow G12 8SJ
Tel. no 0845 166 6028
grosvenor@g1group.com

The Loft is a big and beautiful West End venue with old films flickering on the walls (it's in the roof of the Grosvenor Cinema), trendy yet comfortable seating area and a great atmosphere. Regular events, karaoke booths, private dining rooms, drinks promos and good value for money Italian food complete the scene.

The Sports Cafe Glasgow
292–332 Sauchiehall Street,
Glasgow G2 3JA
Tel. no 0141 332 8000
www.thesportscafe.com/glasgow
glasgowfunctions@thesportscafe.com

The newly refurbished Glasgow Sports Cafe is famous for its unforgettable hen and stag parties. Hens can enjoy a huge range of entertainment. Choose from Wii, race nights, a DJ, a quiz, murder mystery, cocktail lessons, salsa, burlesque or pole dance classes and more. There's always a great party atmosphere.

restaurants & cafés

Arta ££

The Old Cheesemarket, 62 Albion
Street, Merchant City, Glasgow G1 1PA
Tel. no 0141 552 2101
www.arta.co.uk
arta@g1group.com

Lovely private dining rooms, live music and a
nightclub are just a few things that make this
Mediterranean restaurant a great choice for
an evening out. Hen and stag parties are
welcome, and you can book cocktail-making
lessons, as well as a meal and club entry to
make a real night of it. If you fancy something
a bit different, the venue also hosts murder
mystery nights, horror walks and seances!

It's fun all the way at Curryoke Club.

Bibi's Cantina £–££

599 Dumbarton Road, Partick,
Glasgow G11 6HY
Tel. no 0141 579 0179
www.bibiscantina.com

Mexican and American (Tex-Mex) food is
served at this up and coming West End
eatery. The place isn't huge, but the menu is
definitely a crowd pleaser.

Curryoke Club ££

100 Stobcross Road, Glasgow G3 8QQ
Tel. no 0141 248 1485
www.curryoke.com
info@currykaraokeclub.com

Ideal for fun-loving groups, this restaurant
gives you a night to remember, with great,
plentiful Indian food, karaoke, dancing and
the odd comedy night. Your table will be
festooned with hen confetti, balloons and
party hats; it's hen party heaven.

Khublai Khans ££–£££

26 Candleriggs, Merchant City,
Glasgow G1 1LD
Tel. no 0141 552 5646
www.khublaikhans.co.uk
glasgow@khublaikhans.co.uk

Looking for something fun, informal and
genuinely different? Then this is the place for
you. Create your own dishes of food
selecting from a dizzying selection of fresh

veg, herbs, spices, sauces and exotic meats.
The Hen even gets to sit on her very own
throne for the evening.

Rogano £££

11 Exchange Place, Glasgow G1 3AN
Tel. no 0141 248 4055
www.roganoglasgow.com
rogano@btconnect.com

This Glasgow institution was fitted out in
1936, when Cunard's Queen Mary was being
built on the Clyde. It retains the 1930s decor
and classic ambience, and is a gorgeous
place to eat and drink, whether you choose
upmarket bar snacks in the Oyster Bar,
brasserie dishes in the Café or treat
yourselves to a night of fine dining in the
Restaurant, which majors on exquisite
seafood and great French wines.

Tusk ££

18 Moss Side Road, Shawlands,
Glasgow G41 3TN
Tel. no 0845 166 6017

Once you see this South Side venue, with its
selection of opulent and inviting spaces, you
won't want to leave – so it's just as well they
lay on a whole party's worth of entertainment
for you. Book a hen package of a beautiful
three-course meal, cocktail lessons in a
private bar and a bit of karaoke in your own
booth, then let your hair down and dance 'til
late in the club area.

where to party

This is one city where you'll have no problem finding late night bars, clubs of all descriptions and fun, fun, fun on tap. Live music fans will be very happy here too!

You can party the night away at Curryoke Club.

Barrowlands Ballroom
244 Gallowgate, Glasgow G4 0TS
Tel. no 0141 552 4601
www.glasgow-barrowland.com

This has been voted the best venue in the UK for rock and indie gigs. From the Chemical Brothers to The Stiff Little Fingers, the Barrowlands has seen many legendary nights.

Boho
59 Dumbarton Road,
Glasgow G11 6PD
Tel. no 0141 357 6644
www.thebohoclub.co.uk

The Belvedere Booth is a great option for up to 20 guests. You get your own hostess and some complimentary vodka drinks, plus a space to call your own all night. Overlooking

the main venue from your opulent perch, you can pick your moment to go down and mingle with the rest of the crowd. The main venue itself is smart and feels more like a late night bar with a dancefloor than a classic nightclub.

King Tut's Wah Wah Hut
272 St. Vincent Street, Glasgow G2 5RL
Tel. no 0141 221 5279
www.kingtuts.co.uk

A regular stop on any up-and-coming band's first major tour, this hugely popular little venue has live music every night. In the daytime you can have a chilled out game of pool and play your favourite sounds on the juke box, get something to eat and sup down the venue's home brewed lager or a skinny latte if that's more your thing.

O2 ABC Glasgow

300 Sauchiehall Street,
Glasgow G2 3JA
Tel. no 0141 332 2232
www.o2abcglasgow.co.uk
mail@o2abcglasgow.co.uk

Doing what O2 does well – big venue, big
party nights and big gigs.

Sub Club

22 Jamaica Street, Glasgow G1 4QD
Tel. no 0141 248 4600
www.subclub.co.uk
info@subclub.co.uk

After 20 years plus of partying in Glasgow,
the Sub Club still resides deep below number
22 Jamaica Street. Weekend in, weekend
out, you can find the best of the city's music
makers playing to the best people the city
can muster on the best sound system for
miles around.

The Arches

253 Argyle Street, Glasgow G2 8DL
Tel. no 0141 565 1000
www.thearches.co.uk

Another Glaswegian legend, just reopened
after a refurb, this massive club under
Glasgow Central Station continues to offer
top name DJs and live acts to its loyal fans.

The Tunnel

84 Mitchell Street, Glasgow G4 3NA
Tel. no 0141 204 1000
www.tunnelglasgow.co.uk
tunnel@cplweb.com

Kicking the weekend off with a pop, R'n'B,
hip hop and dance mash up and cocktail
promos every Thursday, and keeping the
hedonistic party animals happy until the earl
hours of Sunday, The Tunnel is an original
'superclub' and has been a major Glasgow
venue that regularly hosts big names since i
opened its doors in 1990.

Victoria's

98 Sauchiehall Street, Glasgow G2 3DE
Tel. no 0141 332 1444
www.victorias.tv
info@victorias.tv

If you're looking for risqué fun and frolics,
check out Vicky's Secret, a night held on the
first Saturday of each month, where male
strippers The Hot Boyz take to the stage,
along with 'filthy' comedy from Carrie Jones.
The package for hens includes a two-course
meal, disco and naughty party games. This
fun and high-octane club also hosts The
Sunday Club, Love Fridays and Saturday
party night Infinity. Book a booth in advance
for groups of six or more to get a real VIP
experience at this classy club.

Fantastic light shows and cool scenes are easy to find in this lively city.

leeds

Mill Square (top), City Square (middle), The Calls (bottom).

This big, beautiful jewel of the North has a well-deserved reputation for being a fabulous night out. With world-class clubs, sophisticated bars and a funky, cosmopolitan vibe, could Leeds be your ideal hen destination?

what to do

If you're wondering which city guarantees a great night out, look no further than Leeds. With some of the nation's best clubs and bars, the nightlife is electric.

On the one hand, it's good to know that Leeds was voted Britain's sexiest city last year. On the other, it's discouraging that Jeremy Paxman was named as one of its sexiest men. There's nowt so queer as folk, eh? Still, you'll notice that Leeds is packed with gorgeous 20–30 somethings. What more of an excuse do you need for getting seriously glammed up for your big night out? The shopping in Leeds is great, and you'll find all the big names as well as plenty of boutiques, and the city and its surrounds contains masses of spa, pamper and beauty places.

Once the slap, the heels and the LBD are on, it's off to the centre with your hens for a full-on night on the town. You can either keep yourselves to yourselves or get chatting to other groups and make the most of the friendly vibe in the city.

When the hangover's passed and you're all shopped out, there's still more to Leeds. All the major hen party organisers have activities based here, so you'll be able to book anything that takes your fancy. Also, if you and the girls like walking, riding or cycling, you can't beat the beautiful Yorkshire Dales.

The Corn Exchange shopping centre.

10 good reasons

1. clubbing in fancy dress
2. great cocktail bars
3. top shopping
4. party culture
5. riding in the Dales
6. sphering
7. luxurious spas
8. stylish boutique hotels
9. country cottages
10. friendly and fun

sounds of the city

School spirit Just the sight of the drinks menu at Smokestack on Lower Briggate makes us smile. These guys know their spirits and have a fine selection of brandies, vodkas, gins, bourbons and more, which they lovingly blend into some of the best cocktails on the planet. The bar's cool, dark and slick, with The Roost room upstairs playing funk and soul. Tucked away behind the Roost's bar you can take a Bartending Masterclass and learn how to mix up a storm in a martini glass. A buffet lunch is included, and you can choose how long your lessons last before you hand it all back to the experts and return to the front of the bar where you belong.

PYT Waterfall Spa at Brewery Wharf gives you the feeling of being in some countryside escape when you're actually slap bang in the middle of the city. This ladies-only pamper palace offers various packages, including an evening pass to the Thermal Spa Experience, with hydrotherapy spa pool, Norwegian tropicarium, aromatherapy steam room and other delights, including a relaxation boudoir

and an i-pod filled with mellow tunes to use. If you were feeling pre-wedding stress, wave it goodbye here.

New way home Meanwhile, if you're Leeds local, or you're staying in a Yorkshire cottage – or even if you've slightly dented the budget on your hotel choice – why not bring the pampering to you? The Pamper Party will organise local beauty and massage therapists to visit you and the ladies and give you blissful treatments in the comfort of your very own boudoir. With a few bottles of fizz and some good music, you'll be in seventh heaven.

The lady is a tramp This is not one for ladylike hens we're afraid. But if you're lasses who love a challenge, read on. The Otley Run is an epic pub crawl down the Otley Road, usually done in fancy dress. First, eat a lot. Next, don your themed outfits and get yourselves to Headingley, where the crawl begins with three country-style locals, Woodies, the Three Horseshoes and the New Inn. Don't have more than a half in each. When we say this is an epic we mean it! A little further on is the

Ultimate relaxation at the Waterfall Spa.

POLE FITNESS ACADEMY

Finally, the perfect pole plan for a hen night!

It's you, your closest friends, and all your inhibitions checked at the door. What does that give you? Your own personalized pole party!

Learn the most fun and sexy pole dance moves in just 2 hours:

- ☆ **sensually slither all over the floor**
- ☆ **spin on and climb the pole, maybe even going upside down!**
- ☆ **perform pole tricks and exotic moves**
- ☆ **master a sweet and spicy routine for your own use**
- ☆ **for the finale – a lap dance**

Stripper shoes, costumes and props welcomed and encouraged. If you can't come to us, we can come to you with our portable x-poles.

Contact: 01274 639492 / 07833 102632
trixterspolefitness@myway.com
www.trixterspolefitness.com

Our packages include:
Basic Karaoke
Karaoke with buffets
Karaoke with Cocktail Master Classes + more!
Prices start at just £2.50pp

The Arc, 19 Ash Road, Headingley, Leeds, LS6 3JJ
managers@arcleeds.co.uk
www.arcinspirations.com/arc

For your hen to go **FREE** quote: 'Hen Party Handbook' when you Call 0113 275 2223 or email karaoke@arcleeds.co.uk

Only 10 min's from the city centre.

Authentic Bavarian

A totally unique experience

Down the Victorian stone staircase on Park Row, enter the totally remodelled vaults of the old Bank of England, transformed into a unique drinking and dining experience. **This is truly a real piece of Bavaria in the heart of Leeds and is the new spot for your hen or stag party.**

Steins of the finest German beers served from huge ceramic fonts, along with schnapps and unique German cocktails, all served by waiting staff in classic Bavarian costume make your visit a memorable one.

With the option to buy **your very own keg for the table**, or to sample the huge array of quality beers and tasty Pretzels and Bratwursts to snack on,

The BierKeller is one not to be missed!

For special Stag and Hen packages call 0113 243 2300 or email info@leedsbierkeller.com

www.theparkrow.com

Taps, then it's two modern bars, Arc and Box. Still standing? OK, just keep following the other pissed muppets until you get to Strawberry Fields. Singing...

Make me smile Book a hilarious night at The Highlight on Albion Street – even the most up-tight of your chickens won't fail to find at least some of the jokes funny with fab comedians and a top compere. You'll get food and plenty of cocktails to drink, too.

Drinkin' again If you like beer, you mustn't miss the city's great North Bar. Plonk yourselves down on the long tables to sample a few lagers (they do serve other drinks) and enjoy the great music and fantastic atmosphere in this happy and well-loved drinking den. In March and October the party vibe really gets going with the annual beer fests.

Ride a white horse There is nothing better than horse riding to get you out exploring the Yorkshire Dales. If you're a mixed ability group or total beginners, opt for a residential weekend break at True Well Hall (01535 603292). You'll stay in a 16th century farmhouse or in self-catering cottages, and be given a steed to suit your ability. For the

evenings of nursing your aching thighs there's an old village pub five minutes away. A truly relaxing girly retreat.

Deep kick Universal Dance Creations has a range of dance classes, but choose the can-can party workshop for brilliant hen party laughs, frilly hems and feather headdresses. Your teacher have danced at the Moulin Rouge, no less, and will go through the basic line kicks to more advanced moves with you. Ooh la la! Call 07961 579482.

'been there...'

I booked sphering with Into the Blue. OMG! Hilarious. I would never do it again, but I'm glad we did because nobody will ever forget my hen do! We had a fantastic couple of nights in Leeds, just in late night bars, chatting to stag groups and other hens. It's a brilliant place, Leeds, one of the best nights out anywhere. They just know how to party.

Learn to Can Can with Universal Dance Creations (www.universaldancecreations.com).

where to stay

Self-catering options, both in city apartments and Yorkshire cottages, are good value. But for those who like to be pampered, Leeds is choc full of great hotels.

hotels

Etap Hotel ££
2 The Gateway North,
Crown Point Road,
Leeds LS9 8BZ
Tel. no 0113 245 0725
www.etaphotel.com
H6002@accor.com

This modern hotel chain offers comfortable rooms, which can accommodate up to three people, with a shower, toilet and flatscreen TV. And the next day you help yourself at the great value for money breakfast buffet!

Holiday Inn Express ££
Amouries Drive, Leeds LS10 1LE
Tel. no 0870 890 0455
www.hiexpressleeds.co.uk
reservations.leeds@
holidayinnexpress.org.uk

This three-star hotel is located at Clarence Dock adjacent to the Armouries Museum. It has 130 stylish ensuite bedrooms offering comfort and a good value budget accommodation option. The hotel is 15 minutes walk from the vibrant city centre and the main train station.

Jurys Inn £
Brewery Place, Brewery Wharf,
Leeds LS10 1NE
Tel. no 0113 283 8800
leedshotels.jurysinns.com
jurysinnleeds@jurysinns.com

Just 5 minutes' walk from Leeds city centre and the train station, Jurys Inn enjoys a fantastic central location on the banks of the River Aire. The spacious and comfortable rooms are all ensuite and can accommodate three adults quite comfortably.

✳ shared room without breakfast

£ under £30
££ £30–£60
£££ over £60
pppn

Novotel Leeds Centre ££
4 Whitehall Quay, Leeds
LS1 4HR
Tel. no 0113 242 6446
www.novotel.com
H3270@accor.com

Situated in the centre of Leeds, the hotel is close to shops and the main nightlife areas of Leeds. With Elements restaurant, bar, fitness suite, sauna, steam room and W-Fi, this hotel has all the facilities for a comfortable stay. The main railway station is just a few minutes walk away.

Radisson SAS Hotel ££
No 1 The Light, Leeds LS1 8TL
Tel. no 0113 236 6000
www.radissonblu.co.uk
info.leeds@radissonblu.com

Part of the retail and entertainment complex, The Light, this hotel is right in the heart of Leeds. Easily accessible from major motorway links, the hotel is just 5 minutes walk from the train station. Guests have access to the private Esporta Health and Fitness Club for a nominal fee.

Modern rooms at Holiday Inn Express.

self-catering

Currer Laithe Farm £
Moss Carr Road, Long Lee,
Keighly BD21 4SL
Tel. no 01535 604 387
www.currerlaithe.co.uk

This 16th century farmhouse is set in 200 acres of farmland overlooking the great sweep of the Aire Gap, Ilkley Moor and Ingleborough in the distance. It commands unparalleled views of walled pasture and moorland. An ideal base for any outdoor activities on the moors, this six-bedroomed unit sleeps 12–15 people in a fantastic stone building with beams and open log fires. There are also two additional cottages to rent if your group exceeds 15.

* shared room without breakfast

£ under £30
££ £30–£60
£££ over £60
pppn

Harman Suites 1 & 2 £
48 St Martins Avenue, Leeds LS7 3LG
Tel. no 0871 702 0134

These detached ground floor chalet-style apartments offer good value for money close to the city centre. These self-catering units are well-furnished and fully equipped.

Nostell Priory Holiday Park £
Doncaster Road, Nostell,
Wakefield WF4 1QE
Tel. no 01924 863938
www.nostellprioryholidaypark.co.uk
park@nostellprioryholidaypark.co.uk

Self-catering holiday homes at Nostell Priory Caravan Park nestle in a forest glade within the expansive grounds of the National Trust's Nostell Priory Estate. The holiday homes are comprehensively equipped with cooker, fridge, TV and all home comforts. Electricity and gas is included in the tariff. The park is excellently situated as a base for good walking and exploring Yorkshire. The major towns of Leeds, Wakefield, Sheffield, Barnsley and Doncaster are all within easy driving distance.

The Chambers ££
The Chambers, Riverside West,
Whitehall Road, Leeds LS1 4AW
Tel. no 0113 386 3300
www.morethanjustabed.com
stay@morethanjustabed.com

These sleek, stylish and sophisticated boutique serviced apartments are a haven of calm and five-star luxury. There is also a large room that can be hired out for a private dinner. Apartments are also available at Riverside West on the banks of the river Aire and at Park Place.

Westwood Lodge ££
Westwood Drive,
Ilkley LS29 9JF
Tel. no 01943 433430
www.westwoodlodge.co.uk
welcome@westwoodlodge.co.uk

Choose from four 'listed' cottages situated around the courtyard at Westwood Lodge. Orchard, Applebarn and Coach House Cottages each sleep up to six people. The Old Gallery is larger (sleeps up to 11) and is ideal for a group of friends.

Stunning scenery in the Yorkshire Dales.

THE PARKROW
BAR & BRASSERIE

SITUATED IN THE HEART OF LEEDS is a new bar for a great night out. No expense has been spared to bring this great venue to life, transforming the old Bank of England building into a new trendy nightspot and cool lounge.

SPECIAL STAG AND HEN DEALS are available and range from Cocktail classes and sharing platters, to an elegant three-course meal with welcome drinks on arrival.

EARLY EVENING PIANO AND GREAT SONGS set the tone for the evening, whilst the ambience of the lighting and extensive drink selection help make the whole experience that much more enjoyable.

Our FRIDAY NIGHT LIVE LOUNGE is the place to be seen with the latest local acts performing in an intimate setting for your enjoyment – the perfect setting for relaxing with a cocktail or two or a large glass from our range of quality wines. Join us between 4pm and 8pm for happy hours with some amazing drinks offers.

On Saturday evenings our resident DJ will have you dancing the night away 'til the early hours, playing a mix of all your favourite tunes. Combined with 2-4-1 cocktails for the whole day and night, it's hard not to be enticed in!

For more information call 0113 243 2300 or email bookings@theparkrow.com
www.theparkrow.com

where to eat and drink

Being a party kind of town, Leeds is heaving with pubs and bars, and there is no shortage of great restaurants for all tastes and breakfast cafes in which to recover.

bars

North Bar

24 New Briggate, Leeds LS1 6NU
Tel. no 0113 242 4540
www.northbar.com
info@northbar.com

With the finest selection of beers in the North of England and regular haunt of superstars, such as Sue Pollard, Sylvester McCoy and some of former band Hearsay, North is Leeds' coolest bar for lovers of great beer, music and art.

Revolution

41 Cookridge Street, Leeds LS2 3AW
Tel. no 0800 6300 860
www.revolution-bars.co.uk

The Millenium Square venue is cavern-like. This funky branch of the national Vodka bar chain has a cool patio overlooking the Square and an indoor courtyard for an inside-out experience. Revolution is also at Call Lane in the Exchange Quarter of the city. Recently refurbished, it forms part of the city's most fashionable drinking circuit.

A night out in Leeds has to start with cocktails.

Smokestack

159a Lower Briggate, Leeds LS1 6LY
Tel. no 0113 245 2222
www.myspace.com/smokestackleeds
info@smokestackleeds.co.uk

This dedicated music bar is the only place in Leeds playing funk and soul on a Saturday night. They also feature ska and northern soul on Fridays. You can do a bar-tending masterclass here and learn to make heavenly cocktails from Mojitos to Manhattans.

Strawberry Fields

104 Otley Road, Leeds LS16 5JG
Tel. no 0113 278 4393
www.strawbs.com
strawbsbar@yahoo.co.uk

The 13th bar on The Otley Run is a small, continental-style bar between the two Universities. Naturally it attracts a lot of students, but there's plenty fun to be had at this friendly bar. You can hire out the upstairs bar for a private do as well. And by the way The Otley Run is a mad pub crawl taking in about 20 pubs and bars.

The Arc

19 Ash Road, Leeds LS6 3JJ
Tel. no 0113 275 2223
www.arcinspirations.com
bookings@arcinspirations.com

This contemporary glass-fronted Headingley bar is a stylish place for drinking and eating. You can now book a private karaoke suite at The Arc for night of caterwauling! Combine that with cocktail-making classes or a buffet for a great night with the girls.

restaurants

2 courses + half a bottle of wine

£ under £20
££ £20–£35
£££ over £35

The vast and fabulous Bibi's Italianissimo.

Bibi's Italianissimo ££–£££

Criterion Place (off Sovereign Street),
Leeds LS1 4AG
Tel. no 0113 243 0905
www.bibisrestaurant.com
reservations@bibisrestaurant.com

This glamorous Art Deco styled restaurant
and bar welcomes parties and offers an
amazing dining experience. Executive chef
Piero Vinci serves an extensive a la carte
menu full of Mediterranean dishes plus
traditional pizza and pastas using only the
freshest, highest quality ingredients, sourced
locally where possible.

Fig Mediterranean Grill ££

Alea Casino, 4 The Boulevard, Clarence
Dock, Leeds LS10 1OPZ
Tel. no 0871963 8118
www.aleacasinos.com/alea/leeds
eventleeds@aleacasinos.com
Located next to the Royal Armouries inside
the Alea Casino, the Fig Mediterranean Grill
delivers a clean and simple grill menu that
draws inspiration from the Med,
cosmopolitan Leeds and the surrounding
Yorkshire countryside.

Raja's Restaurant £–££

186 Roundhay Rd, Leeds LS8 5PL
Tel. no 0113 248 0411
www.rajasleeds.co.uk
bikrampalsingh@gmail.com

Rajas has gained a reputation as one of the
finest Indian restaurants in Yorkshire, as well
as the UK. The *Which? Good Food Guide*

has recommended Rajas over the past few
years and more recently, Raja's was voted
one of the top ten Indian Restaurants in the
UK by *The Times*. Raja's is located between
the city centre and the outer residential areas
of Leeds – Roundhay Road is the main road
leading to the city from these areas. It will be
worth the trip we can assure you.

Tiger Tiger ££–£££

The Light, 117 Albion St, Leeds LS2 8DY
Tel. no 0113 236 6999
www.tigertiger-leeds.co.uk
info@tigertiger-leeds.co.uk

The restaurant's cosmopolitan nature creates
an upbeat and lively experience; a modern,
relaxed and naturally stylish environment. The
restaurant at Tiger Tiger, Leeds, is a new
dining experience offering a taste of the east
plus all the traditional favourites. Try delicious
fusion dishes such as Tiger Tiger Katsu
chicken curry and Stir fried Udon noodles or
traditional favourites like Tiger Beer battered
fish and chunky chips or char-grilled prime
sirloin steak.

Viva Cuba ££

342 Kirkstall Road, Leeds LS4 2DS
Tel. no 0113 275 0888
www.vivacubaleeds.co.uk
info@vivacubaleeds.co.uk

Popular with locals and visitors alike, this
latino restaurant serving delicious homemade
tapas, authentic Cuban cocktails and
Spanish and South American wines and
beers gives great service in a warm vibrant
atmosphere.

where to party

Every night is party night in this vibrant city.

organ once was. The award-winning Saturday night Voodoo@Halo has it all: regular celebrity PAs, huge themed events and massive giveaways. DJ Si Edwards and DJ Tango provide the music with a mix of funky house, electro, R'n'B, classics and more...this is clubbing in style.

Evolution

Cardigan Fields Leisure Complex, 9 Cardigan Fields Road, Leeds LS4 2DG
Tel. no 0113 263 2632

A little off the beaten track, Evolution has two rooms each offering a variety of music. It's also home to Sundissential North, which is a huge trance house event running most of the day and night.

Halo

Woodhouse Lane, Leeds LS2 9JT
Tel. no 0113 245 9263
www.haloclubleeds.co.uk
halo@pbr.uk.com

This former church in the centre of Leeds is just up the road from all the main bars. Inside, the club is smart and modern, after a £5 million facelift, and the old church features give it loads of character. The original stained-glass windows, beams, wall features and high ceilings are still in place, which really set it apart from all the other clubs. The DJ plays from way up in the gods where the

Highlight Comedy Club

Bar Risa, The Cube, Albion Street, Leeds LS2 8ER
Tel. no 0113 247 1759
www.thehighlight.co.uk
info@thehighlight.co.uk

Sit back and enjoy nearly two hours of top comedy with four acts, then boogie until the early hours after the show. Food and of course drinks are available and groups of 12 or more get a free celebration pack.

Halo resides in a converted church.

RƎVOLUTION
MASTERCLASS

GET BEHIND THE BAR AND BECOME A COCKTAIL MASTER IN THIS 90 MINUTE INTERACTIVE SESSION!

✪ **COCKTAILS**
✪ **TASTING**
✪ **TOOLS**
✪ **SKILLS**
✪ **GAMES**

HEN GOES FREE!
MINIMUM 8 PEOPLE

QUOTE PROMO CODE 'MARTINI' FOR FREE HEN OFFER
PACKAGES FROM ONLY £24.95 PER PERSON PLUS
NEW PARTY FOOD OPTIONS NOW AVAILABLE

TO BOOK...
ONLINE: REVOLUTION-BARS.CO.UK
PHONE: 0800 6300 860
ASK: A MEMBER OF STAFF

ANY OCCASION, ANY SIZE... REVOLUTION IS THE PERFECT PLACE TO EAT, DRINK & PARTY!

Find us The Electric Press, Cookridge St and on Call Lane, Leeds

Club culture is king in Leeds (above and below right).

New York Disco, a Venetian Grand Ballroom complete with luxurious decor and a stunning chandelier, the seductive Parisian Boudoir, a chilled Aspen Ski Lodge with outside terrace, the First Port Bar, a Wakyama Tokyo Bar and Sydney Harbourside. There are also four exclusive VIP rooms perfect for your party each equipped with state-of-the-art plasma screen, waitress service, tailormade buffets and key card entry system. Oceana just loves themed nights and fancy dress, so you're definitely going to fit in here! However they have a policy ruling out sports wear, hoodies and full body paints...

The Mezz Club

2 Waterloo House, Assembly Street, Leeds LS2 7DE
Tel. no 0113 243 9909

New kid on the block, The Mezz has brought a fresh perspective to clubbing in Leeds. It's a trendy club without being pretentious and it's the people who go there who really bring it to life. There are some interesting events taking place here, including Sinful Sessions – could be an opportunity to say goodbye to singledom in style and rather skimpy underwear...

The Space

The Basement, Hirst's Yard, Duncan Street, Leeds LS1 6NJ
Tel. no 0113 246 1030

This cool and trendy basement club has regular DJ sets getting the dancefloor moving with the latest funky house and urban beats. A great selection of drinks and a vibrant and carefree atmosphere make The Space a popular choice for clubbers in Leeds. Awesome guest DJs include Paul Glasby, Andy Farley and loads more.

Mint

8 Harrison Street, Leeds LS1 6PA
Tel. no 0113 244 3168
www.themintclub.com
info@themintclub.com

This stylish club offers a unique atmosphere and often plays host to the best DJs in the city. You'll love the unique decor complete with polo-mint inspired seating! The infamous unisex toilets provide an interesting, if at times inconvenient talking point and if you get too hot you can always chill in the open-air back room! With new state-of-the-art sound and light systems, Mint Club offers great nights to match its respected reputation.

Oceana

Merrion Centre, 6–18 Woodhouse Lane, Woodhouse, Leeds LS2 8LX
Tel. no 0113 243 8229
www.oceanaclubs.com/leeds
oceana-leeds@luminar.co.uk

Escape to Oceana and discover seven ways to one night out. Arrive early and leave late, explore the themed space and experience five bars and two distinct nightclubs, all under one roof. Inspired by worldwide destinations these include: a Studio 54 style

With 10 shiny new pool tables, air hockey, gaming machines, lounge areas, 50 inch 3D TV's and the **first large-scale 3D projector in the UK**, which measures a whopping 6 metres square! This venue truly is a sporting heaven! With all events catered for, from pool parties to race nights and even Wii Sports parties, all in your own private area and with a large selection of food and drinks menus to choose from.

The multi-channel sports selection is the best around. Shooters is the only bar with such an extensive range of live sporting coverage from all the Premiership games to Rugby and even Ski Jumping! We always show EVERY major sporting event, no matter what time of day or night. The experience and atmosphere here is second to none, so make sure you don't miss out – come down and see SKYSPORTS 3D for yourself!

For special Stag and Hen Packages call 0113 243 2300 or email bookings@theparkrow.com

www.theparkrow.com

manchester

Salford Quays (top), Trafford Centre (middle), cityscape (bottom).

Manchester welcomes in its visitors with a certain smugness. Fabulous clubs, world-class eateries and more good bars than you can poke a twizzle stick at, on top of the footy, the shopping…it's the city that knows it's got it all.

what to do

It's a big, big city and Manchester is one of the UK's top places to party. Whether you're looking for sleekly groomed sophistication or grungy all-out fun, the answer is here.

First for football, second for media and commerce, third fave UK destination for foreign visitors, and taking every medal going for its music scene, you can't argue with the fact that Manchester's one of Britain's greatest centres. It's also absolutely huge, and has a massive young adult population – what with a big media industry, thousands of university students and graduates who won't leave. And that means the city is constantly trying to meet an insatiable demand for more bars, better clubs and world class eateries. All good news for hens coming to Manchester.

The Arndale is the largest city-centre mall in the UK with 240 of all the big-name retailers and fast food places you can think of. If you want clothes by small-name designers, go and have a rummage at Affleck's Palace, with 50 market-style stores. But it's the huge and elegant Trafford Centre, just out of town, that holds the crown for a classy afternoon's lunch and shopping.

And last but not least, Manchester girls are known for being well turned out – hair and beauty are big, so if you fancy a little pampering, look no further than here.

Combine thrills with chills at Alton Towers.

10 good reasons

1. massive club scene
2. good bars
3. shopping
4. spa and beauty places
5. Alton Towers
6. tubing at Chill Factor
7. West-end quality shows
8. range of accommodation
9. student nights and promos
10. nice weather for ducks

sounds of the city

Dammit, Janet When it comes to Rocky Horror, The Sound of Music or Joseph, there's only one thing you want to do and that's sing along. Sing-along-a nights are perfect for a hen party – you get a bit dressed up, get a bit drunk and watch the film, caterwauling along with lots of other people who have an equal disregard for what they look and sound like (although secretly, everyone does want the prize for the best fancy dress). Sing-along-a parties are constantly roaming around the UK and you'll often find one at the Manchester Opera House. Make those classic divas turn in their graves as you Timewarp, yodel or wail the night away.

Piece by piece If you don't fancy a film but you're not averse to a little singing with your supper, Bouzouki by Night is a fabulously fun night of Greek meze dishes and wine followed by Greek dancing lessons from the waiters and a spot of belly dancing. You can stay and dance the night away to disco classics, or make a sharp exit to your next venue if you've had enough feta for one night. Unfortunately they don't smash plates. From experience we can tell you that it's best not to introduce that feature yourself after a beverage or three.

Whole again Anyone for an enema? This and other detox, de-stress and disgusting-sounding but undoubtedly healthy activities may appeal to the hen who's having kittens over the pre-nuptial arrangements. And if they don't, then how about some fabulous massage, manicure, pedicure, facials and tanning to make you all feel like a million squids before your night out on the town? You can find all the health and beauty treatments your heart and other parts desire at the gorgeously calming Inner Sanctuary Retreat in the Northern Quarter. Look out for the Total Indulgence Packages, including Moody Cow and Hangover Recovery.

Rockin' robin The locals rate these as some of the best club nights in Manchester: Sankeys Saturdays, the Warehouse Project, Pure R'n'B Boutique, 5th Avenue for indie – but there are many many more. We say, for hen party laughs, burlesque, cheese and cabaret, it has to be The Birdcage. It's a totally unique concept of club and cabaret.

Get the basques and stockings out; it's time to Timewarp with Rocky Horror Sing-a-long-a.

Love the dogs... Love the Party... Love the Excitement!

HEN & STAG PACKAGES

@ BELLE VUE GREYHOUND STADIUM

You get all of this

THE PARTY PACKAGE

ADMISSION per person
RACE PROGRAMME per person
CHOICE OF FOOD* per person
PITCHER 4pt Pitcher of Beer, Pimms, Archers or Smirnoff
£5 BETTING VOUCHER per person
RACE SPONSORSHIP per group
PARTY PACK per group
GROUP PHOTO per group
TAXI TO TOWN

** Taxi will be to certain areas only. See the websites for drop off preference to your stadium choice.

HEN/STAG PACK Trackside - Min parties of 10 **£25** per person Includes *Fast Food Meal

HEN/STAG DINNER Restaurant - No Minimum **£45** per person Includes *3 Course meal

HEN/STAG VIP Suites - Min parties of 16 **£55** per person Includes *VIP BUFFET

BOOK YOUR PARTY ONLINE NOW

ManchesterHens.com
ManchesterStags.com

OR CALL
0870 840 7550

follow us on
facebook.
twitter

CHECK OUT OUR OTHER STADIUMS AT
www.lovethedogs.co.uk

Let it snow Not far from Old Trafford (which is of course worth a tour if you're a Man U fan) you'll find a little slice of Alpine life in the shape of the Chill Factor^e – Manchester's indoor real snow centre. If you're looking to ski or snowboard, there is a wide range of lessons available for groups, or head for a session on the main slope. The 180m-indoor slope is the longest in the UK and is sure to give your group a thrill! If skiing or boarding isn't for you, then why not try Tubing (zooming down in a rubber tube) or the Luge (a 60m ice slide). As Manchester is generally devoid of snow and big mountains, this isn't exactly a way to explore the local culture, but it's a lot of fun.

It's raining men For all you active hens who like nothing more than a good soaking. Why not have a go at gorge scrambling...it's a bit like caving but with the roof off! Cling to slippery rocks and climb waterfalls while following streams, becks and gorges. The nice people at adventure21.co.uk say you can get as wet or stay as dry

as you like. We say plunge pool jumping is all a part of the fun!

Five o'clock world 5–7pm is a weird time. Too early for dinner, too late to shop. But perfect for cocktails. For some of the city's best, trot round the back of House of Fraser on Deansgate and find Prohibition or Mojo. The latter plays classic rock and packs in a crowd at the weekend, while Prohibition has a friendly vibe, good music and makes for a relaxed few hours. If your night out is focused on the Northern Quarter, tucked away little gem Socio Rehab has some of the best cocktails in the UK and is hugely popular – so you have to get there early to avoid the queues. It's a hard life, isn't it? Be aware of dress codes for cocktail bars and clubs – it's a dressed up scene.

Happy Jealous, actually. The thought of you swanning off for golf, spa and luxury at the stunning Formby Hall makes us a bit sick. The packages are great value – a little golfing, using the utterly gorgeous, spick and span spa facilities, gliding up and down the pool, having beauty treatments, being wined, dined and then going to sleep in the elegant bedrooms – arrghh! When's our next hen do?

Apres-ski Chill Factor^e stylie.

where to stay

You'll find a warm welcome and great accommodation for good prices here. Stay within reach of all the bars and clubs, so that you don't have a huge spend on cabs.

hotels

Arora International ££
18–24 Princess Street,
Manchester M1 4LY
Tel. no 0161 236 8999
www.arorahotels.com
manchester@arorahotels.com

This four-star hotel is contemporary in design while retaining the character of the Grade II listed building. Set right in the heart of the city, it's close to all the attractions and the train station. The rooms feature all the facilities you will need and there is the Obsidian bar and restaurant on site.

Formby Hall Golf Resort and Spa £££
Southport Old Road, Formby L37 0AB
Tel. no 01704 875699
www.formbyhallgolfresort.co.uk
booking@formbyhallgolfresort.co.uk

If you want to get away from the city for some peace and tranquility, head west to the coast and experience some pure luxury at Formby Hall. Stylish and sophisticated, every detail has been meticulously thought about here.

The Hatters Hostel £
50 Newton Street, The Northern Quarter, Manchester M1 2EA
Tel. no 0161 236 9500
www.hattersgroup.com/manchester
manchester@hattersgroup.com
Located in the trendy bohemian Northern Quarter, Hatters offers a clean and comfortable stay in dorms or triple rooms for a very reasonable rate.

Hallmark Hotel ££
Stanley Road, Handforth, Wilmslow SK9 3LD
Tel. no 0161 437 0511
www.hallmarkhotels.co.uk
manchester.reservations@hallmark hotels.co.uk

Close to Manchester airport, this boutique-style hotel offers a lot of luxury for a relatively small price. Relax in the warmth of the decadent lounge bar or totally chill out in the health spa.

* shared room without breakfast

£ under £30
££ £30–£60
£££ over £60
pppn

Elegant luxury at the Hallmark Hotel.

Stay Inn Hotel £

55 Blackfriars Road, Manchester M3 7DB
Tel. no 0161 907 2277
www.stayinn.co.uk
info@stayinn.co.uk

Less than a 10 minute walk to the city centre and handy for Old Trafford and the MEN Arena, this budget hotel offers unbelievable value. It even has free car parking, which is a big bonus. All the rooms are ensuite with TV and Wi-Fi, and there's a restaurant and bar.

The Mitre Hotel £

1–3 Cathedral Gates, Printworks, Manchester M3 1SW
Tel. no 0161 834 4128
www.themitrehotel.net
info@themitrehotel.net
This budget hotel is located in The Printworks – Manchester's huge entertainment complex right in the centre of the city – so you're right on the spot for all the bars, restaurants and clubs you could wish for. Being refurbished as we went to print.

self-catering

Burrs Activity Centre £

Woodhill Road, Bury
BL8 1DA
Tel. no 0161 764 9649
www.burrs.org.uk
burrs@btconnect.com

To take advantage of a wide range of outdoor activities available in Lancashire, base yourselves here in the Burrs Country Park. The bunkhouse comprises five rooms with two, four, six, ten and twelve beds. There's a fully equipped kitchen and dining area. Just bring your sleeping bag for an adventure!

City Warehouse Apartments ££

6–14 Great Ancoats Street, Manchester M4 1LJ
Tel. no 0161 236 3066
www.citywarehouseapartments.com
mail@citywarehouseapartments.com

These modern, stylish apartments are perfectly located in the heart of the Northern Quarter, minutes from Victoria Station and the Shudehill Interchange. All the fully furnished apartments have plasma TVs and DVD player.

Serviced City Pads ££

Tel. no 0844 335 8866
www.servicedcitypads.com
info@servicedcitypads.com

A range of quality apartments sleeping up to eight people are available in several central Manchester locations with this booking agent. If you want to splash out, they have plenty of apartments with wow factor.

✳ shared room without breakfast

£ under £30
££ £30–£60
£££ over £60
pppn

Premier Apartments Manchester ££

64 Shudehill, Manchester M4 4AA
Tel. no 0161 827 3930
www.premierapartmentsmanchester.com
info@premierapartmentsmanchester.com

Well located for The Printworks, the Arndale Shopping Centre and both Victoria and Piccadilly train stations, there's also a metro link stop right opposite. There are 60 fully furnished apartments over four floors in this luxury block.

The Place ££

Ducie Street, Piccadilly, Manchester M1 2TP
Tel. no 0161 778 7500
www.theplacehotel.com
reservations@theplacehotel.com

This loft-style apartment hotel offers the flexibility of an apartment, with kitchen facilities and living room, plus the convenience of a hotel with restaurant and bar on site. Choose from one- or two-bedroom apartments all with Sky TV and Wi-Fi.

The bright lights of central Manchester.

Manchester's Friendliest School of Pole Dance

poletastic

Poletastic is situated in the Heart of Manchester and offers a fantastic range of dance party packages!

The Poletastic Party is the perfect way to kick off your celebration, two hours of dance with the emphasis on FUN!

Prices start at £18pp (t&c apply)

We offer a range of dance styles; Pole Dance, Burlesque, Belly Dance, Cheeky Cha Cha, Salsa, Sassy Street, Cheerleading and Michael Jackson Tribute plus many more!!

Contact us and we will be happy to plan your perfect Poletastic Party!!

www.poletastic.com
info@poletastic.com
07779 332 302
0845 225 8822

PLANNING A HEN PARTY IN THE NORTH WEST?

Then take a look at Manchester Clay Shooting Club. Located just 20 minutes from the city centre, our friendly staff and professional instructors will ensure your hen party goes with a bang!

MANCHESTER CLAY SHOOTING CLUB · WORSLEY

For Details Tel: 07761 409 427 or visit:
WWW.MANCHESTERCLAYSHOOTING.COM

www.adventure21.co.uk

www.adventure21.co.uk

STAG & HEN PARTY ACTIVITY ORGANISERS

abseiling | archery | aquaseiling | bushcraft
canoeing | canyoning | fishing | gorge scrambling
kayaking | orienteering | paintballing
raft building | rock climbing | sailing
target rifle shooting | team building
tyrolean traverse | walking

email: info@adventure21.co.uk
Tel: 01257 474467

where to eat and drink

Head to the Northern Quarter for a little boho atmosphere, stick with the familiar chains of the city centre or try something from a country you've never even heard of.

bars & pubs

Brannigans
27 Peter Street, Manchester M2 5QR
Tel. no 0161 835 9697
www.brannigansbars.com
brannigansmanchester@
cougarleisureltd.co.uk

Open until 3am on Saturday nights (Sunday morning), there's always a great party vibe at this lively bar. Their colourful lit dancefloor is a real centrepiece and when the DJ plays the place really comes to life. There are private areas and rooms available to book for your group – just go to the 'book a party' area of their website.

Mojo
19 Back Bridge Street,
Manchester M3 2PB
Tel. no 0161 839 5330
www.mojobar.co.uk

If you want to get away from the ubiquitous sounds of house and dance music, Mojo's is the place for you. Playing their individual blend of 'real music' and serving up fantastic cocktails, they offer a great night out for lovers of soul, R'n'B and rock'n'roll.

Prohibition
2–10 St Marys Street,
Manchester M3 2LB
Tel. no 0161 831 9326
www.prohibition.uk.com
info@prohibition.uk.com

The high ceilings and intricate wood carving on the bar give an immediate sense of the American Prohibition era, but don't worry they do sell alcohol and there's plenty of fun and good food to be had at this bar and grill.

We love the 70s dancefloor at Brannigans.

Revolution
Arch 7 Deansgate Locks, Manchester
M1 5LH
Tel. no 0161 839 7558
www.revolution-bars.co.uk

One of four Manchester Revolution venues, Deansgate Locks features a massive state-of-the-art basement club, four fantastic bars, dedicated restaurant and chilled-out lounge area. Whether you're relaxing in the lounge or dancing the night away in the club, you're guaranteed to have a great night in this warehouse style bar. There is loads of choice for a hen party here, just call the dedicated party planner line (see website) and they'll talk you through the options.

Socio Rehab
100–102 High Street, Manchester M4 1HP
Tel. no 0161 832 4529
www.sociorehab.com
info@sociorehab.com

If you need rehabilitating in a social environment, this is one place you should visit. If the cool tunes and sumptuous decor don't reel you in, the delicious cocktails certainly will.

restaurants

Evuna ££
277–279 Deansgate, Manchester
M3 4EW
Tel. no 0161 819 2752
www.evuna.com
enquiries@evuna.com

Sample some fine Spanish food and wine in the heart of Manchester. Choose from a wide range of tapas dishes or eat a la carte, alternatively try their signature dish of Sea Bass baked in rock salt and filleted at the table. You can also have a wine-tasting party here, where you can try some of the less well known, but delectable, Spanish wines.

Hard Rock Cafe ££
Exchange Square, Manchester M4 2BS
Tel. no 0161 831 6700
www.hardrock.com
david_atkinson@hardrock.com

It's a worldwide phenomenon, but here in Manchester there's an awe-inspiring collection of rock memorabilia. Choose a party menu for a great value night out, or learn to shake up your favourite cocktails with the resident mixologist.

The Hard Rock Cafe in The Printworks.

'real life'

Learning to mix cocktails at the Hard Rock Cafe was great fun, but tasting what we'd concocted was even better!

The mixology bar at the Hard Rock Cafe.

Ithaca £££
36 John Dalton Street, City Centre, Manchester M2 6LE
Tel. no 0161 831 7409
www.ithacamanchester.com
pa@loveithaca.com

This elegant restaurant serving an eclectic mix of Japanese and Pan-Asian dishes has just been awarded the 2010 HILDA best restaurant in Manchester prize. So if you want a night of sparkling five-star luxury book into Ithaca.

Tiger Tiger ££
The Printworks, 27 Withy Grove, Manchester M4 2BS
Tel. no 0161 385 8080
www.tigertiger-manch.co.uk
info@tigertiger-manch.co.uk

With a restaurant, six bars and a lively club, this is a great place to party. You could start here at lunch time and work your way through the bars – Tiger, Kaz, Raffles, Lounge and The Loft – to the restaurant with an amazing range of dishes and then on to the club for late-night dancing or to Lucky Voice for some serious caterwauling in the privacy of your own luxury private room.

where to party

The relaxed and comfortable bar area at Pure nightclub.

Entourage

Unit 2a, The Printworks, 27 Withy
Grove, Manchester M4 2BS
Tel. no 0161 839 1344
www.entouragemanchester.com
info@entouragemanchester.com

This 800-capacity venue makes up for in style and glamour what it may lack in size. The club is spread over two levels, with a dancefloor on the ground floor and private booths and VIP area on the balcony. There is a range of drinks packages that can be pre-ordered on the website and if one of those doesn't float your boat, you can tailormake your own and the club will happily supply.

Lucky Voice @ Tiger Tiger

The Printworks, Withy Grove,
Manchester M4 2BS
Tel. no 0161 385 8080
www.tigertiger-manch.co.uk
info@tigertiger-manch.co.uk

Lucky Voice is thought by some to be the most liberating, heart-racing, life-affirming private karaoke experience on earth. Sing your heart out with your friends in the luxury of one of the exclusive private karaoke rooms available at Tiger Tiger. Choose from over 6000 songs to sing along to and order your drinks at the mere touch of a button.

Opus

The Printworks, Units 21–23, Withy
Grove, Manchester M4 2BS
Tel. no 0161 834 2414
www.opusmanchester.com
faye@opusmanchester.com

As well as a three-room clubbing venue, Opus hosts the Comedy Lounge every Saturday night featuring some big names and all the up-and-coming stand-up comedians on 'the tour'. There's a variety of packages you can book with different food options, from burger and chips during the show to a three-course meal served in the O Bar before the show, or a hot and cold buffet served in the Chill room before the show. You can even get cocktail-making lessons to complete the night's entertainment.

RƎVOLUTION
MASTERCLASS

GET BEHIND THE BAR AND BECOME A COCKTAIL MASTER IN THIS 90 MINUTE INTERACTIVE SESSION!

- ✪ **COCKTAILS**
- ✪ **TASTING**
- ✪ **TOOLS**
- ✪ **SKILLS**
- ✪ **GAMES**

HEN GOES FREE!
MINIMUM 8 PEOPLE

QUOTE PROMO CODE 'MARTINI' FOR FREE HEN OFFER
PACKAGES FROM ONLY £24.95 PER PERSON PLUS
NEW PARTY FOOD OPTIONS NOW AVAILABLE

TO BOOK...
ONLINE: REVOLUTION-BARS.CO.UK
PHONE: 0800 6300 860
ASK: A MEMBER OF STAFF

ANY OCCASION, ANY SIZE... REVOLUTION IS THE PERFECT PLACE TO EAT, DRINK & PARTY!

Find us at Deansgate Locks, Parsonage Gardens and Oxford Rd, Manchester

Lights and action at Pure in The Printworks.

Pure

Unit 11–12, The Printworks, 27 Withy
Grove, Manchester M4 2BS
Tel. no 0161 819 7770
www.pure.co.uk
info@puremanchester.com

Manchester's one and only superclub can
entertain 2700 clubbers in three different
rooms, plus an exclusive VIP experience is
on offer at The Island club for members only.
At the weekend crowd-pulling DJs play the
biggest tunes on state-of the-art sound
system accompanied by laser lightshows,
stilt walkers, fire breathers, podium dancers
and club visuals.
Friday and
Saturday nights
also feature a
comedy club
where you can get
your night off to
a hilarious start.

The Birdcage

Withy Grove, Manchester M4 3AQ
Tel. no 0161 832 1700
www.birdcagelive.com
info@birdcagelive.com

The number one hen party venue in
Manchester, The Birdcage offers an
entertaining mix of drag queens, showgirls,
male dancers and non-stop DJs that will
have you dancing in your seats. This
flamboyant mix of disco and cabaret is on
every Friday and Saturday night. Parties can
be booked in advance or you can pay on
the door!

The Birdcage will bring some old-fashioned glitz and glamour to your hen party.

newcastle

Angel of the North (top), Millenium Bridge (middle), Laing Art Gallery (bottom).

Newcastle is the UK's most popular stag party venue. Well, girls, we can't have you lagging behind, now can we? With the country's very best nightlife crammed into one lovely city, it's time to get yourselves to Toon.

what to do

Newcastle's nightlife is unparalleled in the UK and you'll be hard-pushed to find a town anywhere in Europe that can beat the party vibe here. It's hen party heaven. Wey aye!

Newcastle has undergone a massive facelift in the past decade – while it was always known that Geordies liked to party, the city's caught up to provide the most incredible selection of pubs, bars, restaurants and clubs. Every taste is catered for, and it's usually easy on the bank balance. The locals may have a reputation for being hard, but that's really due to their ability to go out in sub-zero temperatures wearing almost nothing – you'll find a warm welcome in Newcastle and lots of hen and stag groups partying hard with you.

Apart from the nightlife, the shopping's great over in Gateshead at the Metro Centre, which has over 330 stores and 50 restaurants. The arts centre at Gateshead, the Quayside and the older parts of the city centre have all been revamped and made gorgeous, so it's a great area to look around in the daytime and is fast becoming one of Europe's established city break destinations. You'll find beautiful cafes, galleries and museums, if you're more into sporty action, then check out the horse and dog racing for authentic North-easterly fun.

10 good reasons

1. **brilliant clubs**
2. **the Metro Centre**
3. **Newcastle Brown Ale**
4. **footy at St James' Park**
5. **decent pies**
6. **Collingwood Street bars**
7. **greyhound racing**
8. **the Gateshead arts centre**
9. **little old pubs**
10. **buzzing atmosphere**

Newcastle's grand Grey Street.

sounds of the city

Natural woman Are you a Geordie lass who's feeling just a bit past all this clubbing malarkey? Or maybe you've booked accommodation for a couple of nights, but don't want to party both Friday and Saturday because you'd quite like to be alive on Sunday? Well, here's a top Newkey night in – it'll make you feel like you've taken a one way trip to heaven. Contact The Pamper Party (thepamperparty.co.uk) and they'll arrange for local beauty and massage therapists to visit and give you all treatments. Everyone chips in for shiatsu massage, manicure, reiki, henna tattoos and many more luxurious treats – a party with ultimate chill factor, especially if everyone brings a bottle of fizz or some nibbles along. This is one way to show your friends that you love them. And you know what that means don't you? Wedding presents...

Girls just want to have fun On the other hand...if you're after big thrills and desire large amounts of adrenalin coursing through your veins, take a trip to Cumbria and visit Dave's Adventure Company. The lovely people there will put together a tailormade package of exciting challenges totally bespoke to your hen party. Just tell Dave what you chicks are after and he will do the rest. Whether you want climbing, abseiling, canoeing, gorge walking, ghyll scrambling, archery, caving, kayaking or mountaineering, Dave will fix it up fo you and, with 20 years experience of making adventures, he'll ensure that you're all 100% safe and you have the time of your lives.

Diamonds are a girl's best friend
If you want a quality night with a few choice friends, head for Central Station area, increasingly referred to as the Diamond Strip for its gorgeous eateries bars and clubs. It starts with Revolution on the corner of Collingwood Street and reaches down to include the intimate Madame Koos and the very cool Bijoux. This area is dressed up WAG land, and not the place to pitch up in a novelty hat and order a pint with a straw. If the latter's more your bag then head for the Quayside and Bigg Market for unpretentious fun amid loads of other hens and stags – an unbeatable vibe, good value drinks and an array of bars and clubs to choose from. You know it makes sense.

Bring a the pampering to you with a relaxing party at your house courtesy of ThePamperParty.co.uk.

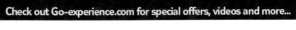

Milkshake Time was when women weren't really supposed to enjoy sex. While we're all a bit more enlightened these days, most of us could still do with some guidance in the art of sweet lurve – and a good laugh at the male genitalia while we're at it. Cue Milky Moments (!!??) foreplay lessons, hosted by Tiger Tiger at The Gate. MMs' private hen parties will show you how to deal effectively with a large appendage, should one arise.

It's oh so quiet The Silent Disco can provide you with a quieter night, if that's what you're after, but you'll probably end up in fits of laughter. Just picture your mates, all headphoned up and dancing away in a silent room. Have a look at silentdiscokit.co.uk.

Spies Your mission: to crack codes, find out who's the genius in your group or take over the town, Monopoly style… with Wildgoose Treasure Hunts you can choose a challenge that will get your brains working and introduce some hilarious competition to your weekend in Newcastle. The huntthegoose.co.uk team can either be there on the day or send you a DIY pack, and you'll spend two–three hours somewhere in the city, finding clues, solving riddles and taking ridiculous photographs, all against the clock. It's the perfect excuse to wear Harry Potter specs or deerstalker hats, if you needed an excuse of course. And yes, you can get a package that ties in with a pub crawl…

The last laugh If you opt for a hilarious daytime activity, be it foreplay lessons, treasure hunting or any number of driving experiences you can get in Newcastle and Gateshead, keep the laughs coming all evening by booking the Hyena Comedy Café. The venue's right in the city centre and you can turn up for great comedians, food, drinks and dancing to keep the ladies happy until the wee small hours.

'been there...'

My memories of Newcastle are a bit hazy. We dumped our bags in the hotel and went out on a cocktail cruise from about 5 o'clock! The locals were dead friendly, we got chatting with quite a few randoms throughout the night, probably because we were dressed as show girls! The bars were fab – really lively and good value. It's a top place to go for your hen.

With a Milky Moments party everyone get a badge with their alias for the evening!

where to stay

Feel like lady muck in your uber cool Tyneside hotel suite or stumble into your B&B in the early hours. Newcastle welcomes the girl-about-town, whatever her budget.

hotels and b&bs

Beamish Park Hotel ££

Beamish Park Hotel, Marley Hill,
Newcastle Upon Tyne, NE16 5EG
Tel. no 01207 230666
www.beamish-park-hotel.co.uk
reception@beamish-park-hotel.co.uk

Situated in beautiful countryside, just one mile from Beamish and only 10 minutes' drive from Newcastle city centre, the Beamish Park is an independently owned hotel with 42 bedrooms. Adjacent to the hotel is a golf academy, including a nine-hole par three course, practice greens and bunkers and a 20 bay flood-lit golf driving range.

Grainger Hotel B&B ££

1–3 Graingerville North, Westgate
Road, Newcastle Upon Tyne NE4 6UJ
Tel. no 0191 298 3800
www.graingerhotel.co.uk
info@graingerhotel.co.uk

Grainger Hotel has easy access to the city centre and makes the perfect base to explore the North East of England. All the guest rooms and suites of this luxury bed and breakfast are tastefully decorated in an elegant style using rich fabrics and ornate furnishings. All rooms are equipped with satellite TV.

Roselodge House £

Benwell Lane, Benwell, Newcastle
Upon Tyne NE15 6RU
Tel. no 0191 274 7388
www.roselodgehouse.com
ijaz.sarwar@btinternet.com

✳ **shared room without breakfast**
£ under £30
££ £30–£60
£££ over £60
pppn

Initially built as a Church, now an impressive B&B boasting 50 luxurious rooms. Sympathetically restored to retain the stunning Gothic architecture, The Roselodge provides comfortable beds at affordable prices. All rates include breakfast and complimentary toiletries. Just 10 minutes away from the city centre, they can accommodate large group bookings up to 30 people.

Royal Station Hotel ££

Neville Street, Newcastle
Upon Tyne NE1 5DH
Tel. no 0191 232 0781
www.royalstationhotel.com
info@royalstationhotel.com

Conveniently located next to Central Station, the three-star Royal Station Hotel combines elegant Victorian architecture with up-to-date facilities. There are 144 spacious ensuite bedrooms and a leisure club with indoor swimming pool, jacuzzi, steam room and plunge pool as well as the popular Destination Bar.

The George Hotel £

88 Osbourne Road, Jesmond,
Newcastle Upon Tyne NE2 2AP
Tel. no 0191 281 4442
www.georgehotel-newcastle.co.uk
info@georgehotel-newcastle.co.uk

This friendly hotel is modern and pleasant providing excellent value for money. Rooms are comfortable with ensuite facilities, triples and quads are available. For large group bookings enquire about special rates. The city centre is just a 10-minute taxi ride away and there's a rank right outside the hotel.

self-catering

Chapel House Apartments ££

Causey Row, Marley Hill, Newcastle
Upon Tyne NE16 5EJ
Tel. no 01207 290992
www.chapelhouseapartments.co.uk
chapelhouseapartments@hotmail.co.uk

These four studio apartments, part of a converted chapel, overlook rolling countryside just 8 miles from Newcastle and 4 miles from the Metro Centre. Each double studio has a fitted kitchen/dining area, ensuite bathroom with shower, independent access and parking directly outside.

Coastal Retreats ££

9 Causey St, Gosforth,
Newcastle-upon-Tyne
NE3 4DJ
Tel. no 0191 2851272
www.coastalretreats.co.uk
info@coastalretreats.co.uk

These five-star luxury self-catering cottages feature professionally designed contemporary interiors with gorgeous soft furnishings and fully equipped kitchens. Guests also enjoy Leisure Club membership for the duration of their stay.

Eland Farm ££

Eland Green Farm, Ponteland
NE20 9UR
Tel. no 01661 822188
www.elandfarm.co.uk
clhs@eland-green.fsnet.co.uk

Just 9 miles north-west of Newcastle and set in idyllic surroundings of 200 acres of grass farm, Eland Farm provides self-catering holiday homes to escape the hustle and bustle of the big city. The farm offers breathtaking views of the Cheviot Hills whilst being within walking distance of friendly pubs, shops and restaurants. Recently converted from a 250-year-old stable block, these three-star cottages give the luxury of modern interiors, but with bags of character.

Hedley Grange Holiday Cottages £

Hedley West Farm, Hedley Lane,
Newcastle upon Tyne NE16 5EQ
Tel. no 01207 232959
www.hedleygrange.co.uk
info@hedleygrange.co.uk

These exclusive barn conversions, Swallows and Woodpeckers, offer stylish, modern accommodation in a perfect rural setting on the border between Northumberland and County Durham. They are set in a secluded garden overlooking a nine-hole golf course. Both have fully fitted kitchens, gas central heating, electric cooker, TV, video, radio, fridge, microwave, iron and use of washer/dryer. Both apartments have safe parking and south-facing furnished patios.

shared room without breakfast

£ under £30
££ £30–£60
£££ over £60
pppn

Newton Hall and Cottages ££

Newton by the Sea, Nr Alnwick,
Northumberland NE66 3DZ
Tel. 01665 576239
www.newtonholidays.co.uk
info@newtonholidays.co.uk

This magnificent Georgian house has nine bedrooms and loads of charm. It stands majestically in 4 acres of beautiful grounds with three accompanying cottages, and is the perfect costal hideaway within minutes of white sandy beaches. The Hall sleeps 18, but can cater for parties as large as 35, if you include the cottages, which are available separately and sleep four–six people. There are nine large double bedrooms in the main house, a fitted kitchen, a dining room with a large table and a drawing room with a full-sized snooker table and a huge world map. Facilities include five widescreen TVs, DVDs and Sky, Wi-Fi and laundry. It is a wonderful location from which to explore this gorgeous part of Northumberland, designated an area of outstanding natural beauty by the National Trust. Newton Hall is less than an hour from Newcastle and 90 minutes from Edinburgh.

where to eat and drink

bars

Bijoux

Mosley Street, Newcastle Upon Tyne
NE1 1DF
Tel. no 0191 260 2378
www.bijouxbar.co.uk
manager@bijouxbar.co.uk

Bijoux bar is the latest edition to the Diamond strip of Newcastle's Mosley Street and Collingwood Street. This intimate and glamorous little bar serves a selection of wines, world beers and fresh cocktails.

There's no shortage of places to enjoy fine wines.

Madame Koos

36 Collingwood Street,
Newcastle NE1 1JF
Tel. no 0191 261 8271
www.madamekoo.co.uk
info@madamekoo.co.uk

This Oriental-styled bar with colourful lanterns and Asian artefacts is a hidden gem just waiting for you to discover the party atmosphere there. The Sneaky Disco plays classic soul, disco, R'n'B, indie, rock and pop, plus all the cheesy choons you could wish for and they're proud of it!

Revolution

Barclays Bank Chambers, Collingwood Street, Newcastle upon Tyne NE1 1JF
Tel. no 0191 261 8901
www.revolution-bars.co.uk/newcastleut

Revolution Newcastle is a luxurious bank conversion with original 30-foot high ceilings, marble pillars and classic wood features. It has cemented itself in the Newcastle scene with a great reputation for fantastic music, a great atmosphere and excellent service. Food is served all day until 8pm with a delicious selection of homemade stone-baked pizza right through until 1am.

The Cooperage

32 The Close, Quayside, Newcastle Upon Tyne NE11 3RF
Tel. no 0191 233 2940
www.cooperage1730.co.uk

One of the oldest buildings in the city, dating back to the 13th century, The Cooperage is full of olde worlde charm. With its reputation for excellent real ales, this pub draws huge crowds, especially at the weekend. Split into several bars and a nightclub, you'll find a lively mix of jazz, soul, funk and latin salsa on most nights at The Cooperage.

Tiger Tiger

The Gate, Newgate Street, Newcastle Upon Tyne NE1 5RE
Tel. no 0191 235 7065
www.tigertiger-newcastle.co.uk
info@tigertiger-newcastle.co.uk

With six bars, a restaurant and a lively club, this is not a place to get bored! A range of different styles across the bars means there's something for everyone and at the weekend the music varies from chart anthems in Tiger and Raffles to the best of the 70s and 80s in Groovy and Ibiza house classics and 90s pop in the White Room.

estaurants

Apartment £££
28–32 Collingwood Street, Newcastle
Upon Tyne NE1 1JF
Tel. no 0191 281 9609
www.apartment-luxebar.com
info@apartment-luxebar.com

This seductive restaurant, bar and members'
club is styled like a Manhattan apartment with
warehouse-sized windows, exposed brick
and solid walnut. East meets West in the
varied and imaginative menu and comes
together to provide a chic and unrivalled
dining experience in this part of the UK.

Frankie and Benny's ££
John Dobson Street, Northumberland
Road Newcastle Upon Tyne NE1 8JF
Tel. no 0191 261 4328
www.frankieandbennys.com

This retro 50s style New York Italian
restaurant and bar always has a great
atmosphere for large group dining. They
even have an online party maker that will
invite the guests for you!

Hotel du Vin Bistro ££
Allan House, City Road, Newcastle
Upon Tyne NE1 2BE
Tel. no 0191 229 2200
www.hotelduvin.com/newcastle
reception.newcastle@hotelduvin.com

Once the home of the Tyne Tees Steam
Shipping Company, it is now a stylish
boutique hotel with classy bistro and bar. The
menu is rooted in classic European cuisine
with a contemporary edge. You'll find
sensibly priced seasonal dishes using locally
sourced produce where possible.

Rocco Bar Trattoria £
22 Leazes Park Road, Newcastle
Upon Tyne NE1 4PG
Tel. no 0191 232 5871
www.roccobar.co.uk
roccobar@live.co.uk

Formerly La Toscana, this new incarnation
continues to serve top-quality Italian cuisine.
Bar Rocco will create a tailormade party
menu for your hen party. Just contact them in
advance to discuss.

**2 courses
+ half a bottle
of wine**

£ under £20
££ £20–£35
£££ over £35

The seductive atmosphere at Apartment Luxebar.

Mandarin Restaurant ££
14–18 Stowell Street, Newcastle
Upon Tyne NE1 4XQ
Tel. no 0191 261 7960
www.mandarin-newcastle.com

For some seriously good Chinese and
Szechaun food, try Mandarin. You can
experience a Chinese feast with one of their
banquet menus, starting at less than £11 per
head, featuring favourites such as BBQ ribs,
Sweet and Sour Pork, Lemon Chicken and
King Prawns in Black Bean Sauce.

Starters & Puds £££
2–6 Shakespeare Street, Newcastle
upon Tyne NE1 6AQ
Tel. no 0191 233 2515
www.startersandpuds.co.uk
eat@startersandpuds.co.uk

Starters & Puds is an exciting new concept in
leisurely eating. They take the best of savoury
and sweet cuisine, mixing it with friendly yet
distinctive surroundings and adding in a
large helping of relaxed ambience. You can
choose several starter dishes like tapas and
share around the table. You'll find this recipe
for a successful eating experience right in
the heart of Newcastle, adjacent to the
Theatre Royal.

where to party

You may be slightly confused by the sheer choice of clubs and bars in which to party your last weekend of freedom away, but if you want fun, you're in the right city.

You can expect some steamy action in Newcastle's top nightspots.

Bambu

13 Grainger Quarter, Newcastle
Upon Tyne NE1 1UW
Tel. no 0191 261 5811
blubambu@pbr.uk.com

Formerly known as Blu Bambu, but now rebranded as Bambu, this is the ultimate party venue. Located in Bigg Market you'll always find a fun party zone occurring here. Find Bambu on facebook and write on the wall for guest list and Q jump entry.

Digital

Times Square, Newcastle
Upon Tyne NE1 4EP
Tel. no 0191 261 9755
www.yourfutureisdigital.com/newcastle
info@yourfutureisdigital.com

This is a club that is serious about its music and the speaker system is second to none. The weekend line up includes Wax:On – a mix of breakbeat, electro and hip hop – on Fridays, while the legendary house night, Shindig, is the main event on a Saturday.

Liquid & Envy

49 New Bridge Street West,
Newcastle Upon Tyne NE1 8AN
Tel. no 0191 261 2526
www.liquidclubs.com
newcastle@liquidclubs.com

With two large club rooms, a VIP area and outdoor area, Liquid & Envy has it all under one roof. Inside you'll find state-of-the-art sound and lighting systems and 360 degree plasma screens providing visuals whichever way you look. You'll find a mix of R'n'B and hip hop playing here on a Saturday night to a discerning clubbing crowd. For a more exclusive experience, pre-book tickets to the VIP area, also known as The Liquid Lounge, there are various party packages on offer, so give them a call and get your last night of freedom sorted in style.

6 A night out in Newcastle is full of surprises. 9

Northern Pole Dance

Looking for a hen do with a difference?

Pole dancing parties are an unforgettable way to celebrate a special occasion so why not round up the girls and prepare to let your inner diva shine...

Northern Pole Dance is the longest running company of its kind in the North East region, dedicated solely to providing pole dancing lessons and parties.

All instructors are friendly, outgoing and above all experienced, thus ensuring that you and your party guests have the best possible time.

All our parties include:

~ Basic lap dancing & pole tricks
~ Chocolates & bubbly for the hen
~ 'Pole Dancer of the Day' award
~ Photo session with your instructor
~ Certificate for all party members

So, what are you waiting for? Book a pole party today and learn how to strut your stuff with style!

Approved Dance School

Contact us on:
T/ 07732 891005
E/ info@northernpoledance.co.uk
W/ www.northernpoledance.co.uk

Nancy's Bordello

13 Argyle Street, Newcastle Upon Tyne
NE1 6PF
Tel. no 0191 260 2929
www.nancysbordello.com
info@nancysbordello.com

Newcastle's only World Music bar and club,
Nancy's is unique. A million miles away from
the corporate scene, at Nancy's you'll find a
melting pot of sounds and scenes bringing
you a remixed version of a nightclub. On a
Saturday night Salsa Viva rules with resident
DJ Coco Vega and guests featuring live
acoustic sessions with a variety of
performers. Dance the night away to the
sounds of salsa, merengue, bachata, cha
cha and latin house. Nancy's also serves up
some tasty food from all corners of the globe
so you have everything you need for an
international night out.

Sea

Neptune House, Quayside, Newcastle
Upon Tyne NE1 3ZQ
Tel. no 0191 230 1813
sea@pbr.uk.com
This stylish nightclub is full of glitz and
glamour and is a popular hang out of WAGS
and local celebs. Top DJs regularly play here
and if you want to chill out you can head to
The Viper Lounge for R'n'B. Alternatively, for a
more exclusive experience, try the VIP room.

Sea nightclub is the place to be seen.

*The light and airy bar at The Attic becomes cool and
seductive after dark.*

The Attic

25–27 Mosley Street, Newcastle
Upon Tyne NE1 1YF
Tel. no 0191 233 1396
theattic@pbr.uk.com

This recently refurbished 1000-capacity
nightclub has swiftly established itself with
the cool set in the city. Arranged on four
floors this funky club is a guaranteed
awesome night out.

World Headquarters Club

Curtis Mayfield House,Carliol Square,
East Pilgrim Street, Newcastle Upon
Tyne NE1 6UF
Tel. no 0191 281 3445
www.welovewhq.com
www.myspace.com/whq (MySpace)
info@welovewhq.com

World Headquarters is an independent club
and proud of it. Here you'll find something a
little bit different to the ubiquitous 'packages'
offered in many clubs. At this club you'll get
more of an underground experience driven
by good music, and it relies on word of
mouth to spread the message. It is laid out
over two floors: upstairs, with its booming
sound system and eye-catching murals, is
the main party scene, downstairs is a more
laid-back affair with comfy leather sofas, a
pool table and the finest selection of whisky
on offer in the city.

⧓ SalSeduce

Newcastle's Best
Salsa Experience

Looking for something different to do for your Hen party?

Look no further...

Salsa is a great way to ignite your celebrations. You will be taught to move to the Latin beats and rhythms of the salsa before dancing the night away in the vibrant city of Newcastle...it is the ultimate Hen Party salsa experience!

Taste all the passion and energy of the salsa in a fun-packed afternoon of dancing, taught by our experienced teachers, offering salsa to suit all abilities.

Relax and enjoy exotic cocktails while you dance and enjoy a memorable experience learning some sexy new moves and sampling some of the cultural secrets Newcastle has to offer.

Visit **www.salseduce.co.uk** for further details, contact Chris on 07862 249846 or email chris@salseduce.co.uk

newquay

It may be a fishing port, but Newquay is up there with our biggest cities when it comes to partying. The town is alive all summer, thanks to surfers, a thriving nightlife and loads of people looking for fun in the sun.

Newquay Bay (top), the harbour (middle), Fistral Beach (bottom).

what to do

Enjoying the general vibe that there's more to life than the 9–5, Newquay is relaxed by day and kicking at night. It's fun all year round, but in the summer you can't beat it.

The UK's surfing capital is one of Britain's most popular hen party destinations – even if you've no intention of dipping your toe in the North Atlantic, the pretty harbour, coastal scenery, party atmosphere and considerable wetsuit-clad eye candy in these parts should tempt you.

And just to tip the balance, Newquay is all about extreme fun, so for hens who want activities – from horse riding on the beach to hovercraft driving – you'll love all the opportunities here for fun and adventure.

There's plenty of accommodation available, but you'll find the best deals out of high season. Winter wetsuits available for hire mean that you can brave the water any time of year! It's not all sandy bunkhouses and tousled tresses, there are many beautiful hotels and self-catering properties in town.

10 good reasons

1. watching the surfers
2. fun and relaxed nightlife
3. unsophisticated fun
4. lovely sandy beaches
5. fresh seafood
6. surfing lessons
7. ice cream
8. the Eden Project
9. beautiful scenery
10. Cornish pasties

Check out the board action down at the beach.

sounds of the town

Hold me, thrill me, kiss me, kill me
Adventure Activities at Lusty Glaze beach offer various rock and sea adventures, and their hen packages are fantastic, especially the Extreme Experience, where you'll spend a morning coasteering or surfing, then after lunch scramble up a cliff assault course, walk a high wire over a chasm and take a high speed zip wire ride…all finished off with drinks on the beach. You can also book a Surf and Spa day or go for the I'm a Sealebrity challenge…believe us, the hen groups fare better than the stags when it comes to the Beach Tucker Trial.

What's goin' down A few miles inland from Newquay is the fantastic new Adrenalin Quarry. Here, you can scream very loudly as you travel at speed down the UK's longest zip wire. Deafen a friend on the twin zip or make it a solo mission as you step off the cliff and zoom over the lake below.

At the bottom of the quarry you can try your hand at hovercraft driving, giving it some serious welly on your solo adventure over land and lake. Just to make a full day of it, there's a karting centre at the quarry too, with Sodi GT2 karts and an 800m track. Kartworld do a great hen package with a proper, Grand Prix-style competition for groups of ten or more, as well as floodlit night karting. Have a look at the website: adrenalinquarry.co.uk.

Soul surfing One thing Newquay's not short on is surf schools. If you want the best quality instruction on offer look no further than the Rip Curl ESF Surf School. They are a level 4 school (the highest standard in the UK) and are walking distance from two amazing beaches. With both surfing and bodyboarding on offer and a complimentary bottle of fizz for hen parties they are a great choice. Learn to pop up and ride that board, or alternatively just cling on tight and try not to drown – it's a brilliant laugh and you'll hire good quality kit that will keep you all warm, no matter what the weather's doing. Tuition is available all year round and you can book a package with accommodation either at Carnmarth Hotel or Bertie's Lodge within walking distance of the sea. Check prices at englishsurfschool.com.

Learn to surf with Rip Curl ESF Surf School.

Knowing me, knowing you It's always good to be shown around an area by people who know and love it, which is exactly what you'll get if you book a hen party through Explore Southwest. This group of surfers, ex-travellers and beach bums have roamed the world and come back to Cornwall because they love it. They'll arrange accommodation, activities, clubs, bars and even eco-friendly transport to lovely Cornwall from any UK address see exploresouthwest.com.

A little less conversation What could be better than riding horses through the waves on a sunny morning in Cornwall? Newquay Riding Stables at Trenance will take you out on gorgeous steeds for a 1–2 hour trek, including that romantic canter along the beach. Cue slow mo and soft focus. If you want something with a little less chat time and a little more action, they do army mornings as part of adventure training. Intrigued? Find out more by contacting the company on 01637 872699. Make sure you do some inner thigh stretches first – you'll be walking like John Wayne if you don't.

I don't want to miss a thing This town is just wall to wall bars, surf shops, restaurants and clubs. Basically, it caters for a relaxed crowd who want to kick back after a day's surfing, so the atmosphere's happy and easy going – and fancy dress is much more common than smart casual round here. Have a simple bar crawl and enjoy the drinks promos, cheap eats and live music all over town.

For Big Nights Out choices include Sailors Club, Berties, Koola or Buzios…for a town this size the nightlife is amazing, so don't be tempted to collapse into bed after a day's surfing – partying hard is compulsory.

Gallop along the lovely beaches with Newquay Riding Stables.

where to stay

When the surf's down and the party's stumbled to a halt, sleep might be a plan. Newquay has masses of choice, but book early or you'll be kipping on the beach.

hotels

shared room without breakfast
£ under £30
££ £30–£60
£££ over £60
pppn

Bertie's Lodge £*
East Street, Newquay,
TR7 1DB
Tel. no 01637 870334
www.bertieslodge.co.uk
info@bertieslodge.co.uk

Berties Lodge is situated above Berties Pub and is an ideal location for any hen party. With a bar below and Berties nightclub on your doorstep plus great views of the beach, there is no better location. It's stylish budget accommodation with bunk beds and shared rooms. *Prices increase in high season.

Carnmarth Hotel ££
22 Headland Road, Newquay
Tel. no 01637 879571
www.carnmarth.com
enquiries@carnmarth.com

Overlooking the world famous Fistral Beach the Carnmarth is a sophisticated option. All the rooms have views of the sea or headland and some even have a private balcony. With the trendy C-bar on hand, it's a popular one.

Hotel Victoria ££
East Street, Newquay TR7 1DB
Tel. no 01637 872 255
www.hotel-victoria.co.uk
bookings@hotel-victoria.co.uk

The three-star Hotel Victoria is situated on the cliffs above the golden sands of Great Western beach with amazing views over Newquay Bay. It suits those seeking a higher class of accommodation with gym, indoor pool, spa and variety of rooms from doubles and twins to luxury suites. Book a surf package with the Rip Curl ESF Surf School.

Reef Island Surf Lodge £
30–32 Island Crescent,
Newquay TR7 1DZ
Tel. no 01637 879058
www.reefislandsurflodge.com
info@reefislandsurflodge.com

This funky retro 70s style surf lodge can accommodate large groups in a variety of rooms. They have secure storage for wetsuits and boards and on site is the Austin Powers style Reef Island bar. Book a package with Reef Surf School.

Tsunami Lodge £
84 Crantock Street, Newquay TR7 1JW
Tel. no 01637 872391
www.tsunami-lodge.co.uk
info@tsunami-lodge.co.uk

Small but perfectly formed this surf lodge offers four-person and six-person bunkrooms with ensuite shower rooms. The clean and comfortable surroundings make it a real home from home. Five minutes to the town centre and only a couple of minutes more to Fistral beach, Tsunami is very well located.

Hotel Victoria overlooking Newquay Bay.

self-catering

AbreakAway £
2 Higher Tower Road, Newquay TR7 1QL
Tel. no 07973 823083
www.abreakaway.co.uk
info@abreakaway.co.uk

A cross between serviced apartments and a hostel, this self-catering option could meet all your needs. Each self-contained apartment has bunk-bedded accommodation (apart from the penthouse with four single beds) with clean linen, an ensuite shower room, a kitchenette with microwave, fridge, crockery and cutlery. You will need to bring your own towels though. A few minutes' walk to Fistral beach and the centre, where all the night-time action takes place. You'll get your own key and there's no curfew!

Airborne Lodge £
98 Fore Street, Newquay TR7 1EY
Tel. no 01637 875648
www.airbornelodge.com
info@airbornelodge.com

This friendly and informal lodge is just five minutes' to the town centre and Fistral Beach. It has high quality twin and dorm rooms sleeping three–eight people. Bed linen is provided and there is a colour TV in every room. A large chillout lounge equipped with self-catering facilities and no curfew makes this a very relaxed place to stay.

Beachwalk Holiday House £
12 Belmont Place, Newquay TR7 1HG
Tel. no 07970 747109
www.beachwalkholidayhouse.co.uk
rich.holder@btopenworld.com

Just a few minutes walk from Fistral Beach, this pad sleeps eight in total luxury, with Playstation 3, iPod docking station, outside surf shower, gas barbecue and other surf break essentials. The minimum booking period is one week and make sure you book early for this popular rental.

Blue Bay Lodges £
Mawgan Porth Cornwall TR8 4DA
Tel. no 01637 860324

✳ shared room without breakfast

£ under £30
££ £30–£60
£££ over £60
pppn

www.bluebaycornwall.co.uk
hotel@bluebaycornwall.co.uk

If you're looking for a bit of peace and tranquility away from the buzz of Newquay itself, this could be the place for you. There are four individual lodges sleeping up to eight people with stunning views of the Vale of Lanhern. All guests are welcome to use the nearby Blue Bay hotel restaurant, bar and facilities.

Smugglers Haven £
Porth, Newquay TR8 4AS
Tel. no 01637 852000
www.smugglershaven.co.uk
kelly.roberts@cranstar.co.uk

Rent a caravan, wheel up in your VW van or pitch your tent at Smugglers for a fun-filled stay. With a heated outdoor swimming pool and the Shakin' Shack Bar to get your party started, it's going to be rockin'.

The Shakin' Shack bar at Smugglers Haven.

Tolcarne Beach Surf Shacks £
Narrowcliff, Newquay TR7 2QN
Tel. no 01637 872489
www.tolcarnebeach.co.uk
info@tolcarnebeach.com

If you want to roll out of bed and into the sea, this is your place to stay. Right on the beach, each shack sleeps four in bunks with bed linen provided. There's a shared shower area and kitchenette on site and a tap outside your shack.

WE'LL GET YOU WET

JUMP OFF A CLIFF ON THE UK'S LONGEST ZIP WIRE. GO WILD SWIMMING & TOMBSTONING ALL IN ONE PLACE

This is 100% no-holds-barred, adrenalin-fuelled fun. Ride The Zip over a beautiful quarry lake, climb dramatic cliffs, jump as far as you dare. Sort the hens from the chickens.

See videos, photos and book your session at:

ADRENALIN QUARRY///.co.uk

AS FEATURED ON CHANNEL FIVE'S GADGET SHOW

Large groups no problem. We go out of our way so you can go over the top. **Call 01579 308 204**

WHILE YOU'RE HERE, MAKE A DAY (AND NIGHT) OF IT
• Get a thirst on at Adrenalin Quarry • Hit our local beaches, restaurants & pubs • Party till dawn in Plymouth clubs...

PLYMOUTH: 20MINS • NEWQUAY 45MINS • LOOE 15MINS

where to eat and drink

Book yer wenches into the Newquay Meadery, or head to the quayside for ultra fresh seafood, before diving into the party vibe that defines Newquay summer nights.

bars & pubs

Buzios

54–56 East Street, Newquay TR7 1BE
Tel. no 01637 870300
www.buziosbar.co.uk
info@buziosbar.co.uk

This award-winning contemporary style cafe bar, which incorporates a restaurant, a club and a pool hall, brings a slice of city sophistication to the North Cornish coast. It's set on three floors and is open 'til 4am in high season. You can also hire it out for your own private do.

Central Inn

11 Central Square, Newquay TR7 1EU
Tel. no 01637 873810
www.staustellbrewery.co.uk
thecentral@staustellbrewery.co.uk

As the name suggests, The Central is right in the heart of Newquay town centre. This lively and friendly pub has a large outdoor terrace, perfect for a sundowner and a spot of people watching after a hard day's surfing. There's a cocktail bar and you can eat here too; later on the DJs get started in the dance bar.

Red Square

11–17 Gover Lane, Newquay TR7 1ER
Tel. no 01637 878823
www.redsquare.co.uk
info@redsquareclub.co.uk

A bar and a club, Red Square boasts the largest Vodka menu in Newquay. So if you're a fan of the Russian tipple, this is the bar for you. They have everything from Absinthe (over 21s only – it's strong stuff!) to Creme Egg flavoured Vodka and about 60 others in between. Vodka lovers' paradise.

The cool bar area at Fistral Blu restaurant.

The Chy Bar & Kitchen

12 Beach Road, Newquay TR7 1ES
Tel. no 01637 873415
www.thekoola.com/the-chy-bar
the.koola@virgin.net

'Chy' is Cornish for 'home' and the relaxed atmosphere here will certainly give you a warm feeling. A cafe bar during the day, The Chy transforms into a lively cocktail bar later on with live DJs. The Kitchen serves modern British food and offers a party menu for larger groups. The homemade 100% pure British beef burger, The Chy Burger, is a smash hit.

Two Clomes

Quintrell Downs, Newquay TR8 4PD
Tel. no 01637 871163

Just outside Newquay, in the gorgeous Cornish countryside, is a real traditional pub serving great food at excellent value. If you want to get away from it all and sample some quality seafood with different specials every day then the Two Clomes is the one. They don't skimp on the portions here and are well known for their wines, so if you've got a good appetite, then come here and enjoy a chilled glass of wine in a quiet setting. If the sun shines on you, dine outside on the terrace.

estaurants

Drinks on the balcony at Fistral Blu watching the sun set is the perfect way to start the evening off.

Fistral Blu ££

Fistral Beach, Headland Road,
Newquay TR7 1HY
Tel. no 01637 879444
www.fistral-blu.co.uk
nfo@fistral-blu.co.uk

With panoramic views of Fistral Beach, the
Fistral Blu bar and bistro has a fabulous
setting, perfect for watching the sun go down
over the Atlantic. The varied menu with strong
Mediterranean influences offers something to
tantalise everyone's tastebuds.

New Harbour ££

South Quay Hill, Newquay Harbour,
Newquay TR7 1HT
Tel. no 01637 874062
www.new-harbour.com
info@new-harbour.com

Fresh, steamed mussels.

To sample some of the freshest locally
caught seafood in a sophisticated
environment, New Harbour is the place to
book. With lobster, spider crab and fresh fish
on the menu they are famous for their 'sexy
fish and chips'. The emphasis here is on
simple food cooked to perfection.

Newquay Meadery £

Marcus Hill, Newquay TR7 1BD
Tel. no 01637 873000
www.newquaymeadery.co.uk
info@newquaymeadery.co.uk

If you want to join up with other hen and stag
parties on your last night of freedom then
book into the Meadery for a night of medieval
munching. The friendly hosts can offer you a
party menu at a price per head to suit your
group. We say let the feasting commence.

Senor Dicks £

East Street, Newquay TR7 1DB
Tel. no 01637 870350
www.senor-dicks.co.uk
info@senor-dicks.co.uk

Mexican food is always a popular choice and
Senor Dicks serves up authentic Mexican
recipes, not just hot hot hot food. Wash it all
down with plenty of Mexican cerveza or the
best Margaritas in Cornwall and you have a
recipe for a night full of spice.

where to party

Get your fancy dress on and hit the town. With multi-room clubs, small venues with great DJs and live acts, and loads of bars and clubs, it's a great place to party.

Radio One's Scott Mills at Berties.

Berties Club
East St, Newquay TR7 1DB,
Tel. no 01637 870369
www.bertiesclub.com
tony.townsend@bertiesclub.com

Anyone who's been to Newquay has been to Berties. It claims to be Cornwall's largest nightclub with a capacity of more than 2000. It's a firm favourite of stag and hen parties with many of the UK's biggest stars playing the venue, from Radio One's Scott Mills to world dance DJ Eddie Halliwell. Berties also has exclusive VIP booths and a VIP room for stags and hens to hire for the evening. It even has its very own party bus, decked out like a disco inside and free limo service running from the town's bars.

Koola
12 Beach Road, Newquay TR7 1ES
Tel. no 01637 873415
www.thekoola.com
thekoola@virgin.net

If you're after live DJs and an electric atmosphere, head to Koola – home of underground music. The industrial-chic decor of this intimate venue on three floors gives it a really edgy feel only surpassed by the DJ line-up. Past events include Ice-T, Groove Rider, Judge Jules, The Kaiser Chiefs and the list goes on. With audio delights from the worlds of hip-hop, drum and bass, through funk and beats to all types of house, alternative rock & live bands, music aficionados need look no further.

The pulsating dancefloor at Pure.

Pure

52 Tolcarne Road, Newquay TR7 2NQ
Tel. no 01637 850313
www.purenewquay.com
info@purenewquay.com

Formerly the legendary Tall Trees, Pure is a brand spanking new incarnation of the South West's no.1 superclub. With ultra cool decor and the best dance music around, Pure offers a quality night out. If there's eight or more of you, why not call ahead and book a table in the club's elegant VIP area: The Island. You'll get the full celeb treatment – priority entry, a table for the night and champagne on arrival. You can even book the Pure Party Bus to transport your group here from Bodmin, St Austell, Wadebridge, Truro, Falmouth and Penzance. Call Pure Transport on 01637 800150 for more details. Also ask about the new comedy club at Pure.

Sailors Club

Fore Street, Newquay
Tel. no 01637 872838
www.sailorsnightclub.com
info@sailorsnightclub.com

Playing commercial dance, hip hop and party anthems, the sailors is a popular destination for clubbers in Newquay. Whether you head straight for the dancefloor, hang out on the balcony above or go for a cheeky concoction in Sailors' legendary cocktail bar, there's

something to please everyone. With plenty of drinks on promotion and very friendly door tax. It's got to be on your map.

The Barracuda Bar

27–29 Cliff Road, Newquay TR7 2NE
Tel. no 01637 875800
www.barracudanewquay.com
newquay@barracudabars.co.uk

It's a bar, it's a club, it's a live music venue and it's massive! Arranged on three floors of fabulous fun, there are plenty of bars doing great drinks promotions, dancefloors, live music, food, pool, fruit machines...frankly, you could spend all day here!

The Beach Niteclub

1 Beach Road, Newquay TR7 1ES
Tel. no 01637 872194
www.beachclubnewquay.com
info@beachclubnewquay.com

With three floors, four bars and two DJs playing every Saturday, this is a club with plenty of choice. Located right in the centre of town and close to the Newquay Meadery and Fistral Blu restaurants, they can arrange hen night packages with both of these restaurants. Alternatively, you can pre-book entry to the club giving you fast track admission to this busy nightspot, so that you can get on with the serious business of partying.

The Ultimate Hen's Guide to... Newquay

The Hotel

3* Hotel Victoria
Pamper packages & pool. Surf lessons
www.hotel-victoria.co.uk   01637 872255

The Restaurant

Senor dicks Mexican & Fiesta Cocktail Bar
www.senor-dicks.co.uk   01637 870350

The Bar

Buzios Bar & Restaurant
Cocktails & late nights
www.buziosbar.co.uk   01637 870300

The Club

Berties Nightclub
Cornwalls largest nightclub
VIP Booths & Guest DJs
www.bertiesclub.com
01637 870369

nottingham

Famed for Robin Hood, lace-making and bicycle-manufacture, you might be tempted to bypass Nottingham. But don't – we've spent a few wild weekends in this kicking city and it ticks all the boxes for a fabulous hen do.

what to do

Fringed by historic forest, Nottingham's got beauty and history, but also boasts fabulous nightlife, superb shopping and more than its share of great pubs. No hoodies please!

Vibrant Nottingham is one of the greatest UK cities to have a wander and shop in – it's full of lovely architecture and arcades, such as Bridlesmith Gate, which dates from the Middle Ages but is now lined with top high street names including Whistles, Diesel and Paul Smith.

Non-shoppers, look for archery in Sherwood Forest (can you resist?), off-roading, blindfold driving, paintball, assault courses and more mentalism – go through a party organiser or visit adranalinejungle.com.

Hockley Village, near the Lace Market, is the local answer to Soho. Here you'll find boutiques, cafés and arthouse cinema. Parties can book The Screen Room – it's the smallest cinema in the world with just 21 seats. You could even line up a little surprise – you can show your own DVDs here (we're thinking home movie horror).

Every July Woolaton Park hosts the Splendour festival – recent headline acts included The Pet Shop Boys, Noisettes and Athlete. Rock City regularly books huge names, from Lily Allen to The Zutons. Clubbing's big in this city, so there's something for everyone. Dress is relaxed, but glam or fancy dress are definitely welcomed.

If wedding planning's left you seriously dry on the humour front, book Funhouse, the Glee Club, Jongleurs or Just the Tonic, or aim for the autumn comedy festival – in its second year and planting funny stuff all over town, with lots of people off the telly, improvisation shows and pub poetry.

10 good reasons

1. great shopping
2. top clubs
3. live music scene
4. archery in Sherwood Forest
5. high wire at Go Ape
6. watersports centre
7. Gatecrasher nightclub
8. Ye Olde Trip to Jerusalem
9. Coco lounge cocktails
10. good enuff for Robin...

sounds of the city

Roller boogie Do you remember roller disco? Any idiot could do it, and it was the only place you could pull at 6mph whilst wearing dungarees. Children of the 70s and 80s, rejoice and get your skates on for Superfunk at Nottingham Trent Student's Union. You'll need to dress funky retro if you don't want to feel upstaged by the young upstart students who are trying to claim roller disco for their own. Push them over and show us some of that backwards criss-crossy stuff. Groovy baby!

My baby just cares for me What do models do when they're not pouting in front of a camera? We've just discovered, to our joy, that the beautiful people aren't just having a rooftop Jacuzzi together at Harvey Nicks – they're actually available to wait on us at parties. Yay! The models from Slaves to Vanity can appear in various states

of dress to hand out drinks and canapés at the venue you've hired for the night. You want greased up, muscle-bound hotties in swimwear? No problem. They specialise in fitness freaks – look at the gallery at slavestovanity.co.uk. Now why can't normal men have stomachs like that? Bah. Slaves to Vanity will provide the models, but they can also organise your whole event – if you're a gal who likes to kick back and enjoy the eye-popping candy, this could be for you.

I'm an ape man As the song observes, modern life can get a little hectic, and you'll sometimes feel primal urges to get into the country – and, possibly, primate urges to get up a tree. Judging by the popularity of Go Ape, where you zip, high wire and swing through the forest, this is normal. It's an easy hop to Sherwood Pines from Nottingham on the bus or train and, once you're there, you'll find yourself in Robin Hood country learning how to swing and holler like Tarzan. Monkey magic starts at goape.co.uk.

Book some eye candy to wait on you for the day.

Row, row, row your boat With great value accommodation, and sports from kayaking, raft-building and sailing to powerboating and whitewater rafting – the National Water Sports Centre iş just ten minutes from Nottingham City Centre and can provide all you need for a fantastic, if damp, hen weekend. Packages include a multi-activity ticket for four activities in one day at just £30 per head. Check out nottinghamwatersports.co.uk.

You are beautiful There are some things we're reluctant to share. But, as it's you... Take a look at Eden Hall (www.edenspa.co.uk). This incredible spa has sumptuous and sparkling facilities. The 'Relaxed Experience' includes use of the salt-water vitality pool, sauna, saunarium, steam, herbal and hot rooms, posh showers, water therapy area, gymnasium, exercise and relaxation classes. You'll be Hank Marvin after all that, so thankfully there's also three-course lunch in the Seventh Heaven Restaurant. Ohhh, we'd give nearly anything to be wrapped in one of those fluffy robes right now!

I wanna sex you up Every month, The Bodega Social on Pelham Street hosts Nottingham's finest burlesque night – The Pitty Patt Club. Admire the likes of Teddy Bare, Cherry DeVille and Pinky Blush as the Deville Dolls Dance Troupe struts into action and shows you what burlesque is all about. If you get a taste for it, drop in to the venue at 1.30pm next day for a fabulous workshop – you'll learn all those balloon popping, bump and grinding moves. Have a look on My Space or call the Bodega box office on 0115 950 5078.

Oh daddy Feeling like a lost little girl with no idea what to do? Never you fret, call the nice folks at East Midlands Chaffeur Services on 0115 822 4003. They can suggest tons of activities, hotels and venues, and set up a tailor-made itinerary. They'll get you discounts where possible, too. This is a local service, so you can guarantee good advice and local know how. The chauffeur will then pick you up, ferry you about, wait for you, and not even tell you off, which makes him even better than your own dad.

> **The Market Square in the centre of town is a great place to head for. There's always something going on and you get a great view of the area from the top of the big wheel.**

Travel in style on your hen party with a limo service.

where to stay

From camping in Sherwood Forest to the chic hotels of Chapel Bar, Nottingham can offer accommodation to fulfil the dreams of any potential hen.

hotels

Holiday Inn Express ££
Chapel Quarter, Chapel Bar, Nottingham NG1 6JSE
Tel. no 0115 941 9931
www.hiexpress.com

Simply walk out of this eye-catching hotel and you'll find yourself at the heart of the city in the Chapel Bar area, home to trendy al fresco dining and vibrant nightlife. With free high-speed wireless internet access you'll have no problems whacking your photo's straight on to Facebook for the stags to see what a great time you're having. Oh and you'll be pleased to hear that the hotel offers a complimentary Express Start Hot breakfast each morning.

Ibis Hotel £
16 Fletcher Gate, Nottingham NG1 2FS
Tel. no 0115 985 3600
www.ibishotels.com

If you're looking for accommodation smack bang in the heart of Nottingham this two-star Ibis hotel could be just what you're after. With 142 modern guest rooms there should be no problem fitting you in. All rooms are air conditioned, offer wireless internet access and satellite TV. After a night on the town you'll be delighted to discover the hotel and it even has a tram stop right outside.

Jurys Inn Hotel £/££
Station Street, Nottingham NG2 3BJ
Tel. no 0115 901 6700
www.jurysinns.com

The three-star Jurys Inn is close to the train station and has a local tram stop close by. The hotel has a bar and restaurant, and the caffeine addicts in the party will be pleased to discover an Il Barista Coffee bar here.

✳ shared room without breakfast

£ under £30
££ £30–£60
£££ over £60
pppn

Expect to be asked for a security bond of £100 per room for groups, which is returnable on check out.

Lace Market Hotel ££
29–31 High Pavement, Nottingham NG1 1HE
Tel. no 0115 852 3232.
www.lacemarkethotel.co.uk
stay@lacemarkethotel.co.uk

If it's pure style that you're looking for then try the four-star luxury Lace Market Hotel, which was formerly a Georgian home. Situated in the heart of Nottingham's trendy Lace Market, the hotel boasts a 2 AA Rosette restaurant (Merchants), glamorous cocktail bar (Saint), and its own Michelin Guide featured gastro pub, Cock & Hoop...what more could you ask for? But if it's a bit of privacy that you're looking for, then you could book private dining for up to 20 guests.

The Nottingham Belfry ££
Mellor's Way, Off Woodhouse Way, Nottingham NG8 6PY
Tel. no 0115 973 9393
www.qhotels.co.uk
nottinghambelfry@qhotels.co.uk

Belonging to the nationally recognised brand of hotels (Q Hotels), The Belfry is located on the edge of Nottingham, five minutes by car from the park and ride into the city centre. With its ultra modern decor, spa facility, health club, free internet access (up to 2 hours) and inclusive of breakfast, it should deliver everything that you might need on a weekend away with the girls. And for those friends that might need to fly to Nottingham, the hotel is just 15 miles from the airport.

self-catering

City Base Apartments £–££

c/o 259 Marine Road Central,
Morecambe LA4 4BJ
Tel. no 0845 2269831
www.citybaseapartments.com
info@citybaseapartments.com

A range of contemporary and comfortable
one- and two-bedroom apartments are
available only a short walk from the heart of
Nottingham's city centre within easy reach of
the main shopping and entertainment areas.

City Pads Serviced Apartments £

111 The Ropewalk, Nottingham
NG1 5DU
Tel. no 0870 850 7995 or 0115 950
2996
www.citypadsservicedapartments.co.uk
sales@citypadsservicedapartments.co.uk

Just a short walk from the heart of the city,
111 The Ropewalk offers the finest
apartments in one of Notttingham's most
desirable locations. These opulent, spacious,
modern luxury apartments provide the
ultimate city experience at an
affordable price. Despite the
luxurious setting, the apartments
still have a 'home from home'
atmosphere to make your hen
weekend relaxing and
enjoyable.

Come 2 Nottingham £

Tel. no 07957 266230
www.come2nottingham.co.uk
steve@steveshouses.com
A wide range of luxury self-catering
apartments, flats and houses in Nottingham
are available at affordable prices through this
website. The perfect way to spend your hen
weekend with friends and family.

Oakerthorpe Manor ££

c/o Derbyshire Country Cottages
Tel. no 01629 583545
www.derbyshirecountrycottages.co.uk
enquiries@derbyshirecountrycottages.
co.uk

Close to Matlock and the magnificent Peak
District, Oakerthorpe Manor is a fabulous little

'stately home' set in exotically planted
grounds and with lots of charming period
accommodation combining with a super
modern kitchen and 'state of the art'
bathrooms. As soon as you arrive through
the electric gates and down the private drive
you will realise that this is somewhere very
special! The Manor just oozes character with
its beautifully tiled hallway, etched glass
panels, corniced ceilings, heavy panelled
doors, fantastic fireplaces and grand
staircase. The lovely hallway, four reception
rooms, panelled games room, four en-suite
and four other bedrooms, dining kitchen and
wonderful large bathrooms make this an
exceptional hen party venue.

Premier Apartments Nottingham £

Ice House, Belward Street, Nottingham,
NG1 1JZ
Tel. no 0115 908 2000
www.premierapartmentsnottingham.com
info@premierapartmentsnottingham.com

These luxury apartments, centrally located,
are the perfect alternative to a
traditional style hotel. They
combine modern elegance and
comfort to offer guests a
relaxing and enjoyable stay.
There is even a secure on-
site car park, which is ideal if
you have hens travelling by
car for the big event. Only a
short walk to the main
shopping areas and plenty of
bars and restaurants nearby, these
are a great value choice of self-catering
accommodation.

Urban Self Catering £

7 The Pinnacle, Cottage Terrace,
Nottingham NG1 5AS
Tel. no 0115 950 9415
www.selfcatering-directory.co.uk

Urban Self Catering apartments and houses
are perfect for a short break in Nottingham
offering a range of accommodation to suit
individual taste and budget. Perfect for a
short stay and centrally located, these
apartments are an excellent option for hen
dos and other occasions.

**✳ shared room
without
breakfast
£ under £30
££ £30–£60
£££ over £60
pppn**

where to eat and drink

With a big redevelopment in the centre, Nottingham has a modern cafe culture vibe. You won't be short of places to eat and drink in this city.

bars & pubs

Revolution

7 Broad Street, Hockley, Nottingham
NG1 3AJ
Tel. no 0115 948 1964
www.revolution-bars.co.uk/hockley

With its dedicated party planners to organise your Hen do, choosing to spend your night in a Revolution bar could take away all the laborious organisational duties and enable everyone to join the fun without any stress. Well located in the fashionable Lace Market area of Nottingham, you can consume your favourite vodka shots and cocktails whilst dancing the night away.

Tantra

20 Victoria Street, Nottingham NG1 2EX
Tel. no 0115 985 9955
www.tantrabar.co.uk
info@tantrabar.co.uk

With love in the air, any decent hen party would coax the hen over to the Tantra coop. This boutique club, with its incense filled atmosphere, low slung sofas and beds to lounge upon, is a real aphrodisiac! Arrive early as lengthy queues tend to build up. It's sassy, classy, passionate and intimate.

The Coco Lounge

3 George Street, Nottingham NG1 3BH
Tel. no 0115 941 8555
coco.lounge@live.co.uk

The Coco Lounge in Nottingham is one of the most popular bars in the city on a Friday and Saturday night. It should provide a great environment for a brood of free range hens with its eclectic interior including big leather couches, a palm tree and an open fireplace. Check them out on Facebook.

Try your hand at mixing a cocktail at Revolution.

The Market Bar

22 Goose Gate, Nottingham NG1 1FF
Tel. no 0115 959 9785
www.myspace.com/wearethemarketbar

Recently voted Nottingham's Best Bar in the Best Bar & Club Awards 2009, this late night basement bar, in the heart of Nottingham's trendy Lace Market, is a place to be seen. The bar is only open from 9pm and you'll need to dress to impress if you want to get in. Playing everything from Electro, House, Techno & Minimal to Hip Hop, Drum & Bass, Dubstep & Jungle there's something for everyone. Check them out on My Space & Facebook.

The Square

6–9 The Poultry, Nottingham NG1 2HW
Tel. no 0115 958 8433

If you're looking for a high octane atmosphere then head to The Squares. Generally populated by weekend revellers in their early twenties and the over-35 crowd trying to recapture their youth, the first thing that will hit you when you enter The Square is the noise; this is not a venue for a quiet chat with your hens. Check them out on Facebook.

estaurants

Bistro L!ve ££

Barker Gate, The Lace Market,
Nottingham NG1 1JS
Tel. no 0845 331 1500 or
115 947 3666
www.bistrolive.com
info@bistrolive.com

you're looking to eat, drink and be
entertained in one venue then Nottingham's
Bistro L!VE could be the venue for you. Being
the largest venue (capacity of 340 people) in
the Bistro chain, you can expect a great
atmosphere for your hen party. They also
offer a party organising service for those
who'd like a little help making it a night to
remember. Open until 2am you can expect
great food, top quality live entertainment and
an atmosphere you won't find anywhere else
in Nottingham.

Canal House ££

48–52 Canal Street, Nottingham
NG1 7EH
Tel. no 0115 955 5011
www.castlerockbrewery.co.uk
canalhouse@castlerockbrewery.co.uk

Located on the bank of Nottingham's canal,
the Canal House is part of a small complex
of pubs and bars based around the canal.
During the summer it's one of the busiest
areas of Nottingham and one of the best
places to go for the start of a night out or to
grab a relaxing drink and a bite to eat too. To
get a seat on warm summer days in the
build-up to the wedding season you need to
bag your spot early!

Chino Latino ££

41 Maid Marian Way, Nottingham
NG1 6GD
Tel. no 0115 947 7444
www.chinolatino.co.uk
nottingham@chinolatino.co.uk

The award winning Chino Latino offers a
sophisticated and elegant dining experience
to your Nottingham hen party. Food is served
to share and dishes are brought steadily to
the table creating an informal yet

2 courses + half a bottle of wine

£ under £20
££ £20–£35
£££ over £35

Indulge in some Asian food at Chino Latino.

sophisticated style of eating and drinking –
the best way to enjoy this unique taste
sensation that is Chino Latino. The distinctive
menu brings together the delicate flavours of
China, South East Asia and modern Japan
offering a contemporary pan-Asian food
fusion. The food is carefully complemented
by a cocktail menu, of course! A classy night
out for you and your hens.

Sinatra ££

8–16 Chapel Quarter, Nottingham
NG1 6JQ
Tel. no 0115 941 1050
www.sinatrarestaurant.com
info@sinatrarestaurant.com

Situated in the new Chapel Quarter of
Nottingham just a stone's throw from the
Market Square this busy bar, bistro and
restaurant has an established reputation for
fine food, great service and stylish
surroundings. Ideal for a light lunch or a
lingering meal Sinatra's Bistro and Restaurant
menus cater for every taste. The bar and
bistro serve light meals, breakfast and you
can simply order drinks from coffee to pink
champagne and cocktails. The restaurant is
more formal and popular for pre-theatre
dining and long lingering meals during the
evenings.

where to party

Dogma

9 Byard Lane, Nottingham NG1 2GJ
Tel. no 0115 988 6830
www.dogmabars.com
nottingham@dogmabars.com

Sitting pretty in one of Nottingham's quaintest streets, Dogma is a force to be reckoned with. Spread over three levels, it's an impressively large space. There's a smallish restaurant upstairs, an immense middle floor with a main bar and a downstairs area, which is where you'll end up dancing the night away. The middle floor is where most of the action happens and even though it's an enormous space, it can get packed to the gills at times, especially at weekends and on bank holidays when they're open until 3am.

Gatecrasher Loves Nottingham

Elite Building, Queen Street,
Nottingham NG1 2BL
Tel. no 0115 910 1101
www.gatecrasher.com

Gatecrasher Loves Nottingham is a three-storey venue with four different rooms boasting state of the art audio and visual equipment throughout. Playing host to live music from some of the UK's most renowned artists and PAs from internationally acclaimed DJs such as Pete Tong and Roger Sanchez, the Gatecrasher phenomenon brings you world-class clubbing. The main auditorium features a huge dancefloor which is guaranteed to be shaking and grooving every weekend.

Я3VOLUTION
MASTERCLASS

GET BEHIND THE BAR AND BECOME A COCKTAIL MASTER IN THIS 90 MINUTE INTERACTIVE SESSION!

- ✪ **COCKTAILS**
- ✪ **TASTING**
- ✪ **TOOLS**
- ✪ **SKILLS**
- ✪ **GAMES**

HEN GOES FREE!
MINIMUM 8 PEOPLE

QUOTE PROMO CODE 'MARTINI' FOR FREE HEN OFFER
PACKAGES FROM ONLY £24.95 PER PERSON PLUS
NEW PARTY FOOD OPTIONS NOW AVAILABLE

TO BOOK...
ONLINE: REVOLUTION-BARS.CO.UK
PHONE: 0800 6300 860
ASK: A MEMBER OF STAFF

ANY OCCASION, ANY SIZE... REVOLUTION IS THE PERFECT PLACE TO EAT, DRINK & PARTY!

Find us at The Cornerhouse & Broad Street, Hockley, Nottingham
All rights reserved - offer can be withdrawn at any time - deposit required - please drink responsibly

Get dressed Grease style for a night out at 70s club Flares and indulge in some Summer Lovin'.

Flares

51 Upper Parliament Street,
Nottingham NG1 6LD
Tel. no 0115 941 2609
www.flaresbars.co.uk/flaresnottingham

Nights out in Nottingham don't get groovier than the permanent party at Flares – the swinging 70s bar and disco famed for making those good times roll. The funky DJ-crafted playlists are guaranteed to get you on the dancefloor. This is the place to get with the groove, dance to great 70s tracks, enjoy a few drinks or book a party package! At the weekend it's hen and stag party heaven – all diggin' it with more funky tunes than you can shake a sitar at. So get glammed up and join the other hens and stags – Flare's is an institution!

Jongleurs

10 Thurland Street, Nottingham
NG1 3DR
Tel. no 0115 950 0120 or
0870 011 1960 (ticket hotline)
www.jongleurs.com
info@jongleurs.com

Situated in the city centre just up from the Market Square, Jongleurs in Nottingham is a great place to celebrate a hen night. At Jongleurs you can eat, drink, laugh and dance all under one roof. Jongleurs provides the best in live entertainment with the top comedians on the circuit. Shows run every Friday and Saturday, so book your tickets for a good giggle.

Reflex

51 Upper Parliament Street, Nottingham
NG1 6LD.
Tel no 0115 941 2609
www.reflexbars.co.uk

The sister to Flares, Reflex is all about the 80s! It's a bar, it's a club, it's a live music venue and it's massive! Arranged on three floors of fabulous fun, there are plenty of bars doing great drinks promotions, dancefloors and live music – it's big hair all the way!

Stealth

Masonic Place, Goldsmith Street,
Nottingham NG1 5JT
Tel. no 0115 822 1313
www.stealthattack.co.uk
info@stealthattack.co.uk

Stealth is a Midlands clubbing institution and Nottingham's number one club. Since opening its doors in April 2004, Stealth's Funktion One soundsystem has been rocked by the world's best DJs and live bands running every Saturday. Stealth and The Rescue Rooms feature two clubs, five rooms, two smoking patios and the best DJs and live bands the world has to offer. Find them on Facebook, my space, twitter and YouTube.

hennightdirect
get your party started here!

Your party solution has arrived

Hennightdirect.com is the largest
independent hen party portal in the UK

We can get your party started with a click!
Choose your city, choose your activity,
choose your party. Let us guide you to an
unforgettable last night of freedom.

Log on to

www.hennightdirect.com

oxford

Oxford skyline (top), Radcliffe Camera (middle), punts (bottom).

It's one of those cities that makes you go 'ahh' when you arrive, thanks to the famous meadows and dreaming spires. But beauty's not just skin deep – Oxford is a vibrant, cosmopolitan, nerdy-yet-funky city with style.

what to do

A beautiful city with lazy rivers, intelligent graffiti, great shops, superb little pubs and restaurants and an unusually high quotient of late night cocktail bars – we lurve Oxford.

Leave your cars at home (the traffic is horrendous) and make it a green weekend, hiring bikes, boating down the rivers and walking to shops, bars and cool little clubs in the city centre.

The student presence is huge. Young people of all nationalities with long scarves and big brains are in the bars, the bicycle lanes and clogging up the queues in H&M. Then there are all the lecturers and academics, clearly too intelligent to brush their hair, in the real ale pubs, delis and bookshops.

Visitors often worry that they will be asked difficult questions about their current reading habits or general knowledge, but relax, a lot of the scruffbags you see out and about are from the old poly, and thus no cleverer than anyone else.

The riverside pubs and boating stations come into their own in the summer. And though some think the Cotswold countryside around Oxford is twee, we reckon England doesn't get much lovelier.

10 good reasons

1. riverside pubs
2. punting
3. cocktail culture
4. student promotions
5. friendly little clubs
6. arty crafty stuff
7. hiring bikes
8. really hard pub quizzes
9. thriving live music scene
10. exploring the Cotswolds

Bikes are the transportation means of choice in Oxford.

sounds of the city

Keep young and beautiful If you feel too young to take golf seriously, take the Mickey with a nine-hole tour of Faringdon Golf Course. This gentle Par three is perfect for those of us who think that golf's basically a question of striding around in Pringle tank tops shouting 'fore' and receiving random applause. There's no need to book – just turn up with or without the Pringle and give it a go. Call 01367 243944.

Summertime You can't really go to Oxford in the summer without punting. Sorry, but there are rules. The River Cherwell, a major tributary of the Thames, wends its way past some of the best Cotswoldy pubs, including the locally loved Victoria Arms in Marston. There's just nothing more mellow than this, particularly if good food and a couple of glasses of Pimms are included. Start out at the Cherwell Boathouse, an idyllic spot and fabulous restaurant that's particularly renowned for its wines. Grab your punt, rowing boat or canoe after lunch (book a 'chauffeur' if you don't trust yourselves at the helm), and drift through impossibly pretty countryside for a few sunny hours.

Tall stories For a less horizontal river trip, Oxford River Cruises will pick hen parties up from various locations in Oxford and take you off for a Mad Hatter's tea party expedition, passing the college backs and meadows and through the scenery that inspired Alice in Wonderland. En route you'll eat cake and drink mysterious liquids labelled 'eat me' and 'drink me' a la Alice. Alternatively, take the picnic trip and disembark for a gourmet riverbank lunch. See oxfordrivercruises.com.

The closest thing to crazy Book your party into one of Oxford's coolest bars, Thirst, for the trendy decor, truly magnificent cocktails and the fact that this is where people come to drink and dance every night of the week. It's known as a haunt for those clubbers who still haven't had enough on a Sunday, possibly because it serves good bloody marys. In fact, Oxford's not short on really good cocktail places with a late licence, another of note being locally-loved Raoul's on Walton Street. Another little beauty is Baby Love, if you think you're cool enough and want to be up 'til 3am.

Pick up a punt at Cherwell Boathouse and head off down river.

Party Bar Risa on Hythe Bridge Street is a great place for a group to eat, drink and kick back, whether you're going upstairs to Jongleurs for the stand up comedy later on or opting for a night on the dancefloor at the classy Bridge nightclub nearby.

Jongleurs itself gets very dark, loud and packed – perfect for a night of rude jokes and stag and hen party debauchery, as after the comedians do their stand up routines the pished and giggling crowd takes to the dancefloor for a bit of a shuffle. It's the Jongleurs effect – you quaff away on those deceptively squash-like cocktails all night, but come midnight, somehow you're not walking straight. It's best to stay with your own kind – even if it does look like the night of the living dead – rather than try to get into another club at this point.

Fire it up If you're in the mood for making a mess, get a few bottles of wine and take the girls off to Unique Creations in Summertown. You'll paint your own ceramics, and you'll be amazed at how relaxing it is. Even if you've got the artistic skills of a hippo it doesn't matter – beauty is in the eye of the beholder so just give it to someone who loves you. Why not make hen party souvenirs for each other? Don't forget to book.

If you're after something a little hotter, why not head off to Banzai Events, near Bicester, for a day of full on outdoor-based activities, such as quad biking, rally driving, 4x4 off-roading, blind driving and reverse steer jeeps. Get competitive with a Jeep Gymkhana or a full on Grand Prix Day. Check it out at banzaievents.com.

Pretty Africa Many of Oxford's best drink and dance emporiums are located underground, Po Na Nas being no exception. With the exotic atmosphere of a Moroccan Souk, albeit one that serves poky cocktails, this is one of Oxford's most respected clubs, known for a great variety of music and a friendly crowd, as well as a bed to lie down on when it all gets a bit much.

Let off some steam in a rage buggy with Banzai.

where to stay

Take your pick from a city centre hotel within stumbling distance of the clubs, a good-value hostel or campsite, or a cute Cotswold cottage for your Oxford hen party.

hotels

Bicester Hotel £££
Chesterton, Bicester OX26 1TE
Tel. no 01869 241204
www.bicestercountryclub.com
reception2@bicesterhotelgolfandspa.com

This chic hotel, close to Blenheim Palace, has an 18-hole golf course and luxury spa all nestling in 134 acres of stunning Cotswold countryside. There are 52 deluxe bedrooms all with views over the fairways or into the designer courtyard. Free use of the gym, tennis courts and swimming pool is included with your stay. To eat, choose between Grays Restaurant and the less formal Brasserie.

Central Backpackers £
13 Park End Street, Oxford OX1 1HH
Tel. no 01865 242288
www.centralbackpackers.co.uk
oxford@centralbackpackers.co.uk

Oxford's premier hostel accommodation, named one of Europe's top hostels 2006–2008, is situated just 5 minutes walk from both the bus and train stations. This comfortable hostel has a high level of security with swipe card entry on all dorms and individual lockers. There's 24-hour access with no curfew and breakfast is included. There's even a BBQ on the roof terrace every Sunday.

Mercure Oxford Eastgate Hotel ££
73 High Street, Oxford OX1 4BE
Tel. no 01865 248332
www.mercure.com
H6668@accor.com

Originally a 17th century coaching inn, this four-star hotel has 63 ensuite rooms and the AA Rosette awarded for The High Table

'been there...'

We got a fab cottage just outside Burford. The first night we stocked up on wine and pizza and had a catch up. On Saturday we went and had a look round Oxford, did a bit of shopping and ate lunch at The Lamb and Flag. Saturday night was best – Pudding Pie came round and gave us this amazing cookery lesson in the cottage, with a three course meal...lush.

shared room without breakfast

£ under £30
££ £30–£60
£££ over £60
pppn

Brasserie and Bar. The hotel is ideally situated for visiting the colleges, punting on the river, shopping and all the nightlife on offer in the centre of the city. The hotel is easily accessible via M40.

Royal Oxford Hotel ££
Park End Street, Oxford OX1 1HR
Tel. no 01865 248432
www.royaloxfordhotel.co.uk
info@royaloxfordhotel.co.uk

The Royal Oxford Hotel is ideally located just 2 minutes walk from the heart of Oxford city centre, and within walking distance of the railway and bus stations. The ensuite rooms all feature free Wi-Fi, fresh fruit and bottled water. Café Coco restaurant is open from 8am–11pm at the weekend.

self-catering

Acacia Cottages ££
Tel. no 0800 234 6039
www.acaciacottages.co.uk
info@acaciacottages.co.uk

At Acacia Cottages they have hand-picked a selection of gorgeous Cotswold cottages for you to choose from. Not only that, but they will organise the whole weekend for you, drawing on their knowledge of the best local hen services and suppliers. So if you want something a bit different to the L-plate wearing ritual try Acacia.

shared room without breakfast

£ under £30
££ £30–£60
£££ over £60
pppn

One of Acacia's gorgeous Cotswold cottages.

Caswell House ££
Caswell Lane, Brize Norton OX18 3NJ
Tel. no 01993 701064
www.caswellhouse.co.uk
amanda@caswellhouse.co.uk

This beautiful historic 15th century manor house is set in the heart of 450 acres of Oxfordshire countryside and is surrounded by rural views with an ancient orchard, walled gardens and extensive lawns stretching down to the moat. Providing luxurious and spacious accommodation for up to 20 guests, Caswell House offers a relaxing, country house atmosphere in the heart of the Cotswolds.

Cherbridge Cottages ££
Hill Farm, Mill Lane, Marston, Oxford OX3 0QG
Tel. no 07976 288329
www.cherbridgecottages.co.uk
enquiries@cherbridgecottages.co.uk

Cherbridge Cottage is part of a 1930s punting station providing contemporary self-catering holiday accommodation just 2 miles from Oxford. The property is set in large secluded gardens with extensive river frontage. Oxford is easily reached by car, cycle track or park-and-ride bus. A private punt and skiff are available to guests throughout the summer months.

Good Lake Barns ££
Church Farm, Shellingford, Faringdon SN7 7QA
Tel. no 01367 710112
www.goodlakebarns.co.uk
info@goodlakebarns.co.uk

Shellingford is a charming small village in the picturesque Vale of the White Horse just 17 miles from Oxford. Goodlake Barns is a series of light and spacious self-catering cottages, sensitively converted and retaining much of the character and charm of the original stone barns, stables and outbuildings. There are three cottages sleeping four, six and eight as well as a studio that doubles as a fifth bedroom for the largest cottage. They are arranged around a courtyard on an organic dairy farm.

Kingfisher Barn ££
Rye Farm, Abingdon OX14 3NN
Tel. no 01235 537538
www.kingfisherbarn.com
info@kingfisherbarn.com

A few minutes from the River Thames in the heart of the most glorious countryside, you'll find Kingfisher Barn. Abingdon is just a 10-minute walk and Oxford is only 8 miles away. This self-catering accommodation is very well presented for a relaxing and comfortable stay. Stratford-upon-Avon, Blenheim Palace, Warwick Castle and of course the Cotswolds are all within easy driving distance.

where to eat and drink

Oxford has a lovely line in riverside pubs serving good British food and drink, but the city centre boasts some swanky bars and party-friendly restaurants too.

bars & pubs

Bar Risa

3–5 Hythe Bridge Street, Oxford
OX1 2EW
Tel. no 01865 722437
www.risa-oxford.co.uk
info@risa-oxford.co.uk

With two floors, two bars and an excellent outdoor terrace, Bar Risa has something for everyone. It's a great place to enjoy a lunchtime meal, an early evening cocktail or a club night. Food is served all day and all night here so you won't go hungry. There are frequent live events including Salsa dancing, Poker and bands; Jongleurs, the world class comedy club, also resides here.

Raoul's Bar

32 Walton Street, Oxford OX2 6AA
Tel. no 01865 553732
www.raoulsbar.co.uk
bartender@raoulsbar.com

Raoul's bar offers a wide range of award-winning cocktails featuring bartender Matt Marshall. Enjoy a cocktail making masterclass here, but make sure you book well in advance, these lessons get booked up very fast. Raoul's has a wonderful varied menu, so why not sample the food while you're there.

The Lamb and Flag

12 Saint Giles, Oxford OX1 3JS
Tel. no 01865 515787

Tucked away in a corner of Saint Giles, you have to look carefully not to miss it. The Lamb and Flag serves great-value traditional pub grub. This historic pub dates back to 1695 and, although it has been extensively remodelled over the years, the rear bars still have the character of an olde worlde pub.

Raoul's Bar in Walton Street.

Thirst

7–8 Park End Street, Oxford OX1 2HH,
Tel. no 01865 242 044
www.thirstbar.com
rob@thirstbar.com

A refuge for city slickers, students and just about anyone who finds out about it. There's something for everyone here. Spacious, lively, trendy cocktail bar, dead centre of Oxford's 'West End', with constant DJ action, Thirst also has a large and pleasant courtyard at rear. There are daily happy hours and even 'stupid hours'.

Victoria Arms

Mill Lane, Old Marston, Oxford
OX3 0PZ
Tel. no 01865 241382
www.victoriaarms.co.uk
victoriaarms@wadworth.co.uk

On the banks of the river Cherwell this country pub has a rural feel, yet it is just a short way from the dreaming spires of Oxford. With large gardens sweeping down to the river, it is a perfect spot in summer, especially if you arrive by punt. You may have seen this famous photogenic pub on Lewis or Inspector Morse!

restaurants

Cherwell Boathouse ££
50 Bardwell Road, Oxford OX2 6ST
Tel. no 01865 552746
www.cherwellboathouse.co.uk
info@cherwellboathouse.co.uk

Situated in the heart of Oxford on the banks of the Cherwell, The Boathouse is a place to relax and enjoy fine wine and fine French dining in a tranquil and picturesque setting. And if the sun shines, enjoy a meal on the fabulous terrace.

Kashmir Halal £
64 Cowley Road, Oxford OX4 1JB
Tel. no 01865 242941

If you're looking for a 'bring your own' (booze not food that is!) curry house, this is the best in Oxford. Kashmir Halal offers great value for excellent quality food. A brilliant choice for big groups, the Kashmir always has a bustling atmosphere and the service is efficient and friendly.

'real life'

We had a great night at The Living Room in the Oxford Castle redevelopment. We were really lucky with the weather and we sat out on the roof terrace which has amazing views. The food was all really well cooked and the cocktails to die for.

The Living Room, Oxford Castle.

2 courses + half a bottle of wine

£ under £20
££ £20–£35
£££ over £35

Who can resist pizza? Head to Mario's.

Mario's £
103 Cowley Road, Oxford OX4 1HU
Tel. no 01865 722955
www.mariooxford.co.uk
mariopizzeria@yahoo.co.uk

For an authentic Italian experience and food like 'mamma used to make' it has to be Mario's. With a great selection of traditional Italian dishes and friendly, attentive service makes this pizzeria trattoria a great place for a large group.

Portabello ££
7 South Parade, Oxford OX2 7JL
Tel. no 01865 559653
www.portabellorestaurant.co.uk
info@portabellorestaurant.co.uk

Dining at Portabello's is a relaxed casual affair whether inside or out on the terrace. Kick back with a chilled glass of Sauvignon and peruse the modern British menu featuring local and seasonal produce.

The Thai Orchid ££
58a St Clement's Street,
Oxford OX4 1AH
Tel. no 01865 798044
www.thaigroup.co.uk
thaiboathouse@btconnect.com

A local dining institution, The Orchid is great for parties. The authentic interior with teak furniture and tropical plants makes an atmospheric environment, but the star of the show here is the wonderful Thai food.

where to party

They'll be spinning the discs at Baby Love.

Baby Love

3 King Edward Street, Oxford OX1 4HS
Tel. no 01865 200011
www.baby-bar.co.uk

Easily Oxford's most eclectic music venue, Baby Love Bar is one of the safest, funkiest and varied venues for world-famous names in pop, house, drum'n'bass, indie and electro, to name but a few.

Clementine's

15 St Clement's Street,
Oxford OX4 1AB
Tel. no 07877 999967
www.clemsoxford.com
info@clemsoxford.com

Situated close to Oxford's famous Magdalene bridge, Clem's is two floors of full-on fun. Upstairs in the newly refurbished cocktail bar experts will mix your favourite cocktail, while you listen to the sounds of deep jazz and funky rhythmics. Downstairs, in the club, fantastic sounds and lighting offer the perfect environment to show off your dancing skills. There's also The Blue Room available for private hen parties of up to 50 people, with waitress service and its own special shots menu.

Escape

9 High Street, Oxford OX1 4DB
Tel. no 01865 246766
www.escapeoxford.com
escape-oxford@hotmail.com

Escape boasts two floors playing a varied mix of music with a selection of guest DJs ensuring a stylish ambience. This luxurious and exclusive venue in the heart of Oxford's city centre combines a bar, restaurant and nightclub. It's a guaranteed good night out.

Lava & Ignite

Park End Street, Oxford OX1 1JD
Tel. no 01865 250 181
www.lavaignite.com
lava&ignite-oxford@luminar.co.uk

With four bars, three dancefloors, state-of-the-art sound and lighting systems, breathtaking visuals and unrivalled entertainment until 2am, Lava & Ignite presents a unique clubbing experience in Oxford.

baby love bar
3 King Edward St, Oxford
01865 200011
info@baby-bar.co.uk
www.baby-bar.co.uk

Bar & Club
Open 9pm-3am Every Day
Available for Private
Parties, Birthdays,
Hen & Stags,
Corporate

baby love bar

baby love bar
3 King Edward st, Oxford OX1 4HS
01865 200011
info@baby-bar.co.uk
www.baby-bar.co.uk

Cocktail Training Hen & Stag Parties!

We demonstrate and train everyone on a few cocktails and then allow you to get behind the bar and make them for your mates! Great fun with lots of Bar drinking games involved! Highly recommended. Great for corporate team building and staff parties also. We also provide Male and Female strippers, Buff Butlers, Kissograms etc for the whole of Oxfordshire and Southeast of England. Pole Dancing classes for Hen Parties are a popular speciality.

Contact 01865 200011 or info@baby-bar.co.uk

A party with a difference!

Po Na Na

13 Magdalen Street, Oxford OX1 3AE
Tel. no 01865 249171
www.eclecticbars.co.uk/oxfordponana/
info@oxfordponana.com

Located in St.Giles at the heart of the
dreaming spires, Po Na Na Oxford is the
most vibrant cocktail bar and nightclub in this
very discerning city. The Souk-style decor
lends an off-beat sophistication and relaxed
atmosphere to every occasion, while the
warm ambience, and buzz from the trendy
regular clientele make Po Na Na the place to
party every weekend. The hottest resident
DJs playing credible music, teamed with
good service, provide the perfect mix.

The Bridge

6–9 Hythe Bridge Street,
Oxford OX1 2EW
Tel. no 01865 242 526
www.bridgeoxford.co.uk
phil@bridgeoxford.co.uk

This busy city centre club fills up early, so
don't be late. The Bridge is split into three
different parts: Anuba (the pre-club bar), the
main club and the lounge. Starting off at
Anuba gives you fast track admission to the
club and you can also hire this place for
private parties. The music at the club is

varied depending on what night you go.
Usually on the first floor there's hip hop and
R'n'B and the second floor plays dance
anthems. In the lounge the music is more
chilled with soulful sounds.

The Cellar

Frewin Court, Cornmarket St,
Oxford OX1 3HZ
Tel. no 01865 244761
www.cellarmusic.co.uk
Located right next to the Oxford Union's
Purple Turtle, this is a less cheesy option.
You can let your hair down and dance as if
no one is looking here. The staff are cool and
the music is always different and interesting.
This is a place for maximum fun.

The Old Fire Station

40 George Street, Oxford OX1 2AQ
Tel. no 01865 297182

The OFS is one of the top party destinations
in Oxford. A classic mix of 70s, 80s, 90s,
chart and cheese makes the weekends
partytastic – heaven for hen and stag parties.
The venue has a long bar with a great
selection of drinks and a good size
dancefloor. You can dance the night away to
all those cheesy choons you never admit to
liking and we won't tell anyone – honest!

Pucker up now girls!

york

Minster (top), Guildhall (middle), Clifford Tower (bottom).

York's the place to go if you're more interested in the paranormal than the paralytic – but with a large 20–40 year old population, the ghosts aren't the only ones with favourite haunts and high jinks on their nightly agenda.

what to do

Famed for it's Viking, medieval and Roman history, not to mention the ghosts, you might think York's stuck in the past. Yet this stunning little city has a thriving nightlife and plethora of great places to eat and drink.

For hen parties, it's a sophisticated choice. The main attractions, shops, bars and pubs are all crammed into the labyrinthine streets, and encircled by the ancient city walls. It's the kind of town where you'll actually enjoy getting a bit lost, as it's full of curiosities and every street corner seems to have a story, a saint or a visiting spirit (and we're not talking guest vodka). Sit by the river or take a boat trip; catch a major art exhibition or picnic by the old abbey ruins; have lunch in a Fossgate restaurant or cocktails and late night laughs at the Evil Eye...

The nightlife is not too twee or stuck in the past – thanks to the excellent university and a young population, York has a fantastic selection of swish bars, ancient pubs and top class eateries, as well as a few good places for dancin' later on.

The Shambles is all cobbled streets and Tudor houses.

10 good reasons

1. charm and charisma
2. cocktails at KoKo's
3. ancient pubs
4. quirky restaurants
5. Yorkminster
6. hiring a boat
7. historic and pretty
8. easy to walk around
9. ghost stories
10. lovely boutique hotels

sounds of the city

F.E.A.R. The world's first ghost tour was started up in York and is still going strong. Funny, chilling and gruesome in turns, the Original Ghost Walk guides walk and talk you around the oldest and spookiest parts of the city and generally aim to scare the bejeezus out of you. We loved it – grotesque tales of locked-up plague orphans, fascinating descriptions of Roman soldiers marching through a cellar, and many other horrible stories and legends bring the city and its past inhabitants to life. The nightly tours start at 8pm at the King's Arms by the river (take a look inside to see how often this place gets flooded, by the way).

You're history York is full of ancient sites, museums, galleries and other attractions. If you only look around two, make them York Minster and Clifford's Tower. The Minster is the largest Gothic cathedral in Europe, alongside Cologne's. The site dates from 627 CE, William the Conqueror was crowned here in 1066, it was trashed in the Reformation, burnt in 1984…. The history's fascinating, but the best thing about it is looking at the tiny gargoyles in the Chapterhouse. Reward yourselves for this cultural injection over the road at Café Concerto. It's the best café in the City – the cake is essential.

Clifford's Tower dates back to William the Conqueror. This small castle keep was where York's Jewish population fled in 1190 to escape violent persecution. They burned themselves to death rather than be captured by their tormentors. The tower's named after Robert Clifford, who was hanged there in 1322.

Take your mind off it with a trip round the nearby York Museum, which has an entire old street as part of its exhibition, or come back to the land of the living with an early bird dinner at the gorgeous 31 Castlegate restaurant. Book in advance, as it's popular.

Party hard Club Salvation, The Gallery and Ziggy's are top York venues for dancing after quaffing in the pubs. Club Salvation leads the way, with nightly DJs playing chart, dance and RnB music to party to. The Gallery is the place for cheese, flirting and fun.

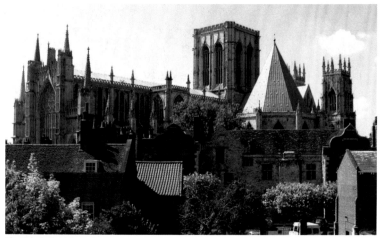

The Majestic York Minster dominates the centre of the city.

Sometimes you just can't make it on your own If you and the ladies like cooking, there's no better way to spend a day (or evening) in York than at The Cooking Rooms. Take a class – from Spanish or Indian cuisine to chocolates or patisserie – or book for a private party and discuss the right menu for you. The people training you are all professional chefs (some are almost celebrity chefs), and by the end of your session you'll be fully skilled up, wined and dined. Even if you've burnt the salad and evaporated the soup, you'll still have a laugh over a wine or two.

Just looking Glam it up with a day at York Racecourse – which has some great hospitality facilities, including four 'dine and view' restaurants. You can book packages, including a box for parties of 16 or more. Rather!

Rock the house Baille Hill House, just outside the city walls, sleeps ten house-trained hens. The big kitchen diner is perfect for dinners together, and with six TVs, two hifis and a video and CD library you won't be bored if it rains. Why not have a civilised soiree in your new home from home – book an entertainer, caterers, hire a model for a life drawing lesson...?

The best entertainment of all, we think, for a stay-at-home hen party is a ThirtyFifty wine tasting night. You'll drink (no spitting out, please) fine wines or champagnes and sparkling wines all night. Learn what goes with what, how to sound knowledgeable about grapes and how to pretend you're not sozzled. Alternatively you can choose to have a chocolate and wine tasting session. They'll arrange a Butler in the Buff or some pampering, too, to really make a night of it. Call 0208 288 0314.

'been there...'

We did the tourist thing... York Minster, the museum, rowing on the Ouse and drinking in as many spooky old pubs as possible. We were staying in a hotel outside town, which is the only thing I'd change as we had to get cabs. I loved the shopping in York, it's such a nice place to wander around. The ghost walk was actually really good and not cheesy at all.

Move yer bloomin' arse! Why not dust off your hat and head to the races?

where to stay

hotels and b&bs

Ace Hotel £–££
Micklegate House, 88–90 Micklegate, York YO1 6JX
Tel. no 01904 627720
www.ace-hotelyork.co.uk
reception@ace-hotelyork.co.uk

Located in the Mickelgate, the oldest part of York, and close to the railway station, this budget hotel is in a grand Georgian building with carved sweeping staircase, panelled rooms and Rococo ceiling. With its own games room, sauna and outside seating area this is a budget hotel with a difference. Choose from 14-bed to twin dorms to suit your wallet.

shared room without breakfast
£ under £30
££ £30–£60
£££ over £60
pppn

Hedley House ££
3 Bootham Terrace, York YO3O 7DH
Tel. no 01904 637404
www.hedleyhouse.com
info@hedleyhouse.com

Just 5 minutes walk from the City Walls and the Minster, Hedley House is conveniently located for the centre. Modern comfortable rooms complement the traditional setting.

Knavesmire Manor Hotel ££–£££
302 Tadcaster Road, York YO24 1HE
Tel. no 01904 702941
www.knavesmire.co.uk
enquire@knavesmire.co.uk

Once the home of the Rowntree family and now tastefully converted to a hotel with indoor swimming pool and quality restaurant. Situated close to York Racecourse, this family-run hotel offers friendly service to all guests and is less than 2 miles from the centre.

Newington Hotel ££
147 Mount Vale, York YO24 1DJ
Tel. no 01904 625173
www.thenewington.co.uk
info@thenewington.co.uk

Positioned on the Royal Approach, close to the racecourse, the Newington makes the perfect base for a visit to York. The modern ensuite bedrooms are comfortable and well equipped; and the indoor heated pool and sauna are the perfect place to relax at the end of the day. Prices include breakfast.

The Bar Convent ££
17 Blossom Street, York YO24 1AQ
Tel. no 01904 643238
www.bar-convent.org.uk
info@bar-convent.org.uk

This somewhat surprising option is a unique choice of B&B or self-catering accommodation. Although not all the rooms are ensuite, they are comfy and well presented.

Georgian grandeur at Ace Hotel.

self-catering

Allerthorpe Lakeland Park £
Allerthorpe Lakeland Park, Allerthorpe,
York YO42 4RL
Tel. no 01759 301444
www.allerthorpelakelandpark.co.uk
info@allerthorpelakelandpark.co.uk

This lakeside caravan and camping park also
has a luxury apartment for rent – Manderlay.
With 50 acres of grounds and lakes,
there is a variety of watersports on
offer here, including windsurfing,
powerboating, sailing, and
canoeing.

Baille Hill House ££
2 Bishopsgate Street,
York YO23 1JH
Tel. no 01845 597614
www.baillehillhouse.co.uk
enquiries@baillehillhouse.co.uk

This Georgian style self-catering cottage is
the only rental accommodation in the centre
of York catering for ten people. With pubs
and bars, restaurants and nightlife just 5
minutes walk away, it's so convenient.

Inyork Holidays ££
11 Walmgate, York, YO1 9TX
Tel. no 01904 632660
www.inyorkholidays.co.uk
agents@inyorkholidays.co.uk

This local accommodation agency brings
together a varied selection of self-catering
apartments and townhouses within easy
access of the city centre all with parking.

Merricote Cottages ££
Malton Road, Stockton on the Forest,
York YO32 9TL
Tel. no 01904 400256
www.merricote-holiday-cottages.co.uk
enquiries@merricote-holiday-
cottages.co.uk

Once a traditional working farm, Merricote
has been sympathetically converted to
provide eight superb cottages, each one with
individual character. Situated in 8 acres of
rural Yorkshire, 3 miles from the city centre,
Merricote is a great base to relax in and to
explore the surrounding area from.

**✳ shared room
without
breakfast**

**£ under £30
££ £30–£60
£££ over £60
pppn**

The Riverside York ££
8a Peckitt Street, York
YO1 9SF
Tel. no 01904 623008
www.riverside-york.co.uk

This luxurious Victorian self-catering
townhouse provides a haven right in the
centre of the city. The spacious and elegantly
furnished rooms, overlooking the River
Ouse, are arranged on three floors.
Accommodating up to six people
and equipped with all the
modern comforts you require,
this will feel like home from
home.

York Holiday Homes ££
53 Goodramgate, York YO1
7LS
Tel. no 01904 641997
www.yorkholidayhomes.co.uk
enquiries@yorkholidayhomes.co.uk

Choose from 11 different properties all
centrally located just minutes away from the
sights and nightlife. The apartments
accommodate two–six guests, but up to 18
can be catered for in several together.

The City Walls.

where to eat and drink

Tea at Betty's, ice cream at La Cremeria, salads at Café Harlequin...there's a café for every occasion here, a pub for every day and a restaurant scene to swoon over.

bars & pubs

Evil Eye Lounge
42 Stonegate, York YO1 8AS
Tel. no 01904 640010
www.evileyelounge.com

It may look like an 'offie', but venture a little further and you'll find a bohemian bar and eatery serving Asian-style food. Famously a hang-out of Johnny Depp...

King's Arms
3 Kings Staith, York YO1 9SN
Tel. no 01904 659435

This is a proper pub serving quality beers and lagers with an unrivalled position right on the riverside. Frequent flooding has made the pub famous nationwide, but when the sun shines, there's no better location in York.

KoKo International Bar
31 Goodramgate, York YO1 7LS
Tel. no 01904 628344
vahe@kokobar.com

If you want good beer, exciting cocktails, excellent wine and champagne, a good atmosphere and interesting people, then this is the place to be! It's a beautiful listed building, believed to be an old monastery. Try KoKo's Ghost cocktail plus many more.

Pitcher and Piano
Coney Street, York YO1 9QL
Tel. no 01904 658580
www.pitcherandpiano.com

With a fantastic riverside location, The York Pitcher and Piano is a great place to enjoy an 'al fresco' drink or even a meal on the large balcony. There's always a vibrant atmosphere here in the evening and you can book a booth for 12–20 people.

The King's Arms pub on the riverside.

Revolution
Coney Street, York YO1 9NA
Tel. no 01904 676054
www.revolution-bars.co.uk/york

Revolution, home of Vodka, knows how to throw a party and has hosted some of the best hen parties. What could be better than getting all of your friends together for one big cocktail party? You can hire a room or book a table at Revolution and why not add on a cocktail masterclass to learn how to mash and shake your own fabulous blends. Then party on to the small hours.

The Living Room
Merchant Exchange, 1 Bridge Street, York YO1 6DD
Tel. no 01904 461000
www.thelivingroom.co.uk
york@thelivingroom.co.uk

With lovely views over the River Ouse, this cool, airy piano bar is an informal place to eat, drink and chill out. With a varied menu and wine list, and over 100 cocktails on offer, There's something to suit everyone here.

cafés & restaurants

2 courses + half a bottle of wine

£ under £20
££ £20–£35
£££ over £35

1 Castlegate £££
1 Castlegate, York YO1 9RN
Tel. no 01904 621404
www.31castlegate.co.uk
nickjulius@31castlegate.co.uk

This elegant restaurant offers a true fine dining experience. Chef, Nick Julius, has created a menu of modern European dishes reflecting the knowledge and experience he gained working in places such as Marco Pierre White's L'Escargot. There is a private dining room available for parties of up to 20.

Bettys Café Tea Rooms ££
6–8 St Helen's Square, York YO1 8QP
Tel. no 01904 659142
www.bettys.co.uk

Inspired by the luxury liner, Queen Mary, in 1936, the York branch of Bettys is resplendent with huge curved windows, elegant wood panelling and ornate mirrors. Sample a hearty English breakfast, a traditional afternoon tea or a three-course meal with wine in Art Deco splendour.

Champagne afternoon tea at Bettys is a must.

Café Concerto ££
21 High Petergate, York YO1 7EN
Tel. no 01904 610478
www.cafeconcerto.biz
coffee@cafeconcerto.biz

Friendly and informal, the musically themed Café Concerto is right opposite York Minster. Serving everything from deli sandwiches for lunch to Swordfish steaks with cous cous on the evening menu, you'll find high quality food freshly prepared to an exceptional level.

'real life'

We had such a good time at The Living Room. Service was fantastic and the atmosphere was buzzing, so we stayed put all night!

The relaxed environment warms up later on!

Fiesta Mehicana ££
14 Clifford Street, York YO1 9RD
Tel. no 01904 610243
www.fiestamehicana.com
info@fiestamehicana.com

Groups of ten or more can order a party menu at this premier Mexican restaurant and sample a variety of authentic dishes, such as Nachos, Chimichangas, Burritos and Fajitas, for the excellent price of £15.95 a head. And if you're the organiser – you eat free!

La Tasca ££
21 Back Swinegate, York YO1 8AD
Tel. no 01904 521100
www.latasca.co.uk
latasca.york@bayrestaurantgroup.com

Share a tapas platter Spanish-style at this classic restaurant, but your fiesta won't be complete without a jug or two of Sangria!

where to party

Head to The Gallery for late night dancing, catch live music at the Black Swan, or take your pick from the city's many beautiful, creaky old pubs – ghosts and all.

Much of York's nightlife is centred on the riverside.

Club Salvation

3 George Hudson Street, York YO1 6JL
Tel. no 01904 635144
www.clubsalvation.co.uk
robyn@clubsalvation.co.uk

The relatively new kid on the block, Club Salvation is a two venue nightspot hosting big-named DJs and live PAs every month. The two rooms are distinctly different with a choice of music in each one. Open until 4.30am on Friday and Saturday nights and with VIP booths available for your private party, the helpful people at Salvation will even organise a limousine to deliver you to the door in style for your extra special night.

Fibbers

Stonebow House, The Stonebow, York YO1 7NP
Tel. no 01904 641413
www.fibbers.co.uk
fibbers@fibbers.co.uk

The top live music venue in York, Fibbers is an intimate and steamy affair. If you want to get hot and sweaty with a load of other indie faithfuls, then this is the place for you. Fibbers also plays host to York's only alternative club night every Saturday – Distortion. So if you want to get away from the usual blend of laser lights and cocktails, give Fibbers a try.

Flares

6 Tanner Row, York YO1 6JB
Tel. no 01904 653283
www.flaresbars.com
info@flaresbars.com

Spread over three floors of this city centre venue, Flares brings you all your favourite 70s hits and disco floor-fillers. Get glammed up in some seriously loud gear and unfeasibly big hair and groove on down to the irresistible soundtrack. They love hen and stag parties at Flares, so contact the venue and find out about the cool party packages they can offer you. If you love ABBA, then Fridays at Flares are for you...it's Mamma Mia all the way.

Get some 70s action at Flares.

Hub Nightclub

53–55 Micklegate, York YO1 6LJ
Tel. no 01904 620602
www.ziggysnightclub.com
contact@ziggysnightclub.com

Currently undergoing a transformation from Ziggys to Hub, this is now the main venue for underground dance nights in York. So if you're into techno and electronic dance music, then this is the place for you. Check the website for more info on the DJs and the music they will be serving up, but expect plenty of heart-pumping beats and big sounds.

The Gallery

12 Clifford Street, York YO1 1RD
Tel. no 01904 647947
www.galleryclub.co.uk
gallery-york@luminar.co.uk

Owned by the ubiquitous Luminar Leisure, The Gallery offers the usual slick and shiny service you'd expect from a nationwide organisation. The very helpful party organisers here will put together a 'club pack' for you with lots of goodies to make your night extra special, all for a small fee of course.

Tru

3–5 Toft Green, York YO1 6JT
Tel. no 01904 620203
www.truyork.co.uk
tru-york@luminar.co.uk

Luminar have got their foot well and truly in the door in York. Tru is a four room venue within the city walls of historic York. You'll find the cream of the local talent DJing here and you can expect a pulsating dancefloor every weekend night grooving to all sorts of music from funky house to cheesy chart.

Vudu Lounge

37–39 Swinegate, York YO1 8AZ
Tel. no 01904 627627
www.vudulounge.co.uk
vudulounge@hotmail.co.uk

This classy cocktail bar has some of the best bartenders in York mixing some quality cocktails. DJ Jed plays here regularly, entertaining an R'n'B crowd 'til the early hours of the morning.

Drinks on the balcony overlooking the River Ouse.

picture credits

Bath Spa Media would like to thank the following for loan of pictures featured in this publication. The reference is given as page number followed by b (bottom), c (centre), l (left), r (right) or t (top) to indicate position where more than picture on the page.

7tl Karaoke Box; 7tr Pop Party; 7bl Riverside Apartment; 7br The Jungle NI; 9t&b Leisure Vouchers; 12tl Butlers in the Buff; 12tc Shaggy Sheep; 12tr Kempton Park; 12bl Piggi T-shirts; 12bc englishsurf school.com; 12br Pop Party; 13tl Leisure Vouchers; 13c Adventure 21; 13tr Beas of Bloomsbury; 13bl Latin Salsa Belfast; 13bc Ascot; 13br Waterfall Spa, Leeds; 14t Leisure Vouchers; 14b Smugglers Haven, Newquay; 18 Pop Party; 24bl&br,25tl&tr Leisure Vouchers; 26 englishsurfschool.com; 29tr Lady Boys of Bangkok; 29bl Leisure Vouchers; 30 Pop Party; 34tl istockphoto©Peter Heyworth; 34tr visitbath.com; 34cl istockphoto©Stuart Taylor; 34c istockphoto©Robert Mayne; 34cr Newcastle Gateshead Initiative; 34bl istockphoto©Craig Swatton; 34bc Cherwell Boathouse, Oxford; 34br visitbrighton.com; 35tl visitcardiff.com; 35tr istockphoto©weinali photography; 35cl visityork.com; 35c istockphoto©Alan Taylor; 35cr bournemouthtourism. co.uk; 35bl Destination Bristol; 35bc istockphoto© Adam Booth; 35bcr istockphoto; 35br www.visit newquay.org; 36t istockphoto©Jason Keffert; 36c istockphoto©Alessandra Litta Modignani; 36b istockphoto©Craig Swatton; 37 Leisure Vouchers; 38 The Sanctuary; 40bl istockphoto©Dmitriy Shironosov; 40tr singalonga.net; 42 Ascot Racecourse; 43t www.partypants.co.uk; 44bl Revolution Karting; 44tr schooldisco.com; 46 Grange Holborn Hotel; 47(all) Haymarket Hotel; 48t&b K West Hotel; 52 The Boundary; 54tl Buddha Bar; 54br Dirty Martinis; 55 On Anon; 58 Jewel Bar; 59 Karaoke Box; 62 Supperclub; 66t,c&b istockphoto; 67 www.visitbath.co.uk; 68 The Makery; 70 www.visitbath.co.uk; 71 belushis. com/bath; 72 Riverside Apartment; 74 www.sub13. net; 73 www.thearchbath.co.uk; 74 www.clubxl.co.uk; 78 www.komedia.co.uk; 80t Belfast Visitor & Convention Bureau, 80c istockphoto©Robert Mayne, 80b istockphoto©Paul Kavanagh; 81l&r Belfast Visitor & Convention Bureau; 82 Latin Salsa; 84 Polercise party; 85 Rezidor Park Inns; 88 Botanic Inns; 87 Rezidor Park Inns; 90 Bambu Beach Club; 92 Belfast Visitor & Convention Bureau; 709t4t,c,b Marketing Birmingham, www.visitbirmingham.com; 93 istockphoto©weinaliphotography; 96 istockphoto© Lev Dolgatshjov; 98 Snow Dome, Tamworth; 100 City-Nites; 102 Marketing Birmingham, www.visit birmingham.com; 103tr istockphoto©Joe Gough; 103bl Ha Ha Bar and Grill; 104 Pleasure Ladies Nights; 106 Sence Nightclub; 108t istockphoto© Adam Booth; 108c Leisure Vouchers; 108b istockphoto©Peter Heyworth; 109 Leisure Vouchers; 110 istockphoto©yang guo; 112 istockphoto©David Dawson; 113 Number One St Luke's Hotel; 114 istockphoto©Stuart Taylor; 116 Brannigans; 117tr West Coast Rock Café; 117bl istockphoto©Dmitriy Shironosov; 118tr Funny Girls; 118bl www.flaresbars. co.uk; 120 The Syndicate; 122t Leisure Vouchers;

122c&b,123 bournemouthtourism.co.uk; 124 Leisure Vouchers; 126 Zorb South; 127&128 Hallmark Hotel Bournemouth; 130, 131bl, 130 bournemouthtourism. co.uk; 131tr istockphoto; 134 The Old Fire Station; 136t,c&b,137,142,144,145bl visitbrighton.com; 138 www.orb360.co.uk; 140 www.madamepeaches.com; 145tr Old Orleans Restaurant; 146 istockphoto©Anna Garmashova; 148 Rendezvous Casino; 150t istockphoto; 150c istockphoto©Marek Slusarczyk; 150t istockphoto; 151 Mandy Reynolds/ ssgreatbritain.org; 152 www.vintageteasets.co.uk; 155 istockphoto; 156 www.premierapartmentsbristol.com; 158,159,160 istockphoto; 162 Destination Bristol; 164t,c&b visitcardiff.com; 163 breconbeacons.org© Nanette Hepburn; 166,168,172&173bl visitcardiff.com; 173tr Leisure Vouchers; 174 istockphoto©Craig Swatton 176 ©DWP-Fotolia.com; 178t,c&b,179 istockphoto; 180 www.createyournight.com; 182 www.irishdanceparty.com; 184,187,188,190 istockphoto 192t istockphoto©Douglas McGilviray; 192c Edinburgh Fringe Festival; 192b istockphoto; 193 istockphoto©Alan Taylor; 194 Harvey Nichols Edinburgh©Grant Smith 2005; 196 Pop Party; 198 Festival Apartments; 180 The Living Room; 201 Khublai Khans; 202t&b Espionage; 204 istockphoto© Dmitriy Shironosov; 206t,c&b Glasgow City Council; 207 Curryoke Club; 208 istockphoto©Miodrag Gajic; 210 Huntfun.co.uk; 214 Sports Café Glasgow; 215&216 Curryoke Club; 218 istockphoto; 220t,c&b, 221 Leeds City Council; 222 Waterfall Spa; 224 Universal Dance Creations; 225 Holiday Inn Express; 226,228,229,230&232 Leeds City Council; 234t istockphoto©Stuart Taylor; 234c&b Marketing Manchester; 235 Alton Towers; 236 singalonga.net; 238 The Chill Factore; 239 Hallmark Hotels; 240 Marketing Manchester; 242 Brannigans, Cougar Leisure; 243bl&tr Hard Rock Café; 244&246t Pure Nightclub; 246b The Birdcage; 248t,c&b,249 Newcastle Gateshead Initiative; 250 The Pamper Party; 252 Milky Moments; 256,257 Newcastle Gateshead Initiative; 258 istockphoto; 260 The Attic; 261 Smuggler's Haven; 262c www.visitnewquay.org; 262b www.visitnewquay.org/Paul Watts; 263 www.visitnewquay.org; 264 englishsurfschool.com; 266 istockphoto©Arjan de Jager; 267 Hotel Victoria; 268 Smugglers Haven; 270&271t Fistral Blu; 271b istockphoto©Ryan Fox; 272 Berties Club; 274 Pure Newquay; 276t,c&b,277,278,280,284,285,286 istockphoto; 290t&c ©Kingpin Media Ltd; 290b Cherwell Boathouse; 291 istockphoto; 292 Cherwell Boathouse; 294 Banzai Events; 296 Acacia Cottages; 298 Raoul's Bar; 299bl The Living Room; 299tr istockphoto©Kai Zhang; 300 istockphoto; 302 istockphoto©Cat London; 304 istockphoto; 305,306,307 visit york; 309 Ace Hotel; 310,312,313tr Visit York; 313bl The Living Room; 314,316 visit york; 314 www.flaresbars.com.

THE CHEAPEST WAY TO THE BEST STAG AND HEN PARTIES IN EUROPE

BUDAPEST **KAUNAS**
PRAGUE **RIGA**
GDANSK **KRAKOW**
POZNAN **WROCLAW**

FLIGHTS FROM SELECTED UK AIRPORT

RYANAIR

win a recording party for 12

with www.songmaker.co.uk

Whether you fancy being a Disco Diva or Abbatastic on the mic, there is no better way to start your Hen Party and get everyone bonded and ready for the night ahead. Simply send your name and address to the email below, and you could win a fantastic fun experience for all standards of singer and ages. The winner can use the prize at one of 70 locations across the UK. There are so many classic tracks to choose from and there is nothing better than watching the hen reach those high notes with a glass of bubbly in hand. Join in on the choruses and sing your hearts out. Make it good, as you may get to relive it when it's played at the wedding!

Send your entry to: competition@cuttingedgeguides.com

Closing date for entries 31/12/11

Terms and Conditions

1. This competition is open to residents of the UK, Channel Islands, Isle of Man and Republic of Ireland aged 18 years or over, except for employees of Bath Spa Media Ltd or Acorne Plc (and their subsidiaries), their families or anyone else associated with this competition.

2. All information detailing how to enter this competition forms part of these terms and conditions. It is a condition of entry that all rules are accepted as final and that the competitor agrees to abide by these rules. The decision of the judges is final and no correspondence will be entered into. Submission of an entry will be taken to mean acceptance of these terms and conditions.

3. Entries should be submitted via email to competition@cuttingedgeguides.com. Entries must be labelled with the entrant's name and image files must be 72 dpi or higher, and between 1MB and 3MB. Entrants should include their own name and email address.

4. All entries must be received by the advertised closing date.

5. All images submitted must be the work of the individual submitting them and must not have been published elsewhere or have won a prize in any other photographic competition. It is the responsibility of each entrant to ensure that any images they submit have been taken with the permission of the subject and do not infringe the copyright of any third party or any laws. Entry to this competition warrants that the photographs submitted are the work of the entrant and that they own the copyright for them.

6. Copyright in all images submitted for this competition remains with the respective entrants. However, in consideration of their entering the competition, each entrant grants a worldwide, irrevocable, perpetual licence to Bath Spa Media Ltd to feature any, or all, of the submitted images in any of their publications, their websites and/or in any promotional material connected

to this competition.

7. Only one entry per person. Late, incomplete or corrupt entries will not be accepted. No responsibility can be accepted for lost entries and proof of transmission will not be accepted as proof of receipt. Entries must not be sent through agencies or third parties.

8. The winning entry will be the one that is judged to be the most visually appealing, original and self-explanatory. The winner will be notified within fourteen days of the closing date of the competition. The winner is required to contact Bath Spa Media to confirm acceptance of their prize within 10 days of notification. In the event of non-acceptance within the specified period, or if the person is not contactable, Bath Spa Media reserves the right to reallocate the prize.

9. The winners may be required to take part in publicity (travel expenses will be paid if necessary).

10. The prize will be available from the date that the results are announced. All prizes are non transferable and there are no cash alternatives.

11. Events may occur that render the competition itself or the awarding of the prize impossible due to reasons beyond the control of the Promoter and accordingly the Promoter may at its absolute discretion vary or amend the promotion and the entrant agrees that no liability shall attach to the Promoter as a result thereof.

12. Bath Spa Media Ltd is responsible for the first part of the promotion, which is the publication and adjudication of the competition. All other facilities connected with the provision of the prize are the responsibility of Acorne plc.

13. English law applies and the exclusive jurisdiction of the English Courts shall prevail.

Benedicta Leigh was born in Hampshire in 1922. After working as a VAD during the Second World War, she trained at the Royal Academy of Dramatic Art, and performed widely in the theatre.

A writer for most of her life, her first full-length work, *The Catch of Hands*, was published by Virago in 1991. A remarkable autobiography, it won the MIND Book of the Year Award. In *Unlock, and Remind Me of the Sea*, she turns her considerable talent to fiction to produce a novel that is as haunting as it is engaging. She has two grown-up children, and lives in Richmond, Surrey.

Unlock, and Remind Me of the Sea

BENEDICTA LEIGH

Published by VIRAGO PRESS Limited, May 1994
42–43 Gloucester Crescent, London NW1 7PD

Typeset by Keyboard Services, Luton
Printed and bound in Great Britain by
Cox & Wyman Ltd, Reading, Berkshire

To David
1929–64

Chapter
One

T HE PARTY RAGED on for some time. She walked home by the shore, and sitting in the kitchen ate scrambled eggs from the saucepan with her christening spoon. Toffee-coloured hair and a small scar near the corner of her mouth due to the mishandling of a cigarette did not satisfactorily proclaim her ability to cause attention, though her appearance brought a reasonable amount of pleasure to a few people.

She attracted, demanded, and sometimes dared the hazard of crying for the bonfire of her life that now and then blistered her. He did not like this. Not because he had a tender heart but rather that he found her inexplicable and thoroughly disliked a great many things about her. He was, he told friends, thankful that they were not married. He also said how guilty he felt saying such things about her, since he was devoted to her and knew she depended upon him. This was hardly true. He did not feel in the least guilty about anything he said about her and he had never been in the least devoted to her, although he liked to think she was dependent upon him. Certainly he was thankful that they were not married, since it gave him scope to show off to other people who admired him.

Emily put on a coat and went out again, leaving the cottage that sometimes accommodated them both as closely as a skin but without its licence.

The sea's hesitation had pitched up a head of spume, and the long spit of sand seemed to her to have shifted shape. A cadaver hung black in her mind, maggots wig-wagging through the eye-holes, and she stood in the cold and watched the spoiling sea and the sand and saw the shape that might, with luck, have been him in death, the ground covering him.

When she got back to the cottage, Morgan was sitting on the step waiting for her.

'You had the keys,' he said. 'I couldn't get in.'

She unlocked the door and followed him in.

'I thought it was you lying there dead as a doornail, but it was the sand and the mist,' she said. 'Must we go back to the green belt tomorrow?'

'Don't be silly, of course we must,' he said, his face a cul-de-sac. Oppressive and incalculable, he did not speak again.

She lay in bed and thought about her mother's dressmaker. Her mother was young then, about twenty, not married yet, and her parents and sisters lived in a London square, the sooty leaves rattling in the rain, the housemaids blind with fatigue stumbling up five or six flights of stairs to bed and no hanky-panky.

And in the late afternoon a dressmaker sat in one of the spare rooms and made dresses for her mother and her sisters, taking the pins from her mouth when she had finished and leaving after she had had tea and seed cake beyond the green baize door.

Emily got out of bed and stood beside the window, and thought of her mother's Marcel wave and saw the mist and the crucifixion through it, and heard the stirring of the planets and the music.

Next morning they drove back to the suburbs and the insistent spring. In the flat she was afraid of the sounds that beat about each room when it rained, but in the cottage the rain glorified her life so that she could bear it even when their minds were brought to siege.

A flight of letters pushed against the front door as they opened it.

'Let me go back,' she said, after the silent unpacking. 'Let me go by myself – I'll get the train, I'll go after breakfast tomorrow, I can get the ten-fourteen.'

Morgan's inclement smile broke her mettle.

'Emily,' he said. 'Be sensible.' And she caught sight of the enemy.

Do not take my soundness and my consideration in the night, the blind frontier.

'Why don't you leave everything to me?' he said. The hair that lifted tenderly from his forehead had reaped for him a harvest of votaries. He was a prude, and a sentimentalist, and like many such, held between his thighs the wrenching need for cruelty, sweetly given, and taken in torment, a butterfly's orgasm.

In the kitchen, planned by Morgan, curtains and wallpaper fragrantly matched. The sunlight possessed his good taste and its yield of seemly vulgarity. He was an occasional actor, and wished for a greater life where lemon trees hung with gold and where he was not damned by Emily's obscure desperation. He had once coupled with Pip, her almost impermeably chic sister, and had found it intensely exciting. He had not told Emily, of course, but often thought of the day he would, and of the pleasure it would give him to do so.

Late in the lee of the afternoon, when he was not there, Emily sat on the bathroom floor and leaned her head against the door and wept, and put her hands across her eyes and sometimes across her mouth and would not let be and could not and felt the falling of it. And lying in a creature's breathing earth, all other sounds forsook the necessary world, except this signature of custody.

At about five o'clock, she picked up the telephone and dialled. Pip's voice came through like a thong.

'Iss?'

'Help me, Pip, please,' said Emily. 'Are you busy? What are you doing?'

'Avocado face-wise,' said Pip. 'Why?'

'For God's sake, Pip.'

'Iss?'

'Pip, I need to talk to you, couldn't I come over? I'm afraid, you see. Could I come tomorrow?'

'No. Avocado now, taking Constance to vet tomorrow. Puppies keep biting her ears. Whined all night.'

'I can't go on not talking about it,' said Emily. 'There's something I—'

'Emily, get rid of him,' said Pip. 'He's a bleeder. Not trimminsely G in B either.' She took a breath and added, 'I shouldn't imagine.' She put the receiver down.

Pip lived alone in a small house in Fulham. She spent a good deal of time on her appearance, and used a taut, compacted form of speech unless in bed with someone, when a remarkable range of dirty talk left her victim greatly overtaxed.

Constance, her Dandy Dinmont bitch, sometimes accompanied her for short pavement walks, otherwise leading a somewhat austere life conducted by her mistress who wore an apron and nylon house gloves when feeding her or stroking her galvanised coat.

Emily did not ring her sister again.

Morgan arrived home in time for dinner, and, charmed by the sight of Emily busying herself in the kitchen, swiftly drew a finger down her spine. She turned, picked up the cup of tea she had been drinking and threw it at him. He backed away. From the table she had laid for dinner she took two plates, two knives, two forks, two large and two small place mats, two pudding spoons and forks and a green Perspex salad bowl bought by him and which now bore several pieces of watercress. All these she balanced in the crook of her left arm and, charging her right hand from it, threw each separate item at his crutch. Quite a lot of dressing and some chopped garlic were all that had attached to it. The tea had missed him and hit the fridge, and some of the watercress fell slowly and sporadically from his jersey to the floor.

He paled. 'Have you taken your tablets?' he said.

'I'll take them now,' she said, and going into the bathroom threw them down the loo. When she came back, Morgan was wiping garlic off his shoes.

'What are we having for supper?' he said.

'Salad,' she said. Morgan got out of the house as quickly as was possible without loss of dignity. He went to the pub first where he had a large brandy, and spent the rest of the evening and most of the night with Pip. He felt he really had to have someone to talk to. Constance, whose ears, protected by pieces of lint and spread upon the floor like cabbage leaves on either side of her reclining skull, seemed most concerned for him. The puppies ate alternately the lint and the ears.

'I just cannot think what goes on in her head,' said Morgan. 'I really do try, but nothing seems to be any good. I mean, I love people, and I can honestly say I have a lot of friends. But she doesn't seem to want people. When we go down to the cottage, she doesn't do anything. Just sits outside watching birds and hedgehogs, that sort of thing. Terribly empty life, quite honestly.'

'Any G in B?' said Pip.

'I don't really think I ought to talk to you about that,' said Morgan diffidently. 'I mean, one's upbringing – I mean it's in really rather bad taste, don't you think? Well you'll understand what I'm trying to say – it's a question of sometimes if you know what I mean, and after all I'm a perfectly normal man and—'

'Then forget it,' said Pip sharply.

Emily arrived at the cottage next morning, the contemplation of solitude like honey for her pleasing. She passed the Drakes' house and unlocked the door of the cottage. The lane was full of puddles and a believer's necromancy told the sky's harmonics.

On the floor of the sitting room she slept, with a cup of coffee beside her and in the air words became numbers and

5

she heard the ring of twelve and the music of three and knew the stepping stones of thunder.

It is you who needs my screaming. I am your pleasure's humiliation but am not roped to your laughter, for I am the limit you will never reach. I am the ring of twelve.

The telephone rang. It was Morgan. 'Why didn't you tell me you were going?'

'Please don't touch me,' she said.

'What on earth can you possibly mean?' he said. 'How can I touch you from here? I simply wondered how you were after that scene last night. I thought you were getting better, but quite honestly I'm not at all sure now.'

'Look after me,' she said. 'Mind about me.' And she said it again: 'Mind about me.'

'Look,' said Morgan, 'I'll come over and have lunch and see how you are.'

'No,' she said, and shook.

'Well, please do take your tablets – you'll feel so much better if you do.' The switchblade of the sentimentalist – I am your inspector and your counsellor, I mind about you, remember the ring-a-roses we used to play.

'Would you feel better if we got married?' he said. Silence lurched between each other's jail. He did not want to marry anyone, yet, poor thing, she needed him to hang on to, to give her some stability in what must seem to her a hostile world.

She said, 'No thank you,' the creep of fear censored by politeness.

'Well, all right,' he said. 'We'll stay as we are. I won't come over, but promise me you'll go and take your tablets and then find something pleasant to do – it makes sense. Ring me any time – I'll always be here and you know I'll help if I possibly can.'

Emily walked out of the back door. Behind the cottage the warm early tangle-buzz of summer's coming

6

restitution, the field-mouse-bent cow parsley, Victoria plum, convolvulus, thump of windfalls in the night, promiscuous blackberries, cram of overgrown undergrowth, kiss of courtesy left by spring, Victorian railway carriage genus Nesbit, convolvulus, acacias bayoneting hair, bay tree between shed and railway carriage, rain, morning storms, no television, the tearing sea and convolvulus and convolvulus and convolvulus, and I will stay here, she thought, until I die.

She went into the shed, took a saw that hung neatly on the wall and started sawing up Morgan's workbench. Since she had never sawn up anything before, she failed, merely producing several small chips of wood and some blood by about four o'clock in the afternoon. She then walked to the village and bought some eggs, bread, milk and a box of chocolates which she opened and started eating on the way home. She felt much revived and looked forward to continuing the work next day, perhaps with greater success.

With this in mind, she walked into the kitchen of the Drakes' house next door where Elizabeth Drake was washing up, and said, 'Would you consider helping me to saw up Morgan's workbench?'

'Certainly,' said Elizabeth. Her young son, who was living in a tent in the hall, said, 'I should think he'd be quite cross if you do.'

'He's away, I take it?' Elizabeth added.

'Yes,' said Emily.

'I'll come and have a look at it first. Are you having difficulties with it?'

'Yes. I can't do it.'

'I see,' said Elizabeth. They got through the gap in the hedge and went into the shed.

'You'll never saw that up,' said Elizabeth. 'You could get someone to do it for you, I suppose, but you might need it. What are you planning? Knocking the whole shed down?'

'Yes,' said Emily.

'I could certainly help you do that, it's like ply, fairly flimsy. Why are you doing this?'

'It's Morgan. I'm afraid of him. Besides, he likes women who wear navy blue frocks with red spots.'

'How extraordinary,' said Elizabeth. 'I can't imagine anyone liking navy blue frocks with red spots. Are you sure?'

'Yes,' said Emily. 'He doesn't really care for women like me at all.'

'But you're very attractive in an eccentric way.'

'Yes, I know,' said Emily, 'but he doesn't like very attractive eccentric-looking, amusing, brilliantly clever women like me, because I take quite a lot of attention from him, which is extremely enjoyable of course, for me and hell for him I'm glad to say. And his mother hates me.'

'*De rigueur*,' said Elizabeth. 'You are not what she had in mind and particularly if out of wedlock. To miss the opportunity of wearing a hat often has a brutalising effect upon women.'

They walked up the Drakes' drive and Emily stood for a moment before getting through the gap.

'Is Morgan likely to be coming over at any point?' said Elizabeth.

'No. I'll stop him. Sometimes I see things and if I'm with Morgan, he says I'm sick and makes me take tablets. I'm afraid of him. I don't tell him anything now.'

'What things do you see?'

'I see music and I see numbers and I see words and I see darkness round him. Sometimes I feel sick. Don't tell anyone. I pretend loyalty, but I dream his torture and death.'

'You're right,' said Elizabeth. 'The shed must go. After the holidays. I'll be comparatively free then. Ring me if you need me.'

Morgan rang at twenty-four minutes past seven to see how Emily had been during the day.

'All right,' she said. 'I've got a slight cold and I'm going to bed early.'

'I rang earlier but there was no answer,' he said.

She said, 'I went out for some aspirin.'

'Are you being a good girl?'

She shuffled her wits and answered, 'Yes. I'm going to knock down the shed next autumn.'

He laughed and said: 'No, I mean really.'

'Well, all right then, the following spring.'

Emily sat in the kitchen, warm with fantasy.

Just me, Elizabeth and a posse of ragged peasants carrying goat's cheese and sawn-off shotguns, and wearing checked shirts and Basque berets. Right, Pablo, we're going in. I have a knife between my teeth and I'm wearing my new black pants in which I look frail and courageous.

The world moved, and memory burned the rocks white and fevered, single trees nailed against the sky's retina. She saw again the crucifixion, and remembered this place. Her hands were damp from it and her life turned from its diagram.

She went out and walked to the sea and stood watching it, and beneath its darkness the transient emerald shoals, the ring and chime and chant of little fishes, a merchant's haul, and the clouds that shadowed it.

Chapter
Two

I N THE MORNING of the house next door, Cork, youngest of
the three children, still slept, though occasionally shaken
by a salvo of hiccups. His thumb was loosely plugged in
his mouth, and beside him on a chair lay his imagined dog,
Raymond, covered with a square of winceyette. Cork's two
sisters, scarcely grown and barely dressed, leaned over him,
willing him to awake and honour the temperate first arrival of
the sun. Alice, tentative, particular, and a little older than the
other two, breathed heavily into Cork's ear: 'Me and Jess are
going to the village to fetch the breakfast bread. Quickly, do
you want to come too?'

Cork's name was Andrew, but upon his sixth birthday he
had asked to be called Cork and his family were agreeable to
this departure from the commonplace. Now, a few months
later, his own name was in occasional use only. This morning,
he took his thumb from his mouth, said, 'Wait for me', and
with his eyes closed, slid from his bed and fought with his
pyjama buttons. His stalk-like neck supported his head as
entrancingly as a poppy's cup, and he smiled at his
worshipping sisters. He was beautiful, but did not yet
recognise any such thing.

On the landing, his mother, naked, passed him, as usual
allowing him to say, 'Why've you got fur down there?' before
habit caused her to answer, 'It conceals certain precincts.' He

11

put his arms round her, touching his ear to the warmth of her stomach.

'Something talking in there,' he said. 'Oh please, let me swim. I want to swim off the spit, and lash my tail.'

'Only if the girls are with you.'

'Why?'

'Because you are awful and because you are beloved.'

'Not belovedest though,' called Jess.

'Listen,' said Cork. 'We're going to fetch the bread. I can swim just two times and the girls can watch me from the shop.'

'Leave her alone!' shouted Jess, flying out of the bathroom disfigured by jealousy. 'Leave her alone, stop doing that to her, don't touch her, she doesn't like you, Cork. Remember what I say.' She gave one terrible sob before leaving instructions. 'Go back to bed, Mummy. I'm leaving a note for you on the kitchen table which says "we of gone to get the bread."'

'That isn't spelt right,' said Alice.

'Get out of this house all of you except Mummy.' Jess pulled Cork from his rock-a-bye refuge, shouting, 'You are never to touch her ever again, or I'll kill you with a big knife. Mummy, it's quite wrong to be bare in front of Cork, it isn't good manners. He's not a baby any more.'

'Yes I am,' howled Cork. 'I am a dear little baby.'

Voices slapping and biting, one colliding with another.

Their mother, Elizabeth, walked into the bedroom, a comfortable burrow, though one where she seldom felt protected. She was angrily watched by Cork.

'Can I come and get in your bed with you and Daddy?'

She said 'no' and shut the door behind her, and Cork, beside himself, shouted: 'I'll never love you again, and I won't ever wait for you again. I'm waiting for good old Raymond, and he's waiting for good old Jesus to come and ride him, although he's been sick so he can't be ridden and he can't come and fetch the bread today – he must stay lying on his chair while I swim and flap my tail.'

All the roots of life were in Cork, and behind closed eyelids he felt the gold of early sunlight and the secret sky, but inside him was the roar of impotence.

Dressed in tender eggshell colours, the girls walked down the lane, followed by Cork, raptly leaping small overnight puddles. Alice, alight with knowledge, said, 'It is wrong to say "we of gone", it's "we *have* gone to get the bread". You wrote it wrong.'

'Please,' fretted Cork. 'Please let me bathe on my own. I've got my bathing trunks on underneath and we needn't tell Mummy. She wouldn't mind anyway because she's busy. I heard something talking in her tummy.'

'No you didn't,' said Jess. 'It was cups of tea inside her, not babies. She doesn't want any more of us.'

'I think I shall start calling her Elizabeth,' said Cork grandly.

The two girls pursed their lips and walked on ahead, but Cork left them, skirted the bridle-path that led to the village and walked down to the beach-tray cabin where Laura the beach-tray lady was snapping the striped blinds up, ready for the Easter visitors. Cork drowned in love for her.

'Marry me,' he whispered, and she said 'Yes', easy and pleasant, the inclination of her mien being always warm and south-westerly.

'Please,' he said and stood watching her, his hands clasped and his heart breaking.

'What is it you want, Andrew?' she said and he answered, 'I want to stand beside you and wear an apron and take the money when the visitors come because you smell nice like apple pudding.'

It was true she sometimes sucked a clove to keep her breath sweet and sometimes for toothache. 'Shall I treat you to an ice-cream before any visitors come?' she said, and he said, 'Yes please' and 'thank you', and she withheld the ice-cream for a moment to give her time to ask, 'Have you had your breakfast yet?' He nodded, a lying nod that each of them accommodated, and his silence thanked her for her sentience, her inferno of crimson hair and her perfect skin. 'When? When marry?'

It is doubtful if she heard him, busy as she was with cups and saucers, and paper napkins. Standing beside her, he absorbed something of her uncommon glory. She seemed to him to be someone of great consequence who had made of him a willing supplicant.

A fine blade of a cat leapt up on to a corner of the counter and stood for a speculative instant before jumping down.

Laura said: 'Your mother says you're not to bathe unless your sisters are with you.'

Cork became possessed, waving his arms and hurling himself about, shouting, 'She didn't say that – I heard her not say it, I can do what I like, we're not visitors like ordinary people – we're different, we live here.'

He threw the ice-cream on the ground.

'I don't want it!' he shouted. 'I was going to give you a present but now I shan't.'

Immediately and unfairly Laura leapt the boundaries of subtlety. 'You're a bad, bad boy to shout at me like that,' she said, her voice dark and out of true. 'Go home. Go home at once and don't come back until you're good.'

Cork saw that the world had changed, and that it had done so with a noticeable absence of charity.

'I'm good now,' he said, to repair the rent that he perceived in his life. He refused the tissue that Laura offered him and said, 'I'm not a baby, you know', and after a moment he said: 'I've got to go now, because I've got a lot of busy things to do. I'll see you some time.'

He turned, and with a deep unhappiness started walking home. Laura had more wisdom than to call him back to her, and Cork felt too raw to go back of his own accord. He was six and a half and it was to be a warm day. A string of gypsies passed him, over from the mainland they were.

At home in the large tyrannical kitchen, Elizabeth and

her husband Joe enjoyed a quiet breakfast of real coffee and a failed lemon mousse discovered by Joe at the back of the refrigerator.

Elizabeth watched him help himself before saying, 'I shouldn't. Not the mousse. It might kill you. And me.'

He emptied it down the sink and said, 'What are you up to today?'

'I'm having an affair with the Dagenham Girl Pipers. Exhausting, of course, but I can't tell you how grateful they are.' Joe moved round the kitchen table and hit her quite a clip on the side of the face with the flat of his hand.

'I was only joking,' she said foolishly.

'I know,' said Joe. 'It's just that sometimes it's quite enjoyable hurting you.'

Cork did not go straight home. He went first to the village junk shop and stole a bracelet, which he put in his shorts pocket. Jess and Alice were already home when he arrived and there were two Coburg loaves on the table.

'Where have you been?' said his mother.

'I've been talking to Laura, given her a good talking to because she was horrid and bit my nose,' said Cork recklessly. 'And I cried, and can I have some wood to make a present for her, so she'll see how nice I really am?'

'I expect so. Ask your Da.' Elizabeth removed from the sole of her shoe a jelly baby which had temporarily anchored her to the floor.

'And can I have a glass of sherry to buck me up?' said Cork.

'He's so sweet when he's good,' mourned Alice, and her mother said, 'Well, he's not good now. You can have wood, Cork, but not sherry.'

'I want to sit on your lap, Mummy,' wept Cork. 'Let me be on your lap and have a sleep so I can be spanking fresh for Laura. Make a lap for me, I'm nearly small, please, Mummy.'

The stranglehold of his voice was her compliance, each

15

restoring the other as he lay nesting, his head nudged into the hollow of his mother's neck. Tears slipped down his cheeks, for the day that once seemed pledged to particular blessings had now betrayed him.

The bracelet fell out of his pocket and on to the floor and Cork closed his eyes against the variable world while his mother rang the shop, explained and apologised.

Conscious of a mild elevation of the spirits, Joe moved towards the door. If his luck were in, he might end up in the nearest intensive care unit, far away from Elizabeth and those damnable children. One last, and perhaps dying, request he directed at her: 'Could you cut my toenails for me?'

'I thought you were growing them.'

A violence rose inside Joe, and a darkness fell upon his day as he realised how near he might be to death, and that he could die without an audience unless he were very careful. He left the kitchen, comforted by the discovery that he had a slight limp which he now hoped to nurture by walking carefully round the garden and perhaps gathering further symptoms to succour.

Cork slept and Elizabeth, with love and fury, called back each birth, each seizure of her territory, each adversary's fists, each interloper. She knew that when the language of war had been relinquished, a swaddled overlord in a pram would be unmasked, waiting to get the upper hand.

Alice stood in the doorway. 'He must be too heavy for you,' she said. 'Shall we put him to bed and let him sleep properly, so that you and Daddy can sit in the garden like real parents? Mightn't it be rather nice?'

'Darling, I think I'll have to leave Daddy. It is difficult to like him. I'm used to him, but it's not enough. He is a custom with me, that's all.' There was no ease in Elizabeth when she said this.

They put Cork to sleep in the nursery and she said, 'Don't talk about it, for God's sake,' thinking: I must tidy up my mind and the sigh in me. She took Alice's hand. Alice did not move.

16

That night it rained heavily, and down the drive water pockets flooded the reflected universe.

During the night Elizabeth's mind wheeled and spun and changed without mercy until she got out of bed. Joe sat up at once. 'What are you doing? What's the matter with you? Where are you going?' he said.

'To look out of the window, to watch the rain. And I have to think about things,' said Elizabeth. 'Joe, wake up. Darling, we never talk about anything and now we need to.'

Joe did not wake up.

Cork came in and stood with his mother watching the curtain of water against the darkness.

'Could Raymond and me come in here with you and you give us strokes?' he said. She said, 'Yes, and tomorrow we will take the bracelet back and everyone will feel comfortable again.'

Cork went out and came back into the bedroom again saying, 'Strokes, please.' From Joe came a deathbed rattle demanding aspirins and a glass of water.

'Get them yourself,' said Elizabeth. 'I'm busy giving strokes.'

Cork said, 'I get a hurt in my inside when I think.'

'A pain?' said his mother.

'No, a hurting,' he said, 'like being frightened.'

'Go to bed, go for God's sake.'

When Cork had gone Elizabeth went downstairs, coldly in her nightgown, and sat in the drawing room with the curtains drawn back, watching the drenched and ruined landscape.

The blindfolding of night sheltered her from her thoughts.

In the morning she looked at herself in the glass and saw no miracle and thought: One day I might cry over that. But not bloody now.

Cork and Raymond had breakfast under the kitchen table.

'Is it because you're frightened about the bracelet?'

asked Elizabeth. Cork said nothing and Jess said, 'Mummy, why does he take things?'

'I expect it's a phase,' said Alice. 'Why don't you take him to a phase-doctor?' She laughed immoderately and Elizabeth said, 'Shut up, all of you.'

The girls blushed and took their Cornflakes into the garden and Joe hastened from the room carrying a cup of coffee and a bottle of painkillers. At the door he did not fail to draw attention to his ulcer, which he said was 'playing up again'.

'I feel as if my life has been rearranged for me, and I can't deal with it. We've got to talk about things,' Elizabeth said and turned her head away and closed her mind.

Out in the garden, Alice said, 'Do you think they like us?' and Jess said, 'I think so. It's each other that they don't like.'

'Mummy said he hit her. Were you there? Did you see him do it?' said Alice, but Jess shook her head.

Cork put his bowl on the draining board and took Raymond for a run in the garden, marking time as he neared the girls, in case they were talking about him. 'I'm going to the village with Mummy this morning,' he said. Jess raised her eyebrows and said, 'You mean you're going with her to take back the bracelet you stole.'

Cork went on marking time without answering, and when his mother called him to go, he said he felt sick and might be sick. But he went with her all the same, saying, just loud enough for the girls to hear, 'Mummy, can we have ice-creams from the shop, just you and me?'

'You can but I won't. I'll give the girls some ice-cream money for theirs when we come back,' said Elizabeth, and the girls exchanged looks. Cork looked darkly at his mother and said, 'When they have theirs, can I have another one so that it's fair?'

'You are a piggy-wig,' said Elizabeth, and they took the bridle-path and what they called the covered way to the village.

Deep green trees, as tall as castles, met over their heads,

splitting the Easter sky and shielding the wood pigeons. Here and there were large and apparently unlived-in houses, their gates swinging, their hedges overgrown.

'If Daddy goes away, can I call you Elizabeth?' said Cork.

'Good Heavens, yes,' she said. She did not goad him to go into the junk shop and confess his crime, since already she felt that an unidentifiable disturbance was abroad and preparing to lay waste the whole family.

A few days passed before Cork went to see Laura again, anxious for fortune's grace, and already sensing beneath his feet the light high meadows of the moon. He did not take Raymond with him. Scraping carrots in the kitchen, Elizabeth saw him swanking off in his best shirt, and said, 'Where are you going?'

Cork came peacocking back. 'I'm going to see Laura, and I'm going to take this for a present,' he said, taking from behind his back two foot-long pieces of wood nailed into an L-shape. 'It's a carving,' he said.

'Lovely,' said his mother, 'it's lovely.' She took it, looked at it, stroked it, said, 'Did Daddy give you the wood?'

'Yes,' said Cork, 'and he gave me the nail and a lend of his hammer, and he said I was an extremely good and faithful servant and much nicer than the girls.'

'Look me in the eye,' said Elizabeth. 'Did he really say all that?'

'No,' Cork said and took the wood from her, watching her and thinking: when I live here alone, I shall sleep in the kitchen so that I can have food whenever I want it.

'I'm afraid, Mummy, sometimes I'm afraid,' he said. She felt the pluck of danger in the atmosphere, and turned as quickly as water starts from a tap.

'I dream things,' said Cork and changed his thoughts. 'I dreamed that Laura would rather have marshmallows than a carving. I think I would rather, too.'

'I'd like a carving every time,' said Elizabeth.

'Are you going away?' he asked, waiting and waiting for the answer or the quietness that could be an answer.

'I don't know,' she said, 'at this stage.'

'I don't want to go with you,' said Cork. 'The girls can go. I want to live here on my own.'

'I see,' said his mother. She watched him touch one of the pine trees for luck as he turned into the lane, leaving, with exhilaration, the warm, dense air in the house.

Laura was sitting in a yellow canvas chair outside the beach-tray cabin. She turned her head as Cork neared her, and each felt the uncertainty of their tenuous friendship.

Cork said: 'I'm sorry', and held out the carving to her and said again, 'I'm sorry. This is so that you'll remember me. I didn't mean to shout, I didn't really.'

'It's nice, Andrew, very nice. Don't worry about the shouting. I was just as bad. Did your father help you make this?'

'My father never helps me with anything,' said Cork. His thoughts planed. 'Can I come and live here with you?' he said.

She took both his hands and said, 'Look, dear, I think I know how you feel, but I'm much too old for you.'

He pulled away from her. 'No,' he said, 'no.' Laura put her hand to his cheek and said, 'You don't want to live with me. Think what your parents would say. They wouldn't like it at all. Have some sense, Andrew.'

Cork felt pain and anger, as though his life had been torn from its purblind sojourn. He said, 'All right then, I won't come back. I won't ever come and see you again.'

He walked quickly away from her and over the shingle and although he felt a little sickness in himself, his mind was sustained by a satisfaction and a balance, as though the entire episode had carried unplanned instructions that he had followed with little consideration.

He walked up the road and as far as the donkey paddock although there were no longer any donkeys in it, and little grass was left. Instead there were large scuffs of bare earth in its exhausted territory and amongst the stony frets of field flowers.

Cork could see that they had already climbed over the gate to the paddock, his sisters and the village girls, the Marys, the Bettys, the Margerys, their faded cotton frocks flying up as they hopped and spun and took hands and sang. They sang 'Poor Jenny lies a-weeping' and 'Wallflowers, wallflowers growing up so high'. Long-ago memories of much earlier singing games, the solitary figure in the centre of the circle, and the simple authentic fear felt by every child.

Elizabeth and Joe were sprawling on the lawn when Cork arrived back. 'When will there be blackberries?' he said. The brambles had snarled his hair as he passed them.

'In the early autumn, darling, when we will have them in summer puddings while the bees still buzz and the swimming's nearly over,' said Elizabeth.

'When can I swim bare? My waggler is still quite small but I'd better be quick because when I'm bigger, it'll be enormous,' said Cork.

'When we're rich, we'll have a swimming pool of our own whatever size your waggler is,' said his mother and fell lightly asleep.

Joe got up. 'I think I'll go in,' he said. 'With a sensitive skin like mine even this early sun can be treacherous.'

'Raymond would like some shortbread and some fizzy lemonade, please,' said Cork.

'I think you ought to stop all this Raymond nonsense,' said his father.

'Joe, goddam you,' said Elizabeth, and as he left she added, 'Have a nice illness.' But inside her a commotion began to grow, for Cork still lived in her, and she would always give him shelter. Once when he was much younger, he had said in her ear, 'Wans I sor a gold bird and it made a cracky noise to me, and wans I sor a ginger dog.'

'He means a fox,' Alice had said. 'I've seen it too but Jess and I don't show off like he does.'

'He's very small,' said Elizabeth, and spooned him up, settling him on her hip where he sat like a potentate.

'A pheasant, that's what I think it was, you clever little monster,' she had said, inexorably loving. 'You clever, clever boy.'

It had indeed been a pheasant, struck by the sun, its feathers a spill of sovereigns.

Cork lay down beside his mother and thought of Laura. He said: 'I am never going to see Laura again. I have decided.'

Elizabeth woke and slept again. Cork thought: when I see the girls, I will tell them. He had left Jess and Alice in the donkey paddock and had come home by himself, passing the little school which he had been persuaded to attend. There he was called Andrew, and not too many allowances were made for his slight backwardness and moments of wisdom.

There were never too many pupils at the school nor too few. As one child left, another arrived and as one season changed hands with the next, so did small newcomers spend their first day stalking Mrs Frame, whose hand was always free to hang on to, and who often had a liquorice allsort ready to put into their mouths should they cry.

'Open your mouth and shut your eyes and see what the fairies bring you,' she would chant, and thus were the weepers eased and strengthened.

It was a warm, shiftless wastrel of a day when summer found its tenancy and the two girls went barefoot. Cork did not do so, for he had new sandals and wished them to be noticed by as many people as possible. Joe mowed the lawn, and Elizabeth was tagged by Cork wherever she went, either in the house or about the garden.

Once he said, 'Don't get a divorce,' and he said, 'Don't. Don't go away.' She thought: I cannot bear any of my children to be unhappy but there is nothing I can do about it.

Cork said: 'The girls talk about it and talk about it until I can hardly breathe,' and Elizabeth thought: They are

22

preparing to make me feel guilty, and she said: 'I will talk to Daddy about it. Let's go into the kitchen. You could make a cake.'

Cork did not want to make a cake, but the cool kitchen tempered the clamour in each of them, and he leaned against Elizabeth.

She thought of the way things were, and he thought of what might have been and perhaps still might be.

He was, after all, a child, and knew only the lunar landscape of his own mind, assuming that others were much the same.

Maybe I will make a cake after all, he thought, as long as I can have all the licks from the basin, even if the girls come in before I've finished.

Elizabeth moved slowly about the garden looking, touching, snipping. She could sense the sea, and the smell of the pines was warm and spicy. A remembered heaviness hung inside her and she knew that the nourishing and cherishing of even one child was enough. Let go. Let it go, that one child, let it finish and let my day end. Retracing Cork's uncertain tempo, her memory held shadows, as though something must break in the going forward of time, and as if a creature were to be taken from her.

These were thoughts as sensational as the calling of the tiger.

The garden showed brilliant in the summer buzz and Joe was taken by a fit of bravura coughing which all but drowned the sound of the mowing machine. He stopped to savour the moment and Elizabeth thought: please God put some sort of spin on my life.

On the way to see Laura at the beach-tray cabin, she passed the empty house, sometimes discovered and played in by children, a house, unlived in and lacking its vital marrow. But I might live there, she thought. I might live there alone.

As she approached the cabin she began to walk quickly and nervously. It was the end of Laura's day, low tide and the huts now empty. On the broad sash of shingle lay driftwood and sea tangle and the brutal pink of a doll's shoe. Beyond the huts, grasses and wild flowers trembled in the vigorous air.

Laura was pulling down the blinds of the cabin, and was neither prepared for Elizabeth's advent nor for her shipwrecked face.

'Hullo Mrs Drake,' she said, but Elizabeth's mind was a murderer's moon, dark and concealing. The haphazardry of anger overran her speech, the avalanche of words promised but not said, nor shouted nor screamed, but stifled.

'You have taken him, you bitch, you have nearly killed him.' Small high-pitched words, thin and raw, were all that came from her, and she knew the fall of the clammy creeper, the climber's testing ground.

'He will die of you,' she said and her mind swam and murmured: I must not die with nothing answered and my world done for, the long ridiculousness of life sped.

Laura watched Elizabeth's face and movements as she turned and walked and turned again, once stooping to pick up a handful of pebbles. She did not feel as though she had expelled some heavy sorrow, but rather that somewhere upon a hilltop a cairn had begun to loosen and roll down towards her, stone by stone, each reaching her and drawing blood before she could avoid the next. 'Bloody leave my son alone,' she wailed, an animal's wail of torment, the deadly note still showing in her voice.

'He's only a little boy,' said Laura. 'He'll mend.'

'Oh no,' said Elizabeth, 'he won't.'

'You silly woman,' said Laura. 'I should bugger off if I were you. You'd drive anyone into an early grave, let alone that poor child.'

She turned and walked up the slipway and Elizabeth watched her out of sight.

A question, a disquiet and a malaise of the senses snatched at her as she went home, and she decided to say nothing to anyone about her encounter with Laura.

In the lapping shade of the afternoon, Cork drowsed, happy with the small creatures that took cover in the willing earth. He dreamed he had bound the Pleiades and taken Andromeda by storm. The little girls lay beneath a tree, head to tail like harmonious fish in a still life, and Elizabeth took off her shoes and felt the coolness of the grass under her feet. 'Where's Daddy?' she asked.

'Lying down thinking about being famous,' said Jess. 'Oh do divorce him, then we can have the house to ourselves. Think of the blissful times we can have. Picnics. And champagne even when it isn't anyone's birthday.'

'I don't think you ought to talk about divorce like that,' said Elizabeth. 'It's a very serious step.' Laura's wintry words had chilled her. I need an enormous wasteland of silence, she thought, to make decisions and discoveries, to put words to my feelings. Then I shall need the curl and spring of the sea. Cork sleeps, and the girls are trying to order my life. I should not worry about anything, but I must, because I am a silly woman.

'I would like cornflowers and a fountain,' she said aloud. Once when Joe had said, 'Why don't you write poetry?' she had said, 'I do, but I leave it in my head where no one can see it.'

Now, with Cork asleep and cornflowers in the offing, she could not think of divorce.

A beetle walked over Cork's leg and Elizabeth put out a hand to flick it away. 'Don't get it away, I like it,' he said, opening his eyes and closing them again.

Summer swung slowly into autumn, with comely chestnuts and late sun.

The smell of the earth captivated, warm and unrestrained. Jess and Alice took the train to a girls' school each day, on the other side of the harbour, and Cork went to the village school.

'Stay, Raymond,' he said as he left the house on the first day, adding to his mother, 'Raymond's lying on my bed today. I said he could.'

'I'll keep an eye on him,' said Elizabeth.

A slant of hail scolded the two girls as they walked home from the station that day, and in it they hopped and laughed, feeling the chart of life so sweetly spread before them.

'Won't it be nice if Cork isn't back yet?' said Jess through the rattle of the weather, and Alice said, 'Yes. He's quite sweet most of the time, though. Isn't he?' It was quite a moment before Jess said, 'Yes.' And the house contained them and their dismissive thoughts.

Few of Elizabeth's collected lives were displayed. She seemed happy but was not; she did not care for her husband but concealed her dislike with reasonable success. Her looks more or less contented her and she did not expect to acquire the folds and galleries that marked an aged skin. She loved her children and worried over Cork, but on the whole an acceptance had settled upon her and therefore upon her family, who were not always looking in her direction.

By the time the two girls had arrived back, Cork was already at home and sitting under the kitchen table.

'He's lost Raymond,' said Elizabeth.

Joe, with dreadful sagacity, said, 'If you ask me, Cork has to make up his mind that his dog is dead and that he must invent another one,' and he cut himself a lavish piece of walnut cake.

Cork unfolded himself from under the table and stood still for a moment. Then he picked up the slice of cake and threw it at his father's head. It missed and fell on to the floor in a shower of crumbs.

The girls, who had been nervously hanging about the garden door in silence, now crept in, anticipation wreathing their faces, and within that silence Cork lifted his fists and hurled himself at Joe, lunging, pounding and hammering, his face streaked with sudden tears. Joe took a step back and Cork lost his balance and fell on the floor. In his head, words swam, some seen written, some heard and now screamed by him on the still afternoon. Jess moved forward, touched him and said to her mother, 'He's gone strange again. I'm frightened.' Elizabeth, shaking, said, 'Let him be, he needs it.'

From the waterfall of words came sentences, and from

the backwoods of his life, Cork felt the tearing of ligaments
and the flowering of wings, and cried, 'This day I will kill you
and your shadow.' And he cried, 'I will win expiation for your
sins, but I will drown your light for ever, for in my head is the
night of hidden music.' Cork got to his feet, and with a kind of
magnificence, threw back his head and from his throat came
the metallic dissonance of a peacock's scream. The blood-red
cry laid open his mother's quick and his father's absurdity.

He stopped, not because of his parents' pallor but for fear
of his own unyielding frenzy. The dynamo began to run down
and he whispered, 'I am the exfoliation of trespasses,' and he
dropped his head. 'I'm cold and I want to fall down and sleep,'
he said. He put his hand in Alice's and she led him into the
bedroom, saying, 'Sweetheart, come on and I'll put you to
bed. Want something to drink?'

'A glass of dry sherry, please, sweetheart,' said Cork,
falling on to his bed. He added, 'Raymond was under my bed
all the time.'

'Cork's showing off again,' said Alice. 'Wants sherry.
Can he?'

'No harm done,' said Elizabeth. 'He'll sleep like a log
anyway, he always does.'

The girls tucked Cork in, and from his bed he called to his
mother, 'Am I rather unusual?'

'I think perhaps you are,' she said. 'Talk to Raymond
about it and see what he says.'

'He can't say things, he's a dog. Dogs can't talk,' said
Cork.

He let his honour ride and, feeling the conflict done, he
slept.

Walking slowly in the garden, Joe and Elizabeth were
also caught by the sense of a battle over but not lost, ready
now for healing and redemption. In the kitchen, Alice and
Jess silently ate walnut cake.

'But where did the words come from?' said Joe.

'I don't know,' said Elizabeth. 'It happened once before.
Something Jess said made him attack her in the same way –

with words – I don't suppose he'll do it again for months, perhaps never.' She stood still. 'Sometimes I don't want to protect him, love him any longer,' she said. 'I want to see the world freshly again, as I did when we were married, and my skin was thinner but not hurt.'

From one of the upper windows a white curtain bellied, like a pennant.

'I love the children,' she said. 'But you are a sentimentalist and they are dangerous, I think.' Joe felt loss, but countered it with a low-key jocularity, by saying, 'Did you ever enjoy being married to me?'

'I don't think so,' said Elizabeth. 'I'm sorry.'

'Couldn't we go on managing as we do now?' asked Joe, and she answered again, 'I don't think so', with the hardness of tears grazing her.

In the soft early evening, Cork woke, slid from his bed and ran to the empty kitchen for plunder, quickly and eagerly eating whatever presented itself for his pleasure.

For his wits' nourishment, he closed his eyes and thought of the abandoned house near the beach, the house in which he planned to live with Laura, whatever the shifts of time brought. 'I will do the cooking and sing a song to her,' he murmured. He sang a song now, and although it had little melody, it had something of a pastoral nature.

Chapter Three

NEXT DAY ELIZABETH said to Emily, 'I don't want him. He's all right, but he's a bloodsucker. There are too many of us. I want to live by myself. Sometimes I dream that he doesn't exist. They're all bloodsuckers. Personally I'm a strangler.'

'Poor little boy,' said Emily.

'I'm not talking about Cork,' said Elizabeth. 'I'm talking about Joe.'

Leaning against a dresser in Pip's kitchen, Morgan said, 'She's a bloodsucker really. Doesn't even want to cook sometimes – says she's tired, well I mean so are we all, but after all one must do something. I'm making some shelves for the sitting room, for instance.'

'Go home,' said Pip. Morgan went back to the flat, buying some smoked salmon on the way. He had just done a commercial.

Emily did not think of Morgan, and felt the balm of safety and put her hand on the plum-tree that in the blue evenings listed and dropped its fruit.

Morgan came down for a week and took Emily back to the flat for a few days to keep an eye on her. 'What have you been doing in the shed?' he said.

'Elizabeth and I are going to knock it down,' said Emily.

'You are extraordinary,' he said.

Elizabeth decided she would make a start on the shed while Emily was away. Cork joined her after school each day.

'We must take everything out first,' he said. 'All the tools, and the bench, and put it all in a special place with something over it in case it rains. Then I think we must start at the end where the door is. It'll make a noise, you know. Still...'

Joe came down the drive.

'What the hell are you doing?' he said. 'When are we going to eat?'

'We're knocking down Morgan's shed,' said Elizabeth.

'Oh, don't be silly,' said Joe, and went back to the house.

'When are we going to have supper?' asked the little girls, coming through the gap.

'Go and make yourselves a sandwich and make Daddy some instant soup and leave us alone. We're doing some work for Emily while she's away.'

Outside the supermarket in East Sheen the Sally Army played. The state of walking exercised Emily's power of thought and she did so every day. A wish to understand the anchorage of her mind further classified her feelings, and sensibility suggested that she might be quite clever.

Morgan did not consider this likely.

'Where did you go? Why do you do these things?' he said. 'If you told me, it would be understandable, but just walking out of the flat without a word seems so strange to me. I mean, once I had to ring everyone we know to see where you'd gone. Why don't you tell me? I just don't understand you. I'll never forget the time when you said you didn't like navy blue. I mean, why not? It's a perfectly nice colour. It's simply that she was wearing a navy blue frock with red spots on – and incidentally her head wasn't shaved like yours – and you had to be different and say that you particularly didn't like navy blue frocks with red spots on. It's true you said it in a whisper, but I know perfectly well that you said it because you just had to be different. And please don't whistle in the street – it's like smoking.'

'It is not like smoking, it's like whistling,' said Emily. 'And I am different.'

'Don't be ridiculous,' said Morgan. 'You are exactly like everybody else, it's just that you have the reputation of being artistic and you think you have to behave and look like that – I mean your family – they're extraordinary – I've only met them once and they hardly bothered to talk to me. It's not that I care, it's simply that I haven't been brought up like that and I don't like that kind of thing. Since they lived in a house like that, I expected some courtesy, at least—'

'They did talk to you sometimes,' said Emily, 'and you don't have to live in a special house to talk to people.'

A late sun examined and reclaimed her life.

'I must go back to the cottage,' she said and got up.

Morgan drove her back to the coast, where she took a ferry. When he got back, he rang Pip, who told him Constance had just been sick in the cupboard under the stairs.

'What was she doing in the cupboard under the stairs?' said Morgan.

'Standing there waiting to be.'

'Have you got any food? Shall I come over?'

'No. Power cut. Fridge off. Food off. Constance sick. Bed, perhaps?' said Pip.

'I don't think so,' said Morgan. 'Not if Constance – is she still in the cupboard under the stairs?'

'Sofa,' said Pip.

'Just as well if I don't come, then,' said Morgan. 'The trouble is that there's no food in the flat except a tin of tuna in vegetable oil, and a packet of spicy chocolate cake-mix with a sachet of icing.'

'Eat the lot,' said Pip, and put the telephone down.

Morgan ate the tuna out of the tin with a teaspoon. He then shook the cake-mix into a cake tin, mixed it with the specified amount of water and poured the contents of the sachet on the top. The icing instantly sank into the cake mixture and was not seen again. He put it in the oven at Gas

Mark 7 and sat down to wait. In about half an hour it had turned black, so he took it out and ate it, and when he had finished, he began to cry.

He cried not because he missed Emily, but because he did not consider this to be a suitable meal for someone like him, nor did he consider the life that he was forced to live suitable either. And the cake-mix was black on top and raw in the middle and the icing had sunk to the bottom.

He felt that he should really be the centre of an amusing and amused crowd of people in bathing suits with drinks in their hands, and that this crowd should include quite a few extremely attractive girls with long legs and not too much lipstick, who would listen to what he was saying, unlike that bleeder Emily who was always intent on impressing people and being different.

The railway carriage leaned, and Emily touched the door of the guard's van. An avalanche of possessors – brambles and convolvulus – spilled over the roof and breathed, 'Disarm.'

In the kitchen next door Elizabeth put on the table a cold chicken, bread, butter and Port Salut, with a note which read 'Cork, Jess, Alice, Joe. Eat this or starve. Home-made lemonade in fridge. I'm eating next door with Emily.'

She went through the gap, and since Emily was sitting outside the railway carriage, said, 'Go and buy some food. It's just warm enough to have supper out here, and we've got to make plans.'

'I haven't any money,' said Emily.

'Consider yourself my kept woman,' said Elizabeth, and gave her twenty pounds.

'Keep talking,' said Emily and walked off to the village.

'You seem to have made an utter Rumpelstiltskin of it,' said Elizabeth when she came back with chocolate cup-cakes, salami, Greek yoghurt from the only good grocer's in the vicinity and a bottle of mineral water from the pub. 'Quite nice, but no bread, no butter? Well, keep the change or give it to the poor.'

'I am the poor,' said Emily, 'and the stupid, but asking him for money makes my stomach turn over.'

'Joe is quite reasonable when it comes to spondulicks,' said Elizabeth. 'But of course he has to spend a good deal on painkillers and the competitions on the backs of Cornflake packets, and books about how to get rich and books about how to avoid the stress of so doing. And naturally he spends a lot on cut-price living.'

'Why did you marry him?' asked Emily.

'It was our old friend, a rebound marriage,' said Elizabeth. 'How did you come by Morgan? He cannot have taken your fancy, surely? How little we know one another.'

The evening was cool and the salami and the yoghurt room temperature. So, alas, was the mineral water.

'Have you a great many friends?' said Emily.

'Not now. I am too bound up with my family.'

'Forgive me for asking, but have you lovers?'

'Not now. The children take up too much time, and I make their clothes as well. Why?'

'Nothing.'

'How would you introduce me to people?' said Emily.

'I should say I got you in a sale, and remark how well you become me.'

'What do you and Joe talk about, if you don't mind me asking?'

'I don't mind you asking. Joe and I talk about divorce a good deal, but we think it would be too much trouble, too expensive, and excoriating for the children.'

'Oh please do, though. Think what a lovely time we could have if you weren't married,' said Emily.

33

'Goodness, what's up with you, you nasty perverted little thing you?'

'I only meant that we would have more time to knock Morgan's shed down.'

'Indeed? I didn't think that was what you meant at all, miss.'

'Please, Elizabeth stop it. Why do you talk like that?'

'I once had an aunt who talked like that. When I was young, I managed to graft bits of her on to myself, but I was ruined by the tap-water of life before I had learned that I was capable of expelling it.'

'She did exactly what she wanted, and, working sometimes in a ramshackle studio in Chelsea and sometimes in another in Rome, she bothered with whom she wished and taught me more than any other person in my life. I talk like she did. But I've changed. I don't always talk like that now. It's the tap-water.'

The evening rode hard away, a black wolf with a moon as white as heat.

Elizabeth went back to the house, where the girls had gone to bed and Joe was watching television. Cork was in the kitchen, sitting on the floor with his back to the washing machine, eating peanut butter out of the jar. Beside him lay four peeled bananas and a bunch of spring onions. 'I'm not at all glad to see you back, you cruel old bitch,' he said.

'Go to bed,' said Elizabeth. 'You're not to speak to me like that.'

'Like what, then? What like speak to you, you old rat, you old fat rat, you huge old fat rat.'

'I am not fat,' said Elizabeth. She dragged him up by his jersey and threw him against the fridge.

'Are are are are are are are,' he said, grabbing and eating a banana on the way. 'Do the shed yourself, you fucking red-eyed farter.' He hit her and climbed out of the window.

This market day gypsy women, seasoned and blooded, walked along the road to the sea carrying baskets of lucky heather, and Cork walked with them.

'My mother's got nasty red eyes,' he said. They said nothing. Their hands were hard and muscular like young men's hands. At the bus stop they waited and Cork walked on. He fancied an ice-cream and Laura wasn't there. The cabin was closed and when he got to the cliff edge he overbalanced and fell, suddenly disturbing a few small stones. The rocks below more or less bisected his face, and in a multiple seizure, all his born days were taken from him.

Chapter Four

L EGAL SUCCESSION AGREED with the little girls, after the shock had worn off.

'Well, I shouldn't imagine he's up in Heaven with the holy angels,' said Jess. 'That's about the most unlikely thing in the world.'

'Be quiet,' said Alice. 'You never know – Mummy's probably feeling quite sad.'

'Hardly,' said Jess. 'She's going to burn all his things. You don't do that if you're sad about your only son dying.'

'Yes you do. It's a purification – absolutely all right, like prayers. It means he's redeemed and we can start again without him only it'll be better. And Daddy'll have a wonderful time because he adores something to show off about, and now that Cork's dead he can show off to everyone all day long.'

Laura got on with things after she had kissed Elizabeth and said how sorry she was about Cork, and after Elizabeth had put her hands over her face and felt little but relief and the lack of shame.

Sometimes she and Emily made love in the grass and afterwards bit into the windfalls that lay about them and ate the seeds of the shepherd's purse and felt the evening shake of pollen and the perturbation of fieldmice. 'I love you because you're rich,' said Emily.

The poor look-out was Morgan's, whose cooking had not

improved, whose television set had failed and whose new barber had buggered up his hair by dyeing it royal blue. He was persuaded that he had suggested the demolition of the shed himself, and this persuasion was fostered by encouraging telephone calls from Emily, who told him how clever he was to think of it. She also thwarted any attempt of his to join her at the cottage by praising his success at housekeeping, reading him cookery recipes over the telephone, and exclaiming over the charm of Joe and Elizabeth who she said she sometimes saw and who were, she added, very good company. But she was perfectly happy on her own, she said.

Morgan added some curry powder and dried onions to a tin of butter beans and heated them up for supper.

The next day he went out and bought a Delia Smith cookery book.

Wage-earners halved, quartered and granulated what remained of the shed, loading the crumbs into a lorry and driving away within three hours and fifty-five minutes. Joe would have liked to help but was prevented by persistent backache and respect for Cork's death. Elizabeth and Emily blocked up the gap in the hedge and bought three hundred daffodil bulbs.

Elizabeth spent little time with her family now and a good deal at the cottage with Emily. At home she made sure that there was enough food in the house for Joe and the girls to exist without her help, and left written instructions for defrosting the fridge and using the washing machine. On successive days she left no money, no directions for the sewing on of buttons or for the unblocking of the sink or the bleeding of the radiators. Instead, she took two bottles of champagne out of the dining room and, leaving a note on the table, went back to the cottage. The note read: Dear Joe, I thought we might separate. Frankly, I've never liked you. Love Elizabeth.

Emily, dazzled by her companion, went out each day, chinking with Elizabeth's money and bought neither chocolate cup-cakes nor salami, nor indeed mineral water, but instead came back with food of a most attractive nature, simple withal and on the whole needing small culinary attention.

The climate, both terrestrial and emotional, was salutary for each of them.

'Tell me who it is you think about.'

'I wrote her eleven letters.'

'Who is it? I know it's someone because occasionally I see her under your eyelids. You have copies, of course?'

'In an exercise book. I threw it away because I never thought – she never answered.'

'What did you never think, you ninny? You'd be surprised at what people will do afterwards. I wish I'd had a hand in your upbringing, Emily.'

'Comfort me.'

'No. You're no more to me than a duenna, a kind of chastity belt in case Joe suddenly starts demanding marital rights.'

'Take my hand then.'

'I don't care to, Emily. I really don't care to. You're such an absolute turd. I used to think you were rather sweet in the days when you bought cup-cakes and ate marshmallows in the bath – darling, don't cry, I must know who you think of and you don't tell me. And it's important that you have a precise record of what you wrote in those letters. And who it is, for God's sake.'

Ever conformity's drudge, Joe rang the cottage first to ask if he could come round and see Elizabeth about her extra-ordinary note. A mouth ulcer slightly impeded his vocal delivery, and he took a tin of lozenges with him when he went.

Emily went and sat in the railway carriage since Elizabeth had said, 'You'd better get out of the way', much as we all do in such circumstances and, finding *The Just So Stories* in the guard's van, she settled down with it.

When Joe reached the cottage, Elizabeth was cleaning

the kitchen windows, much as one might do in such a situation. He smiled, and any rapport there had been between them was instantly usurped by mutual revulsion.

'Now look here,' he said. 'What is all this?'

Elizabeth horribly and unavoidably blushed and her verbal flourish left her. She was, as it were, caught in a half-nelson.

'I don't know what you mean,' she said, as so many of us say when we know pretty well what is meant, and she put her hand to her cheek.

'I need to know exactly what's going on,' said Joe.

'When I told him,' she said to Emily later, 'he said, "But what do you both actually do?" and I said, "More than you, and for longer." It was all extremely dignified, of course.'

Elizabeth had walked back to the house with Joe and stayed there for two and a half hours. When she reappeared she was barefoot and carrying her shoes. Emily, who was desperately eating a piece of bread and butter in the kitchen, said, 'Heavens, I thought you were dead. What have you been doing?'

'Nothing,' said Elizabeth.

'You haven't—' said Emily. 'You couldn't have—'

'Of course not,' said Elizabeth. But she could have and she had. She swallowed and said, 'I needed the change.' But she didn't. It was propinquity.

'Sorry,' she said. But she wasn't in the least.

'I couldn't do that,' said Emily, and wept.

'I expect you could,' said Elizabeth. 'I've always been able to.' It was true.

They were beset by fear yet bound in crisis.

Emily said, 'But it's a most terrible thing to do,' and wept again, and Elizabeth said, 'No, it isn't. We'll have some champagne, and you'll see how perfectly all right everything will be.'

When it was dark but nearly light, Elizabeth said,

'You're as searching as the snow. For God's sake unlock, and remind me of the sea.'

'Have you said the things you say to me to a lot of people?' said Emily, and Elizabeth said, 'Once. Or twice.' But it was a lie. She had said it more than once or twice and would do so again. It was simply like having a second helping when one was supposed to be dieting.

The inconsiderate dawn gave token of her lack of wit. 'You remind me of the sea,' she murmured, closing her eyes, and adding, alas, 'You were wonderful, Joe.'

Emily was asleep, though not soundly, in the railway carriage.

'I can't, you see, get it out of my mind,' said Emily next morning. 'If you'd told me more about it yesterday I might be able to bear it now. Where were the girls?'

'Out with friends most of the time,' said Elizabeth, 'watching a black and white film on the telly with Victor Mature starring, followed by some cartoons and a programme about the Royal Family, and I gather there were some of their favourite commercials. That must have taken most of the afternoon. Then they stayed for hamburgers and Coke, which are much more inviting than the wholesome and delicious provender I still sometimes prepare for them, and I hope, Emily, that you're not going to tell everybody how I ruined your life and made you cry half the night.'

'Was Joe cross about us?' said Emily.

'No,' said Elizabeth. 'As a matter of fact, he's always rather fancied it. Understandably, I think, don't you? I feel much refreshed. Would you like to go to the garden centre today? We could buy a statue of the Medici Venus and some new secateurs. Emily, do stop it.'

'I can't bear it,' said Emily. 'I don't want to bear it, I don't want to think about it. What will happen to my silly life if you do this kind of thing?'

'You will ditch that frightful Morgan and forge an

41

alliance with one of those psychiatrists you go and confess to every now and then,' said Elizabeth.

'This afternoon,' she added, with a shyster's negotiable front, 'I thought I might treat us to a wooden lavatory seat, so much more hospitable than the cold admonishment of plastic. What's the matter?'

Emily sat without moving, in her face a locked invalidation and fear.

She said, 'If you did it only once more, I would never be able to find my balance again.'

'Emily, don't be ridiculous. I've always done it if I felt like it and I expect I'll do it again.'

'Not with me here. Never with me here.'

'Yes, even with you here,' said Elizabeth. 'Well, all right then, Joe was a bit cross about us and you know how nice that always is, so of course I had to. And then you see he likes it if I say no and there's a bit of a struggle. I was a gastronomic haven and I was starving, but I would accept no substitutes. That's probably why it took rather a long time.'

Emily began to laugh and to cry.

Elizabeth said, 'Tell me at once who it is you think about, it was electrifying last night, I almost called out the militia.'

Emily smiled. She said, 'I once fell in love with a German woman dentist. She wouldn't have me. She said, "Listen, you would always be cooking for your Morgan and I would always be in the surgery. It would be most sombre. A little wider, *Liebchen*, if you please. I have to take zis bugger out."'

'Is it her?' said Elizabeth.

'No,' said Emily.

There was a power cut that evening while Joe and the girls were cooking their dinner. It happened just after the pilchards in tomato sauce had burst into flame under the grill.

'Perhaps you poured lighter fuel over them,' said Elizabeth when Joe rang the cottage to ask about candles.

'Where do you keep them?' he said.

Elizabeth said, 'I don't think there are any. I'll bring some up in a minute.'

42

'No,' said Emily. 'Don't go. Please don't. I'll do it.'

She did. Joe said, 'Thanks. How are you, Emily? Which are you, by the way? Male or female? It must have been hell for you anyway – I expect you'll need your tablets. Goodnight.'

'I ran back because I was frightened and I didn't want him to know,' said Emily. 'I feel strange and I haven't got any tablets.'

Elizabeth rang Joe. 'Please ask Alice to post a letter to Emily's GP for a prescription for more tablets. She's writing the note now.'

'Is she upset?' said Joe. 'Not that I'm altogether surprised.'

'Please do what I ask,' said Elizabeth and put the telephone down. 'It's all right, darling, but we're a lot too near that ménage, you see,' she added. 'Sometimes, when I meet people, I think: don't look at me in case you discover me.'

Emily's GP rang the following afternoon and said, "Who are you?" when Elizabeth answered. 'I'm staying with Emily,' she said. 'Can you send her a prescription?'

'Tell her I've talked to Dr Lighter and he wants to see her again first in order to assess her state of mind.'

Elizabeth said, 'I'll get her to ring you,' and rang off.

'Who's Lighter?' she asked Emily.

'The psychiatrist,' said Emily. 'I don't want to see him. I don't want anyone told. I don't want anything done about it. Just the prescription, that's all.'

'What are you talking about?'

'I once told him I really only liked women. I thought you had to tell them everything. He asked me if it bothered me and I said no.'

'For God's sake. What else?'

'Touched me.'

'Where?'

'Between my legs.' The familiar claim of one upon another.

'When?' said Elizabeth. 'How often?'

'About four years ago. I hardly knew you. A few times, I think.'

'What about Morgan? What did he say?'

'He's always rather pleased if anything awful happens to me. That's why I'm frightened of him.'

'You need a gum-shield for people like that. They're wreckers.'

While Emily lay shaking in bed for three days, and Elizabeth started smoking again, the lives of Jess and Alice were exalted by fantasy. They believed themselves to be creatures of great power, possessed of considerable riches and stupendous beauty. Thus did they see sensational futures ahead, and thus did the continuing absence of Cork make bright and pleasant each day of their existence. Further, they engaged the local teenagers in intimate conversation and with them bathed at midnight, none of them wearing a stitch. They also stole money from Joe and bought sweets, make-up and magazines that advocated more graciousness in sexual patterns.

'Although,' said Alice, 'I'd say our mother's sexual pattern is pretty gracious already.'

'Adequate, anyway,' said Jess.

Chapter
Five

J OE LAID IN endless supplies of shampoo, muesli and polythene bags. They ran out of eggs. He bought four dozen size-one eggs and they ran out of muesli and were constipated for weeks. The polythene bags were the wrong size and they ran out of laxatives, painkillers and Elastoplast. The beds were seldom changed and the garden a jungle. Late one evening he found Elizabeth lying face down in the grass, crying.

'I miss Cork,' she said. 'He's at the back of my mind all the time and I don't know what to do.' Joe turned her on her back, broke the universe that lay between her thighs and putting his hand over her mouth said, 'Well, we don't want the news to get out, do we? Emily might hear.'

And he told her that what she really wanted was to come back to him. She said no, and that there were things she wanted now that she hadn't had for a long time, and she asked him if he would ring Emily's psychiatrist and get him to send a prescription for her tablets.

Joe said, 'Why can't Emily ring him herself?'

'She's got flu and a very high temperature,' said Elizabeth, 'and it would carry more weight if you did.' She got up. 'Have you got any soluble aspirin?' she added.

'No,' he said. 'Would you like twenty-five size-one eggs?'

'Not really,' Elizabeth said. 'They're rather constipating if you're not careful.'

'I know,' said Joe, and knocked her flying.

Elizabeth went back to the cottage and said no more than 'I'm sorry' because she was shocked and winded. 'You do understand though, don't you?' she added, and tears fell down her face.

'No, I don't,' said Emily. 'I don't understand any of the things you say and I can't understand the things you do because I could never do them. I feel more frightened of everything when I'm with you than when I'm without you. I feel unprotected. I can't manage what I'm trying to manage and it's not possible to be without you either.'

Her heart broke, though she did not.

But being a fixture, it was fitting that she attempt no form of conveyancing in any direction or in any sense. No contract had existed and the property or properties marked by each on the other could still be viewed without appointment. Moreover, though some interior damage had been sustained, the exchange of robbery had become exceptionally attractive to both, possibly by reason of the aforesaid damage. Thus at various times of night and day they deranged each other's senses and made indistinct their minds by the shores of the October sky. The certain discipline of the seasons gave quarter to betrayal, and soon would bring the importuning south of little birds. Further, the installing of a lustrous wooden lavatory seat was considered of great value, and its frank and steadfast aspect beyond criticism.

But the world was investigative, and an arcane form of blackmail gave it sustenance, alerting these two women, for whom a choice of worry could not exist; and since their mental ability was temporarily clouded by apprehension, any solution had to be suspended.

For from them was exacted a levy of great fear, guilt, misgiving, suspicion, vulnerability and anger, instilling in them doubts of their own values and judgement.

Emily's prescription arrived and was made up. Occasionally she saw a circle with the number twelve inside it in the air, about four feet from the ground.

'Darling Emily, it is time you talked about everything. Describe exactly what Dr Lighter did to you.'

'Well, I don't think I will. I was just going out.'

'Please, Emily.'

'I think I'll make some coffee first.'

'Talk about it, dearest Emily.'

'I thought I might make some bread.'

'Well, we can talk about it while it's rising.'

'I think I ought to do a bit of gardening first.'

'Emily, be stalwart and I will take your hand, but any more of this and I'll beat you to pulp.'

'I'd better lie down, I think I'm going to be sick.'

'Beloved Emily, don't be in such a taking. Tell me exactly, in detail, but first of all tell me this: when you told him about us, did he write anything down? Not that it makes any difference; he has almost certainly told a few colleagues.'

'I thought they weren't supposed to tell anyone. I thought nobody minded about this kind of thing nowadays anyway.' Emily had become white as salt.

'Tell that to the press. It is one of the quickest ways of becoming a household word and they'll go on headlining you for months, if not years. Please allow me to know best, dear Emily.'

'But what we do isn't against the law. Does it really matter?'

'Emily, what makes us not talk about it to other people?'

'But what could possibly happen to us if we did?'

'Nothing perhaps, until the next swathe of people were told. And remember that this kind of thing is often passed from practice to practice. Sensibility hardly comes into it. Nor does the Hippocratic Oath.'

'But we're not famous or anything.'

'Not, my dear Emily, at the moment.'

'Well, I certainly didn't tell Morgan, because I knew he would think ugh.'

'You were quite right not to tell him. Undoubtedly he would think ugh. In fact Joe has always had a tendency to

47

think wow, but will tell no one, since if publicised, it would reflect badly on his manhood. In fact, both ugh and wow are deeply suspect reactions, Emily. Now tell me what Lighter did.'

'I will. I went into the consulting room and he followed me and shut the door. Then he came up to me and put one arm round me and his other hand up me.'

'Far up you?'

'I don't really know – not really. I was frightened. It happened again when I went to see him. I couldn't do anything, I was frightened.'

'You should have told me.'

'I was frightened. I hardly knew you.'

'Emily, you know as well as I do the nature of the hazard. He is making quite sure you feel that if any sort of complaint is made or if you tell anyone at all, the whole lot might come out and everyone in the world would know that you and I make love. If he feels you are becoming a threat, there are other tactics he may employ to keep you quiet.'

'I could have done a bit of gardening in the last five minutes.'

'Emily, please desist from such inconsequential prattle.'

'I'm frightened.'

'Be frightened, but be frightened out loud, and listen to me while you can. It was certainly foolhardy of you to make this touching confession to Lighter, but what he can do further to silence you may be a very great deal worse than you can imagine. Your tablets, for instance. He can change the dosage verbally, perhaps telephoning you, but he will leave the prescription as it is, so that you will take, say, two tablets as he told you, while the bottle-label still instructs you to take one, or vice versa. A moment of indecision and you may take the wrong dosage, which might do you considerable damage. Who would know why? No one. Because he may fudge the case notes as well.

'Perhaps the ultimate in treachery, and one he is able to carry out since he has the knowledge, though of course he may

48

not be conversant with the law relating to toxic side effects, is to fail to warn you of them. Unaware that these are side effects, you will report each one to him (and some are serious) and he will disregard everything you say. With certain drugs the result may well cause a state of confusion amounting to serious mental disorder, and you are likely to end up in a locked cell, with no one the wiser. The side effects of some drugs can be death or brain damage and you can end up in a box, and surrounded by sycophants. All because you love me and money.'

Emily remained bone pale and mute for at least half a minute. At length she asked Elizabeth how she knew all this, and Elizabeth answered that she knew it because she was exasperatingly clever. 'But nonetheless fetching,' she added. 'But now listen, Emily. I have a plan for you, my dearest. You are to go and see Lighter, having made an appointment, and after talking of this and that – the appalling guilt you feel for your worthless life, fantasies about rape, penis envy, other people's appalling fantasies about your worthless guilt, Morgan's appalling penis and his guilt about your guilt, how you envy people who have ladders and appalling snakes who go up them. And then, darling Emily, just mention what he did to you. Something like, "You must have felt terribly unsatisfied last time."'

Emily was crying for the nightmare she could not laugh at, the closing of the world, the numbers she understood and the space that took her away from other people and their darkness.

'It's like a scream in my brain when you show off like that. I feel my mind cracking and my bones powdering. Don't you understand anything at all? Tell me what you want me to do, but not as a joke, not as a joke, because I'm frightened. Believe my screaming, believe I am really here. Please.'

'Emily. Dear.'

'When I was a little girl you could see the seeds in strawberry ice-cream, so you knew it was real. In some ways it has been a fortunate life, but Morgan – I'm afraid of him.

Sometimes the things he says don't sound quite right but I think it's important that I don't tell anyone, and I haven't. I'm tired. Tell me what it is you think I should do.'

They walked outside in the autumn's aberration of light and Elizabeth said, 'I understand', and Emily said, 'It is not quite enough to understand.' 'No,' said Elizabeth. 'I only want to show you how easy it is to trap Lighter. You must do it, though. I can't do it for you. I can't show you what to do like a mother at her child's dancing class, Emily, I can't. Go in, giving him a wide berth, talk a little. And mention what he did to you but be certain what you say cannot be taken as any kind of invitation. Watch, and listen. He has been briefed. He knows that if he says anything at all, it could be taken as an admission and that it may be conceivable that you can bring an action. He will do either of two things and possibly both. He may shout the hell out of you, edging you out of the room as soon as possible, or he may suddenly get up and walk round the room, adjust the position of the waste-paper basket, move some books, straighten the snapshot of his wife and children at a barbecue or otherwise stop you from trapping him into an admission. He must have your silence, and would do anything to take your life. You will know at once that you've got him, but you must be careful. You could be enmeshed in an extremely dangerous conspiracy of silence.'

'Elizabeth, are you quite sure that I can do this properly, and that it will really work?'

'Emily dear, I am not, you understand, a mere camera, I am also a filing cabinet, a tape recorder and a marshalling yard. I have friends who have been through this kind of hell. People don't always survive as well as we are going to and I have learned from them. Please do as I ask you.'

'Come with me. You will come with me, won't you?'

'I will be sitting in the waiting room reading a magazine.'

'You are so clever.'

'I am considered brilliant by many people, although it takes only humdrum intelligence to check any side effects, drugs, legal flummery, etc. in one or two fat paperbacks that anyone can buy anywhere. Dearest Emily, of course I will come with you. I am not a brute.'

'Are you also an advertising agency?'

'Emily, you are the cup-cake of my darkest fantasies. Never before has the icing been so thick, nor the sponge so yielding, never has the paper case peeled away so flawlessly, nor has even that first bite ever been so fulfilling. We are in luck. In Dr Lighter we have upon our plates a man of small intellect, second-rate values and few scruples. I think we might go to Italy for a week or two first.'

'I will buy some clothes.'

'Nothing, I beg you, with puffed sleeves or Peter Pan collars, my dearest.'

Chapter Six

VIETRI-SUL-MARE, a stagger of white houses built against the cliffs of a cerulean seascape, and ready olive trees drowning virtue in the afternoons. Artless, artful Italy, the pickpocket of collectors' evenings and procuress of celibacy.

'By jingo, Holmes, this knocks Baker Street into a cocked hat,' said Emily. 'Are you sure you can afford it?'

'Watson, you still have the greatest of expectations. For you I will buy a cup-cake factory and overturn the medical profession. I think we should always winter in Italy. Nothing restores one so well as doing nothing, for that very nothing that we so seldom do is nonetheless indisputably there to be done. Though perhaps there is an Achilles' heel to be considered; you cannot, for instance, do a bit of nothing, or some nothing, unless you can say, with certainty, that there is still a reasonable amount of nothing put aside for you to do another time should you wish it. Unless, of course, someone else takes your time. It is a comfort to know that no one can take your nothing, since it is nothing.'

'I suppose you think that's clever,' said Emily.

'Moderately, short-arse.'

'I'm crackers about you. Suppose I had an ice-cream?'

'Do, but remember Dryden said, "None but the brave deserves the fair", not, "None but the brave deserves the fat."'

'I'll tell you one thing,' said Emily. 'Fat people can be sultry, but thin people can only be thin people. You wouldn't look marvellous photographed against the Taj Mahal, but I bet I would.'

'You're spectacular and my mind is mislaid. We'll have a light dinner and an early night. Airports are so weakening and there's never anything but strawberry yoghurt in those snack bars.'

It was hamburgers and salad for dinner.

'Say something,' said Elizabeth.

'I have,' said Emily, 'at least I meant to say "Could we have an omelette instead?" but I think I said "Where is egg-hen?"'

'Ask again, in English.'

Emily turned her head a little, and a waiter sped to her.

'I wonder,' she said, clasping her hands, 'if it would be possible for you to bring us each an omelette and some new potatoes on plates that are not cold, but not unbearably hot either.'

'Si signora,' he said and went.

'If you do that again,' said Elizabeth, 'I will keep you waiting tonight. What on earth do you think you're up to?'

'Nothing. I just asked him. Why?'

'Well, it was the sort of vulgarity I do not wish to see again. You are in the worst possible taste, Emily.'

'What, all of me? Every bit of me?'

'Every bit.'

'There must be some bits of me that aren't in bad taste?'

'Very few, and I'm not prepared to discuss them. And I can't imagine why you speak to him in English. You should make some attempt to speak the lingo.'

'Oh, I don't suppose that matters,' said Emily. 'Watch.' She looked over her shoulder.

'Si, signora?'

'Do you think I could possibly have some mineral water

and some ice, please?' said Emily, leaning her cheek on her hand.

'If you don't stop doing that, I'll beat the crap out of you, you little prick,' said Elizabeth.

'Goody,' said Emily. 'Prick is as prick does. By the way, your eyes were too close together last Tuesday.'

'Don't be silly.'

'All right, but I notice they're rather close together today as well.'

'It's not at all funny, Emily.'

'I can't tell you,' said Emily, 'how much I love you.'

'Tell me though.'

'Spoil me rotten first.'

The hotel hung over the cliffs like a lamp, and in the lounge a cabal of German women played cards, one of them with the severely goosed expression of Nancy Reagan.

'Emily?'

'What?'

'What were you wearing when it happened the first time? And the other times, of course.'

'I don't know what you mean.'

'Lighter,' said Elizabeth.

'I don't know, I don't know, I don't want to talk about it now, not here where it's so lovely, and I've forgotten all about it in any case.'

'Emily.'

'Must I? Please.'

'Just quickly.'

'It was in the summer the first time. A frock.'

'Quite. Other times?'

'Well, not trousers. It may have been a skirt.'

'Why not? And how can you account for not wearing trousers? How can you remember it?'

'If it had been trousers, he couldn't have done it, could he?'

'The other times. I suppose you didn't actually want him to do it?'

'No, and I'm going to be sick. Please leave me alone, it makes my head scream when you go on like that,' said Emily.

In the gardens below the balcony burned a reticulation of unknown amber flowers.

The food at lunch being superior to that at dinner, little dressed-up Italian children ate it with their parents on the terrace, as did Emily and Elizabeth.

'Thank God for our daily weather and forgive us our daily bread,' said Emily, and dripping out of the milk-warm sea, ate the sardines, prosciutto, melons, cheese and unbridled puddings that each morning sang in her thoughts and debited her calorie allowance.

'Thank you so much, Paolo, you are so kind and thoughtful.'

'Stop embarrassing everyone, you pulsating little tramp,' said Elizabeth.

'You apprehended me. I wasn't expecting it.'

'I'll wait for you.'

'I've always been here.'

'Did you say you'd always be here?'

'No, that I've always been here. You are beyond the dreams of avarice, and I felt that very same beyond pass my life four hundred years ago.'

But the night-blind white scream of Emily split sleep that night and knocked the living night-lights from the hand of God and sat up Elizabeth.

'What is it, what, Emily what? Tell me.'

Emily's breath banged in Emily's ears, and the curtained Emily snuffed out the other one, the other two or three.

'Morgan,' she said and was sick, and the scarlet runner ran and turned her thoughts, and Morgan fell and the sea of cholera lit the dark of the bitter thief and killed the light of Israel. No no no Morgan no no Morgan.

After the bell had been rung and clean sheets brought, Emily lay in the transparent dawn as fair and simple as honesty and as cool as tranquillity with a glass of water by her bed. Elizabeth sat on the balcony until a thumbnail of light air reminded her to sleep, and to decide.

When she woke, Emily said, 'What is it that happens when we move from life into death? What happens at that moment?'

'Ask me when we are both sitting at the right hand of God,' said Elizabeth.

'I think it has happened to me already.'

'Lie thou there, and have a slight but sustaining breakfast. Tomorrow we will go home.'

'I have nightmares about him, but I am in a prison and am not believed.'

'I have always known it, Emily.'

The flight to familiarity was made pleasant by the anticipation of arrival and the buying of large flagons of scent.

'You are remarkably fortunate, Emily. Not only am I rich but I was also a gymnast.'

'Oh, I say, steady on,' said Emily entranced, and spilled her sherry.

'Nonetheless, Emily, the keeping of the smallest willow cabin I may have made at your gate might mean that you could blackmail me to death. *Ergo*, destroy all such cabins as are still in your possession.'

'I couldn't. Some of them are just shopping lists, like the one that said "Eschew the wholesale purchase of chocolate cup-cakes today, dear child, but remember the urgency of loo paper."'

'Dearest, be calm. Thieves may already have broken into the cottage and settled the entire question for us. I am, as you know, more vigilant than you are. And, Emily—'

'What?'

'Do not allow the word "posterity" to enter your mind at

any point in your life or you will find you are the poorer and others very much the richer for it. I hope I am understood, Emily. Even those of blameless integrity can be prey to such vulgarity.'

'Oh God dispatch my thoughts,' said Emily and wept. The runway swam beneath them, and that night in the cottage she could not breathe or take comfort in familiarity, nor joy in return.

'What is it?' said Elizabeth.

'Something is hurting me. It was all right in Vietri, but now I can't breathe and it has come back and I am sick with it. Maybe I have flu or something. I can only see a sort of blackness, and I can't move away from it. Don't tell anyone, don't say anything, he keeps me in prison.'

'I know,' said Elizabeth, and drew the curtains.

'I'm afraid of something happening to us.'

'I know.'

'Sometimes I hear music, and I think about leaving Morgan and imagine what it must be like to feel safe.'

'I always knew this, Emily, always.'

'Then what is to become of me?' Emily said, for beyond the sleeper and the waker in her there lay a boundary of thoughts and declensions which in turn produced the Decani and Cantoris of her understanding and her life, that was the unsubscribing masterpiece. The choir within her had never ceased singing since the day she was born, and the recognition of evil had there come to rest and cause the occasional dispossession of her wits.

'I'll tell you what is to become of you, young Emily – Chelsea buns which you are going out to buy this instant, while I turn the oven on – they are best gently warm. Go to Beamish and let us hope they have a few left. Wrap up, and when you return refrain from boring me to death with claptrap about what is to become of you. You may be assured of my devotion but stay good or I shall have you thrown from the battlements. I have little patience with my own shortcomings, but that is my affair and yours merely by conjecture and the chance that I am, as usual, showing off. I have noticed you noticing this occasionally and must own to a little confusion at the time, but no more than that. You may cut along now, young woman. Sharpish.'

'But you wouldn't ever leave me, would you?' said Emily.

'I might. I am only an approximation of what people imagine they want and constancy is sometimes subtracted from me by circumstance.'

It was cool in England, and Emily walked quickly to the village, her mind marked by a familiar trellis of anxiety.

While she was gone, Elizabeth rang Miles Copthorne, whose devoted friendship was sustained by an absolute minimum of veneration on either side.

'I'm coming to stay with you, dearest.'

'Oh God, all right. Only for a couple of days, though. Hilary won't be here, he's in *la belle France* with a temperature of 103 and large red blotches all over his face. If you must come, bring me something delicious, I'm horribly underprivileged at the moment because I've got aficionados of the *nouvelle cuisine* coming to dinner. I thought I'd just paint slices of duck in a pool of apricot sauce on the plates and they can simply lick it off. Are you in trouble? Very well then, a Friday to Sunday and then off you go.'

'Constance bit me last night,' said Morgan, finishing the Weetabix.

'It's a wonder she bothered,' said Pip. 'Eat your breakfast and don't use my deodorant again.'

'And I mean I haven't got a shed any more, it was simply knocked down and removed, and they've planted daffodils there. Must have cost the earth, I can't think where the money comes from, I never gave her any in case she spent it. I think she has a few shares, but of course she never used to behave like this. She actually said it was her land and she had a right to destroy anything built on it if she wanted. I mean they seem perfectly happy and if only I could have a word with Joe I might feel I was getting somewhere, but I hardly know him, poor fellow. I mean one knows this kind of thing goes on, but one can't help thinking of it as perversion.'

'Yes?'

'Well naturally I've given it – I've given the situation a good deal of thought and I am, of course, very broadminded.'

'Fancy.'

'I mean, it just doesn't ever sound quite healthy. One cannot imagine what they actually do.'

'Try.'

'I mean when you come to think about it—'

'Do you?'

'Do I what?'

'Often come to think about it?'

'Well, I mean they don't have the wherewithal, do they?'

'What wherewithal?'

'There you are, you see, you simply don't understand what I'm talking about—'

'Go out and buy me a present.'

Beneath Emily's feet was the cool late autumn's world, and across her path the plunge and sprint of a squirrel logged the symmetry of the turning year. 'Kill Morgan,' she said, for the corruption that sidled out of him now demanded voice. This intelligence was not advertised to others but sustained only by herself, and the containing of this knowledge often produced in her the signs of physical illness and great disturbances of the mind.

'Kill Morgan,' she said again, and her thoughts could not turn from this particular self-purification. 'If I could do it myself, I would.' For she had a curious union with another life, yet knew it to be her own. She felt she was of no real concern or account to anyone, perhaps not even to Elizabeth, and yet was able to accept and embrace this thought as though it were absolute knowledge and placed within her without explanation or the need of one.

Yet when she got back to the cottage she said at once, as though some transaction of ideas had only just passed between herself and Elizabeth, 'It was something I recognised in him, but quite slowly, and this was why I couldn't even be in the same room with him sometimes.'

'Then for God's sake leave him, Emily. You are not bound by wedlock, what is keeping you?'

'If I did, there would be no one to tell me what to do, how to bleed the radiators and pay bills – that kind of thing.'

'Emily, desist from this nonsense. At present I pay the bills and bleed the radiators and if I suddenly die, I dare say you would manage perfectly well. Your understandable grief at my death would be assuaged by the welcome knowledge that I have left you a reasonable amount of money in my will.'

'You don't really listen to what I'm saying. You never do.'

'Be quiet, Emily. Next Friday to Sunday I will be staying with Miles Copthorne, of whom you have sometimes heard me talk. We are going to discuss the Lighter business, since that is what is underneath every word you say every day and half each night, and since I was born equipped to deal with such and indeed any other situation. Where are the Chelsea buns?'

'They didn't have any. I got chocolate Bath Olivers.'

'You are very intelligent, Emily. Chocolate is often and significantly craved by the nervous system. I am delighted with your perspicacity. Turn the oven off and the kettle on when you go into the kitchen.'

Chapter
Seven

A FTER ELIZABETH HAD left for Miles's house on the mainland, a handsome dereliction in Hurlingham, Emily rang Morgan and said, 'Could you possibly come over in time for dinner and stay the night perhaps? Elizabeth's away till Sunday, and I really feel we ought to talk. Are you terribly cross with me?'

'Darling, how could I be? I do so understand your little problems. This has been no more than a passing phase, a kind of sickness of the mind, you probably went through the same sort of thing at school, and I'm not ashamed to say that I did. I am here only to help you, believe me, because, Emily, I am aware that you have suffered greatly and that only I can kiss it better.'

'Thank God,' said Emily and putting the receiver down, ate the last two chocolate Olivers.

A familiar fizz of excitement charged Morgan as he put on a scarlet jersey and settled a yellow knitted cap over his cobalt hair. 'Poor child,' he murmured, driving aboard the ferry, 'all that guilt and then having to talk about it. I must be very gentle with her. Thank God I bought some flowers.'

When he arrived, Emily was preparing for herself a supper of bacon, eggs, sausages, fried potatoes, chips, tomatoes, mushrooms and fried bread. To her, opening the front door, he looked like a suppuration, so she shut it again and went back to the kitchen.

Morgan waited outside for a few moments and then knocked on the door and said, 'What on earth are you doing? It's quite cold out here, you know.'

Emily did not answer, and taking her supper into the sitting room, found she had only missed three minutes of *Coronation Street*, and did not miss Elizabeth at all.

Morgan walked round the cottage once or twice shouting 'Emily', but the curtains were drawn and she did not answer. He wandered into the Drakes' garden next door and rang the front door bell. When Joe answered it, he said, 'I can't get Emily to let me into the cottage. I know she's there because she's opened the door once but then she shut it again. She is expecting me. Could I use your telephone to try and ring her?'

'Of course,' said Joe. 'You'll forgive me if I don't offer you a drink, I've just sprained my wrist and naturally I'm feeling a bit queasy. Personally I think it should be in plaster, but I made light of it, so of course the doctor didn't think it was necessary. Do come in, though. I've made a bed up for myself in the drawing room – I have a good deal of pain you see, and it's a struggle trying to get upstairs. But do come in, the telephone's over there.'

Morgan allowed the telephone to ring for several minutes at the cottage, but there was no answer.

'Could you perhaps put me up for the night, do you think?' he asked Joe, who was lying on the sofa with a hot-water bottle. Joe shook his head.

'I don't think so,' he said.

'Why not?'

'I don't really want anyone here.'

'But where are Jess and Alice?'

'I don't know. I never know. Would you mind going now, old chap?'

'All right,' said Morgan. 'Thanks all the same. Good-night.'

He took the car and slept in a Ryde car park, leaving by

the first ferry to Portsmouth, where he had tinned tomatoes on toast at the nearest café and drove home. The flowers he had bought still lay on the seat beside him.

At the cottage Emily put the kettle on, clasped her hands and said, 'Thank you, God, for allowing me to kill Morgan. You are too kind and I appreciate your thoughtfulness. I look forward to hearing from you. Yours sincerely, Emily.'

Morgan rang Pip as soon as he reached the flat in order that she should offer him breakfast. She said, 'For God's sake leave me alone. If you dare to come here again, I'll set Constance on you.'

Joe took two largish sips of brandy and wept into the sofa cushions.

'Oh Elizabeth,' he sobbed. 'Come back to me. You were marvellous when you were pregnant and marvellous anywhere and oh God to think of you in the arms of that little, horrible, swinish pervicant, Embly. After all it's not even proper cropulating, it's just lying doing summing with a frightful twisted pervenute, and you were never a sedutioness, Elizabeth. I used to watch you dress-feeding Cork and I used to think how wonderful that I was an important part of that miracle, oh Elizabeth, to me you were like an angel from Heaven and now you're just a common frawnicator only it's with Embley and that's what I can't forgivable.'

Jess and Alice, who had just come back, glanced at each other.

'Hardly the truth,' said Alice. 'There was no chance of her frawnicating with anyone after Cork was born anyway, nothing but nappies and puke for months. And as for being an angel from Heaven, I think she was a born sedutioness from the word go. Look at that photograph of her playing in the garden with Cork when he was four. That's really what he can't forgivable – the Great Maternal Goddess of Fecundity.'

'You are clever,' said Jess.

'Put the rug over him, and take the brandy away. Oh and

do the washing-up before you go to bed, Jess. I can't possibly face all that tomorrow morning.'

'Well, of course not, you know I'll do it,' said Jess.

'The fact is, Elizabeth, you were an eroticational hazard. And I respect that,' said Joe, and fell asleep.

'I hope you've brought a dressing-gown with you, Elizabeth,' said Miles. 'You know how frightened I am of displayers.'

'Well, I thought I might violate you a little before dinner.'

'Absolutely not, dear. I am Hilary's chosen and apart from a minor lapse fourteen years ago in Brighton, I have always been faithful to him. Come into the kitchen and watch me assemble the kedgeree. I thought at first rabbit stew with a touch of nutmeg, but I kept thinking of their ears and I knew I could never do it. There is a bottle of rather common but perfectly all right sherry behind the salad bowl. I gathered from your voice on the telephone that you and presumably Emily need advice, and I see that you still bite your nails.'

'We have a spot of bother.'

'Go on, first preceding me to the drawing room where we will dislodge Campari from her nest on the sofa, carefully though. Some other cat has attacked her left ear and she is very nervous at the moment. Sit down and tell me without too much detail.'

After listening for some time, Miles said, 'Well, I must say it sounds as if Emily is one of the Great Classical Disaster-Courters, and you are probably making things worse by being perfectly beastly to her. For one thing you must stop all this writhing and sobbing in alien arms, it is both grubby and outdated – mid-Berlin and so on. Imagine the whole thing described in the tabloids as a web of intrigue and you as a travesty of womanhood. Neither of you would ever survive that. On the other hand she probably adores a bit of scourging, particularly from a kind of *déclassée* principessa like yourself. I know Hilary does, he says it keeps him young. Let us leave the subject for the moment and repair to the dining room.'

'How is Hilary?'

'Convalescing with Gillian and Blakey in Shropshire. Apart from that, much the same, still the Balanchine stance, and the black shirt, and still throttled by a gold cross at the neck. Wonderfully old-fashioned, the Josephine Baker era, but a beautiful turn of head even now. He's getting old of course, has to have a lot of little lie downs, especially after you-know-what. I let him blue-arse round the house with the hoover, because he needs to feel useful. He's very restful now on the whole. Still the same air of *bon ton* but of course no taste or judgement. The things I had to put up with when we first met years ago. Terrible stilted food, strips of lemon sole wound round pyramids of rice, covered with a béchamel and garnished with interleaved anchovy fillets. Perfectly horrid. One longed for cottage pie and bread and butter pudding, but it was usually a Bertorelli carcass from the freezer. There is no pudding today, my dear, but I bought some crystallised fruit which is glistening in the other room. We could pick at that.'

'This awfulness that seems to have assailed Emily and consequently you,' said Miles. 'Nasty, but possibly only potentially so. Quite a few of us have probably come across this kind of thing, as you know. No good going to your solicitor, of course, they're only linesmen anyway and terrified of medical conspiracy. You have to deal with it yourself usually. Gillian once said counter-intimidation is the answer, you have to become the *éminence grise* before the enemy does; strategy, be round every corner, anticipate each move and reverse it. I'm sure she was right, because it happened to her once, I'll get her to write to you. And frankly, Elizabeth, the enemy is more frightened than you are because for him the headlines could kill his career, while you and Emily can just go and live in Tuscany; happily ever after, with luck. But when did you last read good publicity for any member of the medical profession? Never, I'll be bound. And Elizabeth—'

'What?'

'At the root of all this with Emily. What is it?'

'Morgan.'

'The chap she lives with?'

'He is evidently a frightener, possibly not quite normal. She is absolutely unable to tell me much, only that she is afraid of him. She has nightmares about him, can't bear being too near him and is sometimes physically sick if he so much as crosses her mind. But she says she can't leave him because there would be no one to tell her what to do and in any case no one would ever believe he is not perfectly lovely in every way. It is utterly comprehensible to me yet absolutely unexplainable to other people who only see the topsoil. That she doesn't have any money simply seals the lid on her hopes of getting away from him. It is evidently this situation that has locked her into the psychiatric system so irrevocably, and although I have tried to help and have made suggestions, she seems caught between two lethal charlatans.'

'For God's sake, poor creature.'

'Emily is not a poor creature, Miles. She is a creature of great fortitude, and this is what makes it all so impossible.'

'What is the name of this psychiatrist she thought she had to confess to?'

'Doctor Lighter.'

'From the northern region possibly and with, perhaps, a kinship to the Thuggee. One wonders if there is a touch of the Raj apparent in Emily that might explain things. After all, in any decent massacre, the bridge-playing memsahib would be the first to be cut down, Swan and Edgar, cream shantung and all.'

'Miles, I sometimes wonder whether you are extraordinarily clever or merely ridiculous.'

'Mrs Holmes, I think you may congratulate my astuteness in either possibility, though I have a few additions to make to what I have already said. You were perfectly right in your advice to Emily, but there are one or two points of artistry in which the medical profession is able to excel. Complicity between Lighter and Emily's GP will mean that the fudging of record cards may be almost certain, and this is, of course, extremely serious. However, it would only come to light in the event of an investigation, a pipe dream that we all share on these occasions. Have another apricot. To me they often call to mind the pleasure it might be, were one to eat a baby.'

'I think perhaps a plum, my dear Miles. They have a darker nature.'

Against the weak next-morning sun, Emily saw the cross and in its shadow knew the other life, and under the eaves of consciousness lay her despair of light. For the numbers she sometimes saw were concerned with colours and were to do with this other life she knew existed, and which took indefinite form and often stood to her right and slightly behind her. A sense of twin, she sometimes thought, and felt that these formations had cared for her since she was about five years old.

'I shan't bleed for you,' she said and broke the waiting silence within her. But a colonnade of thoughts rose up and faced her.

Gillian's letter to Emily arrived three days after Elizabeth came back. It read:

Dear Emily,

Miles thought it might be helpful to you if I wrote and described what Blakey and I found out when we had a spot of trouble some time ago, which frightened us both quite a lot. It's extremely easy to become a threat to the medical profession in a situation like yours and this is often when plans to silence or even liquidate you may be drawn up. One of the things you begin to realise quite early on is that you are offered no treatment whatsoever beyond the odd prescription, which naturally you should not accept without question. However, there are rather more sinister attempts that may not be so obvious. Something that Blakey discovered when she was a nurse and later on a GP's receptionist was a kind of sabotage that was evinced in a patient's record notes – information that was passed from doctor to psychiatrist to specialist to doctor, in your case it would be something like: 'This patient is anybody's during an internal examination. Mind out and make sure you have a nurse present as witness.' Letters from your doctor to a specialist could well read: 'This patient keeps alleging that she was sexually assaulted by a psychiatrist. Obviously a troublemaker. Be careful.'

Drugging patients is quite a common way of keeping their mouths shut and of course a very easy way of doing so. Elizabeth was quite right to warn you about this, since there are several drugs whose side effects are serious enough to cause severe mental disorder if ignored, or even to dispatch one, since iatrogenic death is nothing new, and no questions are ever asked. Beware of rigged 'Inquiries' and forged record notes.

One of the things you can do is to become familiar with the signs of chicanery during a consultation. In the trade, these are known as 'Fear of Proceedings Displays'. The medical profession does not breed wonderful actors and a doctor's fear of the law is extremely easy to spot. Fear of anything makes one's voice move into a higher register – think of that moment when someone says merely: 'I wonder if I could have a private word with you' or the moment when you can't put off opening your bank statement any longer – these are the times that can grasp your stomach and squeaken your voice, and of course doctors have a great deal to fear. Therefore mark first the pitch of the voice behind the desk and the interruptions, hesitations, contradictions and disclaimers that attempt to stop you trapping the doctor into any form of admission, and to bludgeon you into silence. Since doctors and all members of the profession can be accused of assault if they even touch a patient without consent, erroneous prescriptions for potentially dangerous drugs are the easiest and most popular way of damaging and thus suppressing troublemakers and if the odd patient dies, who cares? No one will ask questions.

Be of good cheer, Emily, for the extraordinary behaviour that I and, of course, Elizabeth have described is an admission in itself, and the doctor or psychiatrist is in the soup already. But since there is a somewhat below-average intelligence among medics, he or she will fail to realise it.

Blakey says that your dedicated GP, for instance, is admitting to, let us say, endless falsified medical records or records not kept at all, prescriptions changed without vital blood tests, new medication cropping up without notice, precautions disregarded, side effects withheld and so on.

Apparently, my dear girl, your records will consist of extremely unpleasant defamatory statements concerning your private life and in particular any sexual inclinations he can invent about you, these last being of great interest to other doctors, who will enjoy reading them and will privately recall them whenever you meet.

It is worth mentioning that in your present position you will be refused an internal examination because this can be taken as sexual assault, and you have already suffered that in truth and are now a threat. In fact, however ill you feel, and however dangerous your symptoms, you will get no help from any doctor or psychiatrist because they have all been primed. If you die, tough.

But take heart, Emily, and take notes. The ploys

that Elizabeth and I have described mean that it is not you who are in their hands, but they who are in yours. You do not have to do anything a member of the profession advises unless you are, broadly speaking, incapable. By the way, many solicitors are part of the network, so don't bother with them – you'll simply be led down a carefully prepared blind alley, and it'll cost you. Publicity is cheaper than legal action, and is both immediate and destructive – just what we want.

One last thing. The knowledge that if you do open your trap, all your past may 'come out'. They bank on this to keep you quiet. Do you really care? Decide.

What I'm saying is that you and Elizabeth will really have to deal with an ugly and frightening situation yourselves. It is a question of calling their bluff in any way you can (do not put anything in writing, of course).

Yes, certainly there are good and scrupulous doctors, we know that from experience. But many others are kudos-seekers and jacks-in-office, and are therefore easily corrupted. Get them and good luck. But be wary.

If you're a good girl, we'll tell you how to survive death some time.

Yours, Gillian and Blakey

Emily wrote back on a postcard: 'In a way, I think I have. Emily.'

For she had always known she was in the front line and first to feel the shock of sudden fire open her mouth and close this life, and that in the awaiting love was her insistence and serenity accounted for yet almost never given expression.

She was thirty-nine and Elizabeth forty-three, and there seemed now a shortness of time ahead of them, its filament perhaps inescapably worn thinner. Yet it was stronger than it had ever been, and in the warehouse of her mind, spare and empty, Emily killed Morgan again, and wrote upon shopping-list paper: 'Accept me and then accept me, and in that acceptance take my life, Elizabeth, but keep nothing I have ever written to you, or there will be no chance for either of us.'

An hour later, Elizabeth picked it up and said: 'What's all this? I've already said it could cause difficulties if we kept each other's willow cabins, and you don't often write to me anyway.'

'I am perhaps seeing ahead,' said Emily. 'It's just that I have to do some thinking, and I wondered if you could go back to Joe and the girls for a week or two.'

'My dear Emily, what on earth do you mean? Think how you would hate it if I did. Would not the idea of a spot of how's-your-father between me and Joe be extremely upsetting for you?'

'Duck's back, Elizabeth, I assure you.'

'Emily, I am very much put out to hear this. Please pull yourself together and tell me exactly what you have in mind. At present you are simply wasting my time.'

'Elizabeth, my dear, I have come to certain conclusions, and to that end there are decisions to be made, in which you have little part. I must therefore be alone. If you are not busy now I wonder if you would bring in some more logs – by tonight we shall need them – and it would be lovely if you could do the shopping today. After all, you won't be here after tomorrow.'

'Won't I?'

'Well, not for a bit, anyway.'

'You are beginning to sound like me, Emily.'

'Perhaps I am you.'

'Yes, perhaps. But you didn't really mean duck's back, did you?'

'Absolute duck's back, my dear Elizabeth. Peccadillo-wise I'm not interested. And while I am about it, I suggest you do not take off all your clothes at once in bed. You tend to look like nothing so much as a pound or two of hake lying there.'

Elizabeth silently went out to the log-pile, skinned her knuckles and brought in three logs.

73

'It is not quite enough, we shall need at least three more if we are to have a comfortable evening. When you have done that, we can both relax and perhaps you would care to read me one of the Norse sagas. I am particularly fond of the part where a messenger brings Halgerda news of her husband's death, and Halgerda answers: "All will be glad of that." Simple heartfelt stuff that we can all reciprocate.'

'Emily, I am doing my best to understand what is going on in your mind, but I cannot help feeling you ought to go and see Dr Lighter. I am beginning to wonder whether your story about him touching you up is not absolute fabrication.'

'I shall be seeing Lighter next Wednesday morning and staying afterwards with Pip.'

'I am glad to hear it, Emily, I really am. I will of course come with you, as I promised I would, but I cannot go on upholding you if you behave in such an extraordinary way. Frankly, who do you think you are?' said Elizabeth.

Emily moved in a little and smacked her face. Elizabeth did not move or speak until she said, 'I can't think why everybody always seems to want to hit me', and sobbed once.

'You distract people, that's why. You have distracted me for months, and I can feel the most terrible absences in you which I will not belong to. At present I know I must be alone because it is the only way I can work. I don't need your support when I see Lighter because I only trust my own values. Please, Elizabeth, understand, and go as soon as possible after breakfast. At a given time, I will make clear my willingness to have you back, and until then do not ring me or otherwise make overtures to me. You have never given me the chance to find out anything at all about myself, and that is what I have to do while you are not with me. And a spot of how's-your-father between you and Joe won't hurt me anyway.'

It was not what Elizabeth wanted to hear, and Emily's sleek, well-sanded words set up a wince of pain in her.

In ones and twos persisting leaves forsook the tree whose

axis rocked beneath November gales, and earlier summers were but thinly remembered. Next day, a winding-sheet of mist enclosed the cottage and the house next door.

Chapter
Eight

'HAVE YOU COME back?' said Joe, as Elizabeth walked past his breakfast and sat down.

'No,' she said. 'I'm here for a week or two and I'm going to sleep in the schoolroom.'

'Can I do anything?'

'The garden. Couldn't you have got someone to do it?'

'Well, I know how you love gardening, so I was hoping you might be able to deal with it.'

'Where are the girls?'

'I'm not sure.'

'Get them to sweep up some of the leaves. It's too late to do anything else now. How are you managing otherwise?'

'I miss you.'

'Well, of course.'

'Do you know if there's any paracetamol in the house?'

'Why should I? I haven't been here.'

There was an unfavoured look about everything, and a fewness of memories debilitated the house more than the silence within it.

'It's because you haven't been here for so long,' said Joe, following her from room to room.

'I believe that none of us was ever here,' she said although it was only about a year's worth of differences that she felt.

'I wish you'd really come back, I mean really come back,' he said.

'In the spring I'll do something about the garden,' said Elizabeth. 'But it will not be possible to really come back. Not now.'

'We can eat together while you're here, I suppose?'

'I will cook myself a small nourishing meal every now and then and I shall take it upstairs to eat. You can do the same thing, of course, only you will eat it down here.'

'I suppose there's no chance that—'

'There is no chance of anything else whatsoever at any point during my sojourn here. You do not value me enough, Joe. And in any case I see that your wrist is out of action.'

Elizabeth sat perfectly silent for a moment and then took a long, indrawn breath.

'It is like a war,' she said. 'No one knows where anyone is, nor who they once were if you find them.'

They did not speak again for some time.

Soon after she had met Morgan, and had been sent by her doctor to see Dr Lighter because she kept seeing numbers and hearing music, Emily began to see words as well.

These usually appeared in front of her but above and slightly to the right of her eye level. They were almost always written in a brownish colour, not unlike terracotta, as though perhaps a conté crayon had been used.

Sometimes she saw whole paragraphs and often made a note of them, and occasionally wrote herself as much as an entire page as though the words were being dictated to her. When she looked later at what she had written, she found she had no recollection of having written it at all – it was as though it was the work of someone else.

She had a strong constitution, but often felt deadly tired after this sort of writing had taken possession of her, sometimes falling asleep the moment she had put down her pen.

The figures she saw often concerned dates, and since she could not do sums, she was confounded into curious calculations which appeared to have no attachment to these dates yet somehow made some sense to her. Sometimes these date-calculations made her physically sick, and she had to stop.

She had never dared tell Morgan about any of these things, nor did she say much to Elizabeth, but there were people in her family who had had like experiences, and when she was a young child she thought everyone had them.

After Elizabeth had left the cottage, Emily luxuriated in bed for some time. She had no decisions to make because she had already made the two most important, of which one was to deal with Lighter, and the other was to spend the following hours lying about in Pip's house eating junk food and peppermint creams, and watching late-night movies on the television.

'Now tell me, Emily, are you still worried about this sexual problem of yours?' said Dr Lighter, settled and expansive.

'Oh no,' said Emily. 'Not now, not after the wonderful things you told me last time, and all those other times. I think about them quite a lot when I'm by myself and my friend isn't there. I felt we really began to understand each other a little more each time I saw you and that's exactly what I said to her about you – I said, "I can talk to him about absolutely anything and you should hear the things he says about the kind of person I am, and how he would like to paint me." My friend was quite jealous because she's terribly possessive, you see. How about you, though, did you enjoy it as much as you seemed to?'

Lighter moved a pencil on his desk and said, 'I'm not quite sure what you're talking about.'

'Well, all that talking, of course. I don't often have

anything to do with men, so it was really fascinating, the things you thought of, and of course you use your hands so beautifully. Although I have to admit I felt terribly depleted afterwards, didn't you?'

'Pardon?'

'I mean talking to a man all that time – it's so exhausting. My friend says men are mostly boring, but I told her you were magic. Do you know what I sometimes think – well, I suppose it's a sort of fantasy, really, but what I think is that it would be quite exciting if there were some sort of investigation, and everyone knew about it, because only you and I would really know what happened while we were talking. I mean they'd never find out because I only told my friend and her friend, so it would be just allegations really and we'd be all right.'

Dr Lighter rose and moved a photograph of his thirteen-year-old god-daughter Aurora on the mantelpiece. He had forgotten to turn on his tape recorder, and slept ill beside his stocky wife that night.

The drawing and quartering of Dr Lighter was to have a beneficial effect on Emily's daydreams for some time to come.

'I noticed the word "investigation" caused him considerable alarm,' she said happily to Elizabeth a day or two later. 'On the other hand the term allegation seemed to revive him slightly, poor fellow.'

'Very well done, Emily. I am pleased with your progress and your courage shall not go unrewarded.'

'You patronising weasel, I'm as good as you are any day.'

'No one,' said Elizabeth, 'is as good as I am.'

'Except me.'

'Except no one, Emily. I am the ruler, you are the ruled, I am the rich, you are the poor, and as my grandfather once said, it is sometimes necessary to grind the faces of the bourgeoisie in any case. At such times, exceptions do not exist.'

'Except for me.'

'Be very careful, Emily.'

'Except sometimes, when the apparent doing of nothing can often result in quite a lot. Aren't you proud of me? Next Wednesday I am going back to London to deal with something else, and without any help from you, Fatso.'

As far as Elizabeth was concerned, a strange disengagement of the spirit, though not of the heart, had taken place in Emily, in spite of what appeared to each as a perfect restoration of the fellowship of love. She felt a change begin to work in her, like the rising of a good elastic dough, and elation filled some part of her, neither settling nor fighting but striving and moving and winding in her as if it were the preparation for some directive.

It was a time for movement in her life. The raw local wound that she sometimes felt took the rockface of her resistance, and the music in her was rough and beseeching.

I have to go on, I must go away, but not yet, not yet, she thought, as if certain territory awaited her, though without impatience, without a mite of urgency, for though she knew it could not be too soon, she knew too that it would never be too late.

'I feel as if something is my fault, but I don't know why and you won't tell me,' said Elizabeth. 'Don't finish with me, don't, Emily. I would find it impossible to bear, and as it is I am sad and baffled and frightened by you.'

Emily shook her head and said, 'Don't be. Whatever happens to us both, we will always have meeting-places. It is simply that I have to find out more about myself and a half-knowledge is isolating me for the time being. I know I have a slight unremarkable clairvoyance, but there is a great deal more that I need to have explained.'

'I see, but I don't understand, darling Emily,' said Elizabeth.

'I've discovered there is someone I need, that could tell me what it is about me that seems to be so wrong to other people. I must find out, you see, find out what it is, whether there really is something wrong about me, or whether it could

81

possibly be something else – perhaps even something wrong with the others. Of course, I know I'm different, but oh God everyone is different. It isn't enough just recognising that much, I have to know much much more. Shall we have cups of tea, shall I put the kettle on?'

'I'll do it,' said Elizabeth.

'You don't have to, just because of me being different and infuriating.'

'No, I don't have to, but maybe I'd feel better if I did. Dear Emily. You are infuriating, though.' A small not altogether difficult silence lay between them.

'Well then, I will be going to see her – to find out what I can about myself next week. On the mainland. You needn't worry about it,' said Emily.

'Who is it?'

'I haven't met her yet.'

The knock of words sounded in Emily's head and wrists. Inside her was a city she did not know and so could not recognise, although it had always been there, changing only in age, and in it was the blood and smoke of battle and the fall of diadems.

In Vietri-sul-Mare, among the olive trees and the resonating children, there was a thunderstorm. A frequency of these being usual, candles were always ready to be dispensed from the reception desk, to counter, in little, the immediate fusing of all lights and the death of power for many hours. Food could not be cooked or kettles boiled, nor, without a battalion of candles, could Scrabble be played. However, wine was accepted with pleasure, and plates of salami, melons, bread, butter and cheese were put upon the dining-room tables. Some guests became friends, some remained steadfastly silent. The young went to bed early, and so did the old.

Emily and Elizabeth were not in Italy for that particular thunderstorm, but had been so on another evening, and had sat upon their balcony, transfixed by the potent glory of the lightning, and the darkening sea that crouched beneath them.

Chapter Nine

S NOW LAY ON Cricklewood, and in its diamond light were villas and little shops and the Jubilee Line, and above them the sky was as chancy as a young girl's promise.

Emily crossed the road and a tracker's marks followed her. 'Perhaps I am to be shriven,' she thought.

Little children took handfuls of snow and ran away without throwing it. There was a harmony in their lives, and they felt it with the gathering of each day and the prescribing of their nights.

'Perhaps I am not worth the shriving even,' thought Emily, but in this there was little or no account of the spirit that had so often and so lately disturbed her senses.

'My name is Emily,' she said when Mrs Barrett had opened her front door and stood before her. 'You very kindly said I could come and see you. I am a little late because I couldn't find the house. I'm sorry.'

'It is perfectly all right, my dear. I see the milkman has not been yet, so if you like milk in your tea, I am afraid you will be unlucky,' said Mrs Barrett as Emily followed her upstairs. Her accent was not altogether English. Once a student of Jung's and now in her eighties, she remembered him with love and admiration.

The house enclosed Emily, and Mrs Barrett's forthright figure gained a chair facing her. The room was owned by a great deal of dark furniture, and there was little light, the curtains being drawn against the lambent afternoon. A neat black cat with a white belly stretched and rumbled and made nothing of Emily's presence.

Mrs Barrett was a percipient, and had, in any case, met a few Emilys before. She smiled and waited. On the wall behind her head hung a mandala.

'I had to put all the furniture out of another room and into this one,' she said and did not explain, only adding, 'It was necessary.'

'I was told—' said Emily.

'What were you told, my dear?'

'Well, I was told you might be able to explain what is wrong with me,' said Emily, 'if you don't mind, and if it isn't a nuisance.'

'It is not a nuisance and I don't mind at all, but what do you think is wrong with you?'

'I don't know. Most of the time I think nothing is really wrong with me.'

'Tell me a little more.'

'I have to go to a psychiatrist.'

'Who told you you had to go to a psychiatrist?'

'My doctor.'

'Who knew you well enough to suggest this?'

'Not really. I don't think he knew me at all well.'

Distinctions could no longer fall away, and thus did loyalty to Morgan, fear of Lighter and devotion to Elizabeth become simple. With these surfaced the visions, the numbers, the music and at last, desperately, two voices she had heard and had not dared admit to hearing. All these were perhaps pickings for the curious, for tomb robbers, and were losses for those who thought themselves victors, and many of the questions Emily asked were answered by herself though she was not entirely aware of this.

'And you told all this to a psychiatrist?' said Mrs Barrett.

'Not Morgan and not the voices,' said Emily and sat pulsing as silently as the ambiguous hare.

'And I have no doubt that you were given tablets. Am I right?'

'Yes.'

'I will make peppermint tea for us.' Mrs Barrett left the room, and the cat noted Emily, but no more than that. Certainly no more than that.

I am not the I that I thought I was, decided Emily, shadowed by an enormous wardrobe with an eiderdown on top of it. She got up and looked out of the window. Quiet snow fell. I will never get back tonight, she thought, and when Mrs Barrett came back, asked to ring her sister and Elizabeth.

'Where are you?' asked Elizabeth.

'Cricklewood. I'm spending the night with Pip, though.'

'What are you doing in Cricklewood?'

'Nothing to do with you, buster.'

'Are you sure you can't get back? You know I don't like being alone.'

'Go and bandage up Joe. Goodbye.'

'Listen to me, my dear,' said Mrs Barrett. 'You must not be alarmed if I tell you that you are very strongly psychic, because this only means "of the spirit" and all people are that of course. The trouble with you is that you have little extra differences and senses which are suspect to some people who do not understand the things you see and hear. I have quite a few people like you, who are always rushed off to psychiatrists who of course have no idea how to treat them and so stick labels on them because it is convenient and stops them from taking up time. There is nothing wrong with you, nothing that crying and talking won't put right, and if you can't do that with Elizabeth then come here. In any case I will do some tests, and for these I need you to write your name on a piece of paper and to take just a little piece of your hair. I have always scissors.'

85

'Am I explained then?' said Emily, as they began later to discover each other.

'You don't need to be explained. Come again and we can talk more.'

Snow followed snow, and had canopied the cottage when Emily arrived back the following day. Her footsteps gave susurrus to silence, and in the outlawed garden trees dressed in white embraced one another's branches and became one in winter's long communion with the earth.

Elizabeth was lying on the sofa reading when Emily opened the door and said, 'I am very strongly psychic', with a certain amount of bravado in her voice.

'In that case,' said Elizabeth, 'you will know that in an effort to clear the snow from the step, I slipped, fell and damaged my ankle about four hours ago. Three of these were spent in St Luke's casualty department where there were of course a great many other people already, and the fourth lying here awaiting your return since I am unable to move. Be good enough to make me a cup of Darjeeling, and if, as I suppose, you finished the Rich Tea biscuits on Sunday, I must ask you to procure more from Satterthwaite's. And Emily—'

'Yes?'

'*Prontezza.*'

'You mean now?'

'I forgot you didn't speak the lingo.'

'It was you who didn't speak the lingo. But Elizabeth—'

'My dear?'

'I am very strongly psychic.'

'That is of little account to me since I am in considerable pain. I was made to feel somewhat *de trop* at the hospital, as though I were wasting the time of the entire workforce.'

'But strongly, Elizabeth, strongly.'

'To Satterthwaite's, dear child, and with all possible *prontezza*, or in your language, "now-ness". Further, we have nothing for dinner, and since I am being excessively brave, I suggest you bring back something delicious and put it on my bill. Let us have done with psychicness for the present. Do not stay upon my words.'

Within both of these women was held the office of love, which would endure beyond let or barrier; and at any time and in any place, each could make application for pasture from the other without division of any kind.

Emily came back from Satterthwaite's with six eggs and a packet of chocolate cup-cakes.

'Oh Emily,' said Elizabeth. 'Dear Emily, come here.'

'Wait a minute, wait. We could have an omelette, and then cup-cakes with ice-cream for pudding, so don't be cross, but in case you are, I've got a present for you.'

'Emily, don't go away.'

'I am away already.'

'Wait for me, though, wait for me, dear Emily.'

'I have to wait anyway.'

'Come here please, come here. Why were you so long getting eggs and cup-cakes, why have you got a present for me? Come here.'

'I am here. But I fell down on the way back, and I thought you might like the stone I tripped over, to make certain you never ever dare to forget me, you devious postulating rat.'

Emily held out the stone, large and wet from snow. 'Come on,' she said. 'Come and get it.'

'I can't. My ankle is agony, I told you. Did you hurt yourself falling down?'

'My side a bit, that's all. Oh Elizabeth, just tell me one thing. Tell me you're crackers about me, like you used to. Tell me you can't live without me, tell me that.'

'I never said that. You did. I can perfectly well live without you, my dear child. I can simply go back to Joe and the girls.'

'I know that. I have always known it. Don't you want your present?' said Emily.

'I'm frightened. Once it was you who were frightened.'

'Believe everything I say. Once you didn't. What's wrong with your ankle?'

'Nothing much, only a strain, it was because I missed you. Emily—'

'Yes?'

'Say you give a monkey's for me.'

'I do. Say you're in a constant two-and-eight over me.'

'I am.'

An invasion of light from the snow outside gave splendour to the room.

'Beg, then,' said Elizabeth. Emily shook her head and handed her the stone.

'No admittance,' she said, knowing that Elizabeth had already taken much from her, and that she had allowed it, a distraction of judgement having been compelled by love and its attendant silliness.

'You never asked me about being very strongly psychic,' she said.

'Oh Emily, nor I did. Tell me all about it,' said Elizabeth.

'I don't want to.'

A certain landscape rose in Emily's thoughts, the taste of it bitter and thin as ruin and the pillaging of occupation.

'I don't want to,' she said again, and feeling the uncovering of herself too meagre to secure and too great to set at liberty, added, 'I will not be distracted by you', and leaving the cottage, walked slowly down to the seashore.

Scuffs of melting snow littered the sand, and upon it the back and forth of the waves had left inscription that in the low tide and the banked sky was music and speech and a greatness of promise.

Emily stood there for only a few seconds before walking back. As she opened the door, Elizabeth looked up and said, 'You couldn't ever really have meant duck's back, could you? Not really?'

'Only a little,' said Emily, and the armoured cry of endurance broke and took hold and beat against her, a cry of survival. 'I would never, never forgive you if you did it again. Not ever that.'

Elizabeth was still.

'I made an omelette,' she said.

'When, for God's sake?'

'While you were out. I thought I heard you coming.'

'Then throw it away, you maniac.'

There hung between them a grotesque silence. If you can wait, then wait for me, Elizabeth. Bring back my life again and again, and so bring back the engine of my being, which is yours.

'I have to go away,' said Emily, 'or you must.'

'Was I perhaps just a bend in the road for you?'

'Dear, dear Elizabeth, I believe you may have been. Perhaps only at the beginning when my noticing was blurred by you and I couldn't pick things up without dropping them and couldn't use my mind without it slipping through my fingers.'

And her mind said: you were a kind of me that forbade likeliness and yet was sensible of recognition. Our territory is not the same, but we are each marked by the same ploughshare and even by the differences in our growing-time. 'Where will you go, if it has to be you?' she said.

'I suppose,' said Elizabeth, 'I suppose I will go back to Joe. Where will you go, if you decide it is to be you?'

'I will stay here because it is the only place where I can be alone.'

'Then I will have to go. Emily, oh please. Don't let this happen, don't. It is not bearable for me.'

'You are ridiculous, my dearest, and have been the complication of a lifetime for me. Furthermore, you silly girl, you have wrecked the possibility of a perfectly good dinner by making an omelette half an hour ago and leaving a day's washing-up for me. You never taught me how to bleed the radiators and you didn't show me the way to pay a bill—'

'You just pay it,' said Elizabeth faintly.

'That's not enough. I saw one once. What are all those little boxes that say "total" and stuff?'

'It just means the amount.'

'Amount of what? Crap? You know perfectly well I'm

not able to live by myself because I've got no money and no expectations until you die and it can't be too soon for me and I didn't say that before because I felt delicate about it.'

Elizabeth put her hands over her face. 'I'm sorry about the omelette,' she wept.

'Forget that, you never do anything, you never touch the garden in case you break your nails, you don't do the shopping, you've forgotten how to cook, and now you've hurt your bloody ankle—'.

'I know, I'm sorry, it wasn't my fault.'

'...and I bet you've slept with Joe more often than you've ever let on.'

'Well yes, I know, but I really didn't mean to, I mean honestly I didn't.'

'Why did you do it, why did you do such a terrible thing? And your nose is running.'

'Oh Emily, it wasn't a terrible thing, I just didn't think about it, you see we often do that if there isn't anything else to do. Which there wasn't. I mean sometimes. Well I mean almost always. Well always, really. When I was there, of course.'

'Yes, of course. Oh Elizabeth, I wish I could say that for me you were just a border skirmish.'

In the bird-black night Elizabeth said: 'I'm sorry.'

'You silly, silly girl. But you must go, all the same. And I will stay. Don't try and advance your case or softly buy my attentions or dig my grave too soon or too deep.'

'When we're dead, what's the difference, what will be the odds?'

'The odds will be the difference, I dare say,' said Emily, knowing that they would slip into each other's death simple and clean as they slipped now into each other's skin without murmur of explanation or the taut expectation of two strangers. Change change, my mind, but never change my substance.

In the bright midwinter's day, Elizabeth said, 'We could go away and live somewhere else. Together. It would be lovely, like it was in Italy.'

And Emily said, 'No.'

'But I'll never do it again.'

'You will, wherever you are. Elizabeth, you have already absorbed my life and I will not be consumed by your inability to stay good.'

'I'm sorry, I'm sorry. What about your being psychic? Please tell me about it, it was my ankle that made me so awful.'

'You need no telling, and there's no telling in me now, anyway.'

'When must I go?' said Elizabeth, after a moment.

'After Christmas. Some time after Christmas.'

'What are you going to do about money?'

'Come to you, of course.'

'Creep. What about radiators?'

'I'll ring you, and you'll come and bleed them.'

'Creep. Can I come and have tea with you?'

'If I invite you. But not unless.'

'Will you come and dine with me and Joe ever?'

'Never. I am not a necessity to you, and I need to have no one else's values but my own to consult.'

The circle of their lives was tied, and, turning, thus became charged and completed. The certain proximity of these lives, and the familiar glory of its certainty left no other summit to be touched, nor octave to be caught and sung.

Chapter
Ten

I N SPRING THE sun burned early in the sky, and winter's pledge to Easter's honour gave direction to the land.

Elizabeth, walking down to the cottage, saw the door open and Emily standing outside in her dressing-gown.

'You've got bare feet. Catch your death.'

'Probably. Dearest, what do you want?'

'We're going away. Moving.'

Emily felt the skin taken off her and the coldness of it, and the foot-pad on her left.

'I know,' she said. 'I had a dream.'

'I miss you,' said Elizabeth. 'Even next door.'

'Say it again.'

'And again?'

'Yes, for ever. You were the only thing that ever happened to me,' said Emily.

'I said no, I didn't want to, I said I couldn't, but I am part of Joe and the girls again and we are going. It is the thinking that I cannot bear, all the time it happens, I'm not able to think what I'm doing at all. They don't know, of course. Emily, stop me. Stop me from the damnation of loyalty.'

'You don't talk like you used to.'

'Of course I don't, cloth-ears, I was showing off for you. Keep me here, Emily. Please.'

'I can't stop you or keep you.'

'Well, let's go out to dinner somewhere and talk about it.

We can't really make any decisions yet.'

'We?'

'You and I.'

'Dear Elizabeth, I am not part of that you and I any more. But we can go out and eat, as long as you give me the spondulicks for a new frock.'

'You shyster.'

At dinner, Elizabeth said, 'I have the most awful sadness in me. We could have had Christmases.' A small tumult began to speak in Emily and she was silent.

'Do you remember what it was that made you first take such a shine to me?' said Elizabeth.

'Maybe I was attracted by the fact that I would never be able to trust you.'

As Emily said this, the remembered attraction and distraction rose in her, and with it the peril and devastation of war, and the changing seas that they now found in each other.

'What was it like? What time of day was it? Was it dark or light when you noticed these extraordinary feelings you had for me?'

'It was nearly dark. I noticed you had a somewhat dishonest personality and it's possible that this had some pull for me that I needed.'

'Needed?'

'Wanted. Perhaps wanted. It was like a kind of peril,' said Emily.

On a mild, well-natured hazelnut of a day, Elizabeth and Joe sold their house. 'Joe thinks it will help me to forget Cork,' said Elizabeth.

'It's possible,' said Emily. 'But I don't think it is a need for you.'

In each was recovered the measure and temperature so early locked in their year's joyful confederacy, and Emily knew the lament beyond Elizabeth's words. 'I am never able to be alone, never, and I am not able to think about us. It is terrible,' said Elizabeth. And indeed there was little freedom in her, for turning from the thrall she had so happily embraced, she now found the bondage that had seasoned much of her life no longer commendable, perhaps even valueless.

Emily sighed and said, 'Take your begging-bowl away, darling Elizabeth. Do you wish to confess to any dubious connections with other people lately? It is not necessary for me to be privy to them, of course, a simple yes or no will be enough.'

'One or two.'

'You see how impossible you are. I could never bear it and that's why you do it and have always done it.'

'Only partly.'

'Of course.'

'But you will think about me, won't you? And talk about me sometimes?' said Elizabeth.

The blazoning of spring's establishment took holy orders from the skies, and from the sun a link-boy's guidance fell, and Emily said, 'I will talk about you, dear Elizabeth, and think about you. I will tell people about us and say you were an impulse buy I never regretted. And I shall tell them you were the Egypt of my life's great alteration. And even then, I shall tell them. For we are not perishable.'

Also by Benedicta Leigh

THE CATCH OF HANDS

'An extraordinary piece of writing – brilliantly funny, perceptive and tragic all at once' – *Monica Furlong*

WINNER OF THE MIND BOOK OF THE YEAR 1992

With the piquant wit of Colette, the lyricism of Laurie Lee and a passion all her own, Benedicta Leigh tells the story of her life – a life made remarkable by her determination to rescue it. Born in the 1920s, to parents who allowed her delightful eccentricities and dreams of glory, her childhood and adolescence were a restless seeking out of life.

But after her beloved father's death during the Second World War, and the suicide of her lover some years later, came the first of many shattering breakdowns. It is twenty years later that, with an undeniable force of will, Benedicta Leigh bravely takes up the sword to tackle the nightmares, and to loosen the knot within herself. Extraordinarily perceptive, *The Catch of Hands* is written with powerful candour and a painterly skill. Benedicta Leigh's is a unique voice, full of beauty, longing, pain and courage.

BROKEN WORDS
Helen Hodgman

'Helen Hodgman combines acute observation with a
surreal imagination to give a stylishly bizarre account of
the lives of a group of urban women now: *Broken Words*
is funny and poignant, a vivid evocation of the cruelty
and beauty of life'
– *Shena Mackay*

In this extraordinary novel we discover the seedier sides of
Clapham Common life as we meet Moss, her young son Elvis
and her lover Hazel, scraping by on the DHSS. Then Moss'
ex-husband tips up, pursued by the cult he has abandoned
and Hazel's ex, Le Professeur de Judo, begins to think
murderously of her back in Vancouver. We meet Walter, too,
walking his dog Angst on the Common, and Buster and
Beulah from the Women's Design Collective, their offspring a
result of the milkman's sperm donation (swapped for a rare
Beatles' bootleg). Finally, there is the Bogeyman with his
chipped junkie eyes who Elvis shadows, dizzy with love.

As the sun rises and sets beyond the distant towerblocks and
snow falls on the Common, the balances of people's lives shift
and strain . . .

A bizarre black comedy of contemporary urban life, *Broken
Words* is written with sparse elegance and a fierce wit. This,
Helen Hodgman's third novel, is a *tour de force*.

ROPE TRICKS
Jocelyn Ferguson

'Part murder mystery, part *bildungsroman, Rope Tricks*
is a portrayal of innocence corrupted. Extremely funny
and deeply touching, it transgresses boundaries and
gives us a brand new heroine' – *Sara Maitland*

George Sondberg is brought up by her brilliant, reclusive,
physicist father in weird isolation in the highlands of
Scotland. Her foray into the real world, when she is sent to
London at seventeen, forces her to confront fragments of her
unresolved past: the mystery of her mother's early death, her
father's amputated academic career, and his alias as a writer
of successful pornographic novels. Under the guardianship of
her pretentious but prosaic godmother, Luria, George's
illusions and expectations about paternal love, sex and
fantasy are variously altered by a series of curious encounters
and terrifying interludes.

This enthralling first novel of immense lyrical imagination
flirts boldly with provocative themes – pornography and
fantasy, reality and illusion.

AQUAMARINE
Carol Anshaw

'Startling and vibrant . . . Surreal in its structure it is a dream of a novel' – *Erica Wagner, The Times*

With striking ingenuity, *Aquamarine* explores the intricate ways early choices, made impulsively or agonizingly, reverberate throughout a life. Jesse Austin, on the verge of turning forty in 1990, is inhabiting three equally plausible lives: married, pregnant, living in her home town of New Jerusalem, Missouri and having an illicit affair with a maverick skywriter almost half her age; lesbian English professor in New York bringing her lover back to Missouri on a visit; divorced mother of two, running a down-and-out swimming academy in Venus Beach, Florida. Each is haunted by the moment she can't get back to, the moment hidden behind the aquamarine, when she lost the gold medal for the hundred-metre free-style at the 1968 Olympics to a fatally seductive Australian swimmer named Marty Finch.

With wit and wry affection, Carol Anshaw explores the unlived lives running parallel to the ones we have chosen.

THAT'S HOW IT WAS
Maureen Duffy

**'[She] creates the world of her childhood and
adolescence so that one can feel, smell, and taste it'
– *Doris Lessing***

Paddy is illegitimate, the daughter of yet another Paddy, Irish
and IRA who abandons her English mother, Louey, at her
birth. This is the story of that mother – frail but with an
indomitable spirit – of that daughter and of their life together,
seen through the clear eyes of Paddy as a child and as an
adolescent. Set in wartime England, wonderfully evoking
working-class life of that period, the subtle changing
relationship between Paddy and Louey is movingly conveyed
in a novel which is really a love story, but this time telling of
the love between parent and child.

Also by Maureen Duffy

THE MICROCOSM

'A highly disturbing and original novel' – *Daily Telegraph*

At the House of Shades, Matt, a bar-room philosopher, tries to make sense of the disparate lives which cross here -- of Judy who saves herself and her finery for a Saturday night lover, of Steve the gym teacher who dreads a chance encounter with a pupil in this twilight environment, and of Matt herself, who needs these vicarious exchanges despite the security of her relationship with Rae and her sense that this lesbian sanctuary is a prison too, enforcing the guilt and estrangement of the city streets beyond. Elsewhere there are women such as Marie, trapped within an unwanted marriage and unable to admit her sexuality, and Cathy, for whom the discovery that she is not 'the only one in the world' is an affirmation of her existence. With its innovative structure and style, perfectly mirroring the voices and experiences of women forced by society to live on the margins, *The Microcosm* remains as powerful today as when originally published in 1966.

THE OTHER WOMAN AND OTHER STORIES
Colette

'Her prose is rich, flawless, intricate, audacious and utterly individual' – *Raymond Mortimer*

The colours and scents of the Parisian world provide the backdrop to Colette's subtle and ruthless observations of the loss of childhood magic, the insecurity of solitude and the stresses and strains between husbands, wives, lovers and mistresses. With their emphasis on the unexpected, telling detail, these stories invite us to witness such scenes as the blossoming of one dutiful wife under the furtive touch of a lover and the immodest innocence restored to another by a simple mask and concealing costume. Reverberating with wit and psychological acuity, *The Other Woman* is a supreme example of Colette's ironic understanding of human beings at their most intense and vulnerable moments.

NOVEL ON YELLOW PAPER
Stevie Smith

'Unlike any of her contemporaries, beyond fashion . . .
an original' – *Financial Times*

Pompey Casmilus works as a secretary for a prestigious
magazine publisher, and scribbles down -- on yellow office
paper -- her wonderful thoughts. She muses about anything
and everything that enters her highly original mind: Nazi
Germany, the Catholic Church, sex education . . . But most of
all she thinks about love: love for friends, and love for Freddy
-- for Pompey is young and in love, but must she marry? *Novel
on Yellow Paper* (1936) introduced Stevie Smith's loquacious
alter ego and heroine Pompey Casmilus. Her idiosyncratic
voice is heard at its most characteristic in a novel which casts
an acute sidelong look at London life in the thirties. It
remains one of the most distinguished fictions of this century.

Virago also publish OVER THE FRONTIER and THE HOLIDAY.

THE VET'S DAUGHTER
Barbara Comyns

'The strange off-beat talent of Miss Comyns and that innocent eye which observes with childlike simplicity the most fantastic or the most ominous occurrences, these have never, I think, been more impressively exercised than in *The Vet's Daughter*' – *Graham Greene*

Alice Rowlands is the daughter of a bullying veterinary surgeon. Her world is Edwardian South London at its most oppressive, its harshness softened by the innocence of its victim who here relates, in her own vivid and uneducated words, the story of her girlhood and the growth of her fatal occult powers. Longing for romance and excitement Alice is trapped in a life which is dreary, restrictive and lonely – made bearable only by the kindness of her dull suitor, Blinkers, and briefly, hopelessly and rapturously by Nicholas, a handsome young sailor. Through the eyes of Alice we watch strange events unfold – events which lead her, triumphantly dressed as a bride, to Clapham Common and her moment of final ecstasy.

The pathetic yet monumental personality of Alice dominates this distinguished and unusual novel, a formidable literary creation at once humorous, bizarre and immensely touching.

Virago also publish OUR SPOONS CAME FROM WOOLWORTHS, SISTER BY A RIVER, THE SKIN CHAIRS and A TOUCH OF MISTLETOE.

A FAVOURITE OF THE GODS
Sybille Bedford

'A writer of remarkable accomplishment' – *Evelyn Waugh*

One autumn in the late 1920s, a beautiful woman boards a train on the Italian riviera. Her name is Constanza, and she is *en route* to Brussels and a new marriage. With her is her young daughter Flavia, who is going to England for the education she has always wanted. An odd, almost meaningless incident interrupts their journey, and Constanza makes a seemingly abrupt and casual decision that changes the course of both their lives. Yet perhaps the pattern had already been set by Constanza's own mother, the American heiress Anna, who years before had left home for a strange marriage with an Italian prince . . .